Early Life

Kitchen Bitch

Kitchen Bitch

LIFE LESSONS FROM CAROL'S KITCHEN

By Carol Frazzetta

Cover photo courtesy of the *Staten Island Advance*.

Printed in the United States of America

First Printing, 2019

ISBNs:
Print: 978-0-9773900-1-4
Digital: 978-0-9773900-2-1

Library of Congress Control Number: 2019910560

For rights inquiries, contact Maria Giudice
maria.giudice@hotstudio.com

www.hotstudio.com

For my daughter Terri,
an exceptional, unselfish woman
who gave her heart and soul
for our business.

I love her very much
and miss teaching and cooking
with her every day.

TABLE OF CONTENTS

Early Life

A Catered Affair

Carol's Cafe

So Long, Farewell

The Frazzettas

MY PATERNAL GRANDPARENTS, Salvatore Frazzetta and Adele Natali, arrived in the United States of America on August 4th, 1905, after travelling over from the Enna Province of Sicily, and their hometowns of Valguarnera-Caropepe and Raddusa. They came to the U.S. on the passenger ship SS *Perugia*, that had set sail on July 21st from the port of Palermo, Italy. They brought with them their two children: Maria (Mary), age two, and my father Alfonzo, who was only eight months old. As with all other immigrants coming into the United States, they passed through Ellis Island, before going to live at 179 Bleeker Street in Manhattan.

Wedding photo of my
parents: Mary and Alfonzo.

My mother's father, Stefano Prinzi, came to the U.S. on the passenger ship SS *Carter Prince*, from the town of Santo Stefano di Camastra, in the Province of Messina, Sicily. He sailed out of the port of Naples, Italy, in 1899 when he was 25 years old, with just $10 in his pocket. The ship's manifest listed his occupation as a "barber," and said that he was going to live with his brother Carlo, at 25 Monroe Street in Manhattan. I don't know much more about my maternal grandparents because my mother didn't speak much about them. What I do remember, is that I loved my grandfather Prinzi very much.

My mother, Mary Frazzetta, was a tremendous influence on my love for food. Her love for cooking and baking was what made her happy. I never saw my mother read a book, but I did see her cut recipes out of the Sunday *Daily Mirror*, a newspaper that no longer exists. I loved to sit at the kitchen table and watch her cook. I would lick the bowls. My favorite bowl was when she made lasagna: the fresh ricotta mixed with the mozzarella and dribbles of her delicious Sunday tomato sauce. That was heaven on Earth to me.

My mother, my father, and my grandmother Adele.

My mother never had an opportunity to be a child. Mom took care of her family at a young age because her mother was not well. As the oldest daughter, she not only took care of her father's candy store, but also worked in a sweatshop, sitting at a sewing machine and sewing slipcovers, hour after hour.

My mother met my father, Alfonzo Frazzetta, when she was 15 and he was 18. My father was a very handsome, charming young man (or should I say "boy"). He had just been released from a Catholic home for boys, where he had been raised from the age of nine. His mother, my grandmother Adele (and I use that title loosely), put her four children in separate homes after her husband died at the young age of 32.

My grandfather Salvatore was an architect and artist, and he loved to cook. In Sicily, my grandfather's family was very successful. He grew up on the family's farm, having his own horse as a child. Until the day he died, my father loved telling me stories about his father's horse. When my father was only nine years old, his father became very ill with an ear infection, and died suddenly. After my grandfather died, my grandmother couldn't (or wouldn't) take care of her children. As a result, my Uncle Bill was put in one home, and Aunt Mary and Aunt Violet in another. My father was the last to be put into a home, and the way my grandmother placed him in the Catholic home affected my father and his brother and sisters for the rest of their lives. My father went home one day and found his mother wasn't there. He wandered the streets looking for her.

My parents fell in love, despite the great resentment of my father's mother, Grandma Adele, who wanted an educated woman for her son.

Friends of Grandma Adele took him in, or so he thought. The next day, the police came to the door and brought him back to the police station. The police then took my father to a strict Catholic home for boys where they shaved his head to prevent the spread of lice. My father never got over that humiliation.

My father lived in the home until his mother came to get him because he was finally old enough to work. My father received one Christmas card from his mother the entire time he was in that home. He treasured that card dearly, and showed it to me many times. It was wrinkled and yellow, and I secretly wanted to cry every time he showed me, but I knew how much it meant to him. It was no more than two sentences long. She said she could not come, and had written something like, "I wish I could be with you."

My parents fell in love, despite the great resentment of my father's mother, Grandma Adele, who wanted an educated woman for her son. My father wanted, and needed, a mother. The day of their engagement party, Adele locked my father in his room. He was a wonderful athlete, so he climbed out the window and jumped down a few floors. They married, and had their first child (my brother Frank) exactly nine months later. Next was my sister Adele, then me (they had wanted a boy), and finally my sister Jeanne—a pregnancy kept secret from me and everyone else.

When I was growing up, my mother Mic (that's what everyone in the family called her) did not use child psychology—she just hit me! It's funny, but I don't remember her hitting my delicate, hypochondriac sister Adele, or my genius brother Frank. Perhaps it was the difference in our ages. Or was it because I was stronger, or chubby, or fat?

All the Frazzetta children were born in the house, except my sister Jeanne. You see, my mom was 39 years old, and I guess you had to stop having sex at that age. The first time I was told my mother had a baby was when I woke up one morning and asked where my mother was. They told me she went to the hospital to have a baby. The next time I saw my mother 10 days later, she was sitting in the living room with the whole family, breastfeeding my sister Jeanne. I felt so in need of affection, and wanted my mother to hold me, but no one noticed.

Soaking up the sun in my baby carriage.

My brother, sisters, and I were born many years apart; my brother Frank is ten years older than me, my sister Adele is five years older, and my sister Jeanne is nine years younger. This does not make for close family relationships. My mother was caretaker to her sisters and brothers, and all of their children too. The entire family all lived on the same block. The main house was owned by my grandparents, where they lived along with my parents, my brother and sisters, and my Aunt Winnie and her family.

We lived in a one-family house, but none of us complained. Our rent was $50 a month. My brother, who they discovered was a genius artist before he reached 10 years of age (drawing cartoons on a blackboard), slept on the porch, which was also his studio. My sister Adele and I slept on a sofa bed in the living room, Jeanne slept in a crib in my parents' bedroom, and my grandmother and grandfather had the other bedroom that connected to the kitchen. My favorite aunt, Winnie, who was from England, lived with her

My brother Frank, my sister Adele, and me.

husband, my Uncle Sammy, their two daughters, and Winnie's adopted little sister in the basement of our house.

My mother's room was the kitchen, where she cooked and baked for all of us. Her two brothers, two sisters, and all of their children came to that house every day. Every holiday was celebrated together, with lots of food, music, vegetables, and flowers from the garden. And of course, my grandfather's homemade hearty red wine. My grandma, Anna Prinzi (my mother's mother), did not cook anymore because she was anemic and delicate. I did not know that at the time and wasn't told that she was ill. I remember that my grandfather would make her some concoction, with meat in a colander, dripping into a bowl. I asked what it was, and they told me that she needed iron, and she would drink the broth.

On a bike by my house.

Grandma Prinzi (we called her Grandma Prince) was funny, loving, kind, and generous, and never forgot to give us presents. She gave me the affection that I longed for. She sat in a rocking chair in her long dress that covered the bottom of the chair. Whenever I was in trouble (which was often) I would hide under her dress. My mother would look for me, and I guess it was a game, because my grandmother would giggle and say she didn't know where I was. She died when I was nine, and it was the first time that I saw my mother cry. In the church, they played Ave Maria. I remember crying, and still cry to this day when I hear that beautiful music. All I know is that I loved her very much, and how I missed her when she was gone. I still think of her now.

It wasn't until 50 years after Grandma Prince's death that my mother told me about her life, and that was only after I had asked her. My grandmother was an excellent cook, sewed beautiful clothes for the whole family, knitted, and crocheted. My mother said she had the hands of an angel. I did not know that my grandfather did not know how to read, so my grandmother read to him every day from an Italian newspaper. My favorite family times were the holidays, and all the food on the table.

Of all my mother's children, I was the only one who loved to shop for food with her. There were no supermarkets near where we lived. My mom did not drive, so we walked or took a trolley. She went to the same stores

A day at Bay 3 - Brighton Beach in Brooklyn with my parents, Frank, and Adele.

every day. Nick the butcher, Don Cheech the vegetable and fruit man, and Mr. Mesquite's grocery store. My favorite place was the chicken market in Sheepshead Bay. The smell of the place, with the rabbits, ducks, and chickens scurrying around. How I loved to pick out the chicken, run after it, catch it, and weigh the chicken, holding it by its feet and standing on the enormous old scale covered with straw. Then I would hand the chicken to the butcher, and they would weigh me again, to tell how much the chicken weighed. I would watch as they cut off the chicken's head, and in the backyard, as they plucked the feathers, I would watch them fly everywhere. There was no protest from me. I was hungry and I knew the chickens were raised for food. The feet were my favorite part, and my mother used them in her chicken soup. After the soup cooked for hours, I would chew and suck on the bones so I could eat the marrow. My mother wasted nothing.

How I loved her chicken soup, with soup greens and tiny pasta, and her chicken cacciatore with hard-boiled eggs and sweet sausages in a plum tomato sauce, served with fusilli pasta covered with freshly grated Romano cheese on the side.

To feed our family, my mother would take leftover spaghetti, put it in a large frying pan, and cook it until it was crispy and black on the bottom. Then she would invert the pasta onto a plate and slide it back into the pan to cook it on the other side. Beaten eggs were added and grated Romano cheese. This was her spaghetti frittata and she made this many times while I was growing up because it was a delicious and inexpensive meal.

One of my fondest memories from my childhood was when my brother Frank and my mother came to my class at P.S. 209 on my birthday. My mother brought a platter of her delicious spaghetti and meatballs in Sunday sauce, and my brother drew cartoons on the blackboard with colored chalks. The teacher never erased his drawings and they were still there when I graduated. I felt so much love on that day.

My Chicken Cacciatore.

Chicken Cacciatore

Prep Time: 45–60 minutes

Cooking Time: 1½–2 hours, that includes browning the chicken, cooking the sausages and boiling the eggs

Yield: Serves 4–6

2 organic chickens (3–4 pounds each) cut into 24 pieces in total

Kosher salt and freshly ground black pepper

⅔ cup extra virgin olive oil

4 tablespoons unsalted butter

1 lb. sweet sausages or a combination of hot and sweet sausages. *Note: if you think your guest will not like hot sausage, just use the sweet.*

2 large onions, chopped fine

Sugar to taste

½ teaspoon red pepper flakes

2 red or yellow bell peppers, sliced into 8 wedges

12 cloves garlic, minced

4 large shallots, minced

Fresh Serrano chiles to taste. *Remember, it should please everyone. I like to start with a teaspoon of minced chiles. Taste the sauce for spice and see if it is what you want. You can always add if needed.*

About ½ lbs. mushrooms, sliced or quartered (your choice). *I like Shiitake; use only the cap and save the stems for a mushroom stock.*

Fresh basil leaves, to taste

Fresh oregano leaves, to taste. *Just the leaves.*

Italian parsley, chopped coarsely, to taste

1 cup of dry red wine of good quality

1–2 cups of tomato concasse *(fresh ripe plum tomatoes, peeled, seeded and chopped into ½" cubes)* **or diced canned tomatoes of the best quality**

4 28-oz. cans Italian plum tomatoes, left whole

6–8 large hard-boiled eggs. *Place eggs in a 4-quart saucepan and cover with cold water, 2 inches above the level of the eggs. Bring to a full boil and shut the flame off. Cover the pot and set a timer for 13 minutes. As soon as the timer rings, pour off the hot water and run cold water over the eggs for 5 minutes. Add ice cubes to the pot, stir the eggs around and peel off the shell. Store the eggs in a bowl, covered with cold water in the refrigerator until needed.*

Wash the chicken pieces in cold water. If you prefer not to use the neck, back, liver, or gizzard, set aside for another use (these are my favorite parts). Dry the chicken very well on several layers of paper towels. Season chicken with salt and pepper.

Add enough olive oil (about ⅛ inch thick) to cover the entire surface of a large, heavy, preferably cast-iron frying pan. Heat the oil over medium heat with a lemon wedge in the pan.

continued

Chicken Cacciatore, *continued*

When the lemon wedge starts to sizzle, add the first pieces of chicken, one at a time. Wait for the previous piece to sizzle before adding the next one. Do not crowd the pan. If all the chicken doesn't fit, use two pans or do one batch at a time. If your oil starts to smoke, pour it out and use fresh oil (do not wash your pan). Sauté the chicken until just golden brown on all sides. The chicken will not be cooked through. It will finish cooking in the sauce. Remember that the white meat needs less cooking time than the dark meat, so plan accordingly. When done, set aside in a single layer.

Place sausages in another frying pan and cover with cold water. Cover and bring to a boil. Lower to a simmer, keep covered, and cook for five minutes more. Throw the water out or save and use as part of your pasta water (if serving fusilli pasta on the side). You can also use reserved sausage water to thin your sauce the next day.

Place sausages in the same pan you cooked the chicken. Sauté with a teaspoon of olive oil until golden brown. Prick the sausages a little if they start to break. When done, set aside.

Add fresh olive oil to the pan if necessary and the unsalted butter. Add sliced onions, and sprinkle with sugar, red pepper flakes, and a large pinch of kosher salt. Cook the onions slowly, about 20 minutes, until sweet and golden.

Add sliced bell peppers to the onions and cook for about five minutes, stirring frequently. Add garlic, shallots, and Serrano chiles (if using). Cook about three minutes. Add mushrooms and sauté until fully colored. Season with salt, pepper, and sugar. Add fresh herbs to taste. Set aside.

Deglaze the pan with red wine and reduce until almost gone. Put all the ingredients back in the pan and add the tomatoes. Cook slowly for about an 1¼ hour, uncovered. Add peeled hard-boiled eggs in the last 10 minutes of cooking (just to heat the eggs through). Add fresh herbs to taste and adjust seasoning to suit.

Serve with cooked fusilli pasta on the side, covered with some of the sauce. Freshly grated Parmesan cheese for the pasta. Garnish with fresh basil leaves.

NOTE:

- I like to make this in quantity and freeze it in portions. Do not freeze the hard-boiled eggs. I make them fresh when I serve my portions.

My Mother Mary's
Sicilian Spaghetti Frittata

Yield: Serves 4

4 eggs

2 teaspoons of water

Freshly grated Parmigiano Reggiano cheese

1 cup of fresh mozzarella, cut into ¼ inch cubes (optional)

Kosher salt and freshly ground black pepper, to taste

Fresh basil and Italian parsley, to taste

Leftover spaghetti with tomato sauce (about 2–3 cups)

Extra virgin olive oil, as needed

In a bowl, beat eggs well, with water, freshly grated cheese, salt and pepper, to taste. Remember, salt is already in the leftover spaghetti.

If you have a non-stick 10-inch frying pan, or cast-iron frying pan, it is preferable. Heat a couple of tablespoons of olive oil in the pan with a sprig of parsley or basil leaves. When it sizzles, the oil is ready.

Add the leftover spaghetti with the tomato sauce, and flatten it out like a pancake. Fry until it is golden brown and crispy. Turn with a large spatula and repeat on the other side. You may need to add a little olive oil.

Pour the beaten eggs on top. When the eggs starts to set, sprinkle with mozzarella. You can turn over or place under a preheated broiler.

The eggs should be golden brown. Sprinkle with fresh herbs. Remove from the pan and place on a warmed plate. If you feel it is oily, place on a plate lined with paper towel. Remove from the paper towel and place on a warmed plate.

Serve warm or cold.

Refrigerate leftovers. I love to serve this with a green salad and crusty bread.

NOTE:
- Any leftover pasta with tomato sauce will do.

A Sweet Influence

FOR THOSE WHO GREW UP in Brooklyn, there was nothing as sweet as Ebinger's cakes. A family-owned bakery that opened in 1898 and expanded into 54 stores, they were famous for their Blackout Cakes, Crumb Cakes, Yellow Cupcakes filled with Lemon Curd, Chocolate Cupcakes filled with white cream, Chocolate Chip Cookies, breads freshly baked and sliced to order, Huckleberry Pies, and all of their German-style pastries, which were consistently delicious. It wasn't just the cakes, it was the boxes, the way they tied the string, and the Ebinger ladies who worked there.

My mother said they used to come out of the store to pinch my rosy cheeks as I sat in my carriage. Little did I know what an influence Ebinger's would be in my life. I was sad when they closed their doors in 1972. What's even sadder to me is that all of Ebinger's recipes for their fabulous baked goods died with the owner, who didn't share them with anyone while he was alive.

At Carol's Cafe I developed a line of desserts called "Ode to Ebinger's." It took a year alone to work on my version of their famous Blackout Cake. I taught the recipes that I developed at Carol's Cuisine Cooking School, and continued to see what I could create from my memories. My customers in the restaurant who had loved Ebinger's were thrilled and continued to encourage me.

One of the Ebinger's bakeries in Brooklyn.

Ode to Ebinger's New York Crumb Cake

Yield: Makes one 9×12 inch cake

2 tablespoons vegetable oil

4 cups all-purpose flour, plus more for dusting pan

½ cup granulated sugar

2½ teaspoons baking powder

½ teaspoon salt

1 large egg

½ cup milk

2½–3 teaspoons pure vanilla extract (taste for seasoning)

1 cup light-brown sugar, firmly packed

2 teaspoon ground cinnamon, or to taste

Freshly grated nutmeg, about ½ teaspoon

¾ cup unsalted butter (1½ sticks), melted and cooled

confectioners' sugar for dusting

Place rack in center of oven, and heat to 325 degrees.

Lightly brush a 9×12 inch baking pan with vegetable oil. Dust with flour, and tap to remove excess. Set aside.

To prepare the cake batter: In a medium bowl, sift 1½ cups flour together with the granulated sugar, baking powder, ¼ teaspoon of the freshly grated nutmeg, one teaspoon of the cinnamon, and the salt; set aside.

In a second bowl, whisk together egg, milk, vegetable oil, and vanilla. Using a rubber spatula, fold dry ingredients into egg mixture. Spread batter evenly into prepared pan, and set aside.

To prepare the crumbs: In a medium bowl (*do not* sift flour for crumbs), combine remaining 2½ cups flour, brown sugar, the remaining nutmeg, and cinnamon.

Pour melted butter, gradually, over flour mixture, and toss with a rubber spatula and two big forks until large crumbs form.

Sprinkle crumbs over batter, and bake, rotating pan after 10 minutes.

Continue baking until a toothpick comes out clean, about 10–15 minutes more.

Transfer baking pan to a wire rack to cool. Dust with confectioners' sugar.

Using a serrated knife, cut into three-inch squares.

Store in an airtight container for up to three days or wrap tightly in plastic wrap, store in refrigerator, and then serve at room temperature. You can also double wrap and freeze it for up to a month.

Ode to Ebinger's Carol's Blackout Cake

Cake

Yield: Makes one 9-inch round cake

3 ½ ounces unsweetened chocolate, chopped

1 can (8 ¼ ounces) julienne beets (only an expensive brand, do not buy store brands)

¼ pound (1 stick) unsalted butter, at room temperature

2 ½ cups firmly packed light-brown sugar

3 large eggs, at room temperature

2 ½ teaspoons pure vanilla extract, or to taste

2 cups all-purpose flour (Pillsbury or Gold Medal)

2 teaspoons baking soda

½ teaspoon table salt without iodine

½ cup buttermilk (room temperature)

Baking pans: two 9×2 inch round aluminum baking pans

Preheat oven to 350 degrees. Grease bottom and sides of pan with Pam Baking Spray, carefully, spending time on the bottom and sides. Place strips of parchment paper on bottom only. Spray again and dust with sifted cocoa. Bang out excess and set aside.

Melt chocolate, carefully, in double boiler over hot water. Leave over hot water, off the heat, while preparing the cake.

Drain beet juice into small bowl. Set aside. Place beets on cutting board and chop into very small pieces or use a food processor. Chop, pulse on and off until small pieces form. Add to beet juice and set aside.

With a flat beater, beat room-temperature butter, brown sugar, eggs, and vanilla in a large bowl of electric mixer at high speed. Beat about 10 minutes and scrape down occasionally. It should be fluffy and light. Reduce speed to low and beat in warm melted chocolate. Scrape down until chocolate is incorporated.

Sift together flour, baking soda, and salt onto wax paper or into a bowl.

With mixer on low speed, alternately beat flour in fourths and buttermilk in thirds into chocolate mixture, beginning and ending with flour. Mix quickly, just seconds, and scrape down, beginning and ending with flour, until just incorporated. Add beets and juice, and mix on medium speed until blended, about one minute. The batter will be thin and you will see pieces of beets.

continued

Ode to Ebinger's Carol's Blackout Cake, *continued*

Divide the batter equally between the two prepared pans. Weigh them for perfection! Bake in the 350 degree oven for 25–30 minutes or until toothpick inserted in center comes out clean with a touch of chocolate still on the toothpick. Do not over bake or cake will be dry.

Cool cakes in pans on wire racks sprayed with Pam, for 10 minutes, and invert onto racks. Cool completely. If desired, cake layers may be wrapped in plastic wrap and foil, and frozen.

If using the cakes for Blackout Cakes, trim the tops of the cakes to even out the layer and reserve the trims for crumbs. It is easier if cake is partially frozen or frozen.

Meanwhile, make Carol's Chocolate Pastry Cream. Pastry cream must be at room temperature to decorate cake. It is difficult to spread on the moist cake if it is too cold and hard.

Decorate layer cake with chocolate pastry cream. Traditionally the cake was two layers. You can make the cake three layers and reserve the fourth layer for more crumbs. If you do that, the servings should be smaller. Fill the layers, carefully dividing the pastry cream. Do the sides and top with the pastry cream. Sprinkle with the cake crumbs. Refrigerate until ready to serve.

Sprinkle crumbs with a little sifted confectioners' sugar to accent the crumbs before serving. I like to take the cake out of the fridge about a half hour before serving. It brings out the intense chocolate flavor.

Note: Be careful with the crumbs or they will stick together. Chill or freeze them before chopping into crumbs.

Chocolate Pastry Cream recipe on next page.

Carol's Chocolate Pastry Cream

6 tablespoons flour, very carefully measured; be sure to level off your measuring spoon

1½ cups whole milk

1½ cups heavy cream

⅜ teaspoon salt

1¼ cups sugar

12 large egg yolks

1 vanilla bean, split and scraped or 1 teaspoon pure vanilla extract, or to taste

16 ounces of semisweet chocolate, carefully melted and kept warm over double boiler

Combine the milk and cream.

Combine flour with a small portion of the milk and cream mixture to make a paste. Stir with a whisk until smooth. Gradually add the remaining milk and cream mixture.

Place in a heavy three-quart saucepan. Stir in salt and sugar and vanilla bean. If adding vanilla extract, add it at the end. Cook over medium heat, stirring until mixture becomes as thick as a medium white sauce.

Temper the egg yolks. Whisk the yolks till smooth and add, a little at a time, one third of the white sauce. Whisk quickly so it does not curdle. Whisk back into the remaining white sauce in the saucepan.

Place back on the heat over a low flame and stir continuously until it comes to a boil. Do not stop stirring, just check for the bubble, so that it has come back to a boil and thickened.

Have ready a bowl of ice with another bowl in the ice. Place a strainer over the bowl and strain the pastry cream. Stir warm chocolate into mixture with a whisk. Taste for seasoning, and add vanilla extract, if desired.

Cover with plastic wrap and refrigerate until cold and thickened. It is now ready to fill and decorate the cake.

East or west,
Home is best.

Miss Miller

THE FIRST COOKING TEACHER in my life was Miss Miller. She was the cooking teacher at P.S. 209 in Brooklyn, New York. It was 1951 and I was in the eighth grade. Miss Miller was tiny but mighty. She wore her gray hair in a tight little bun. Her dress was covered with flowers and she wore orthopedic shoes.

Opposite: The actual drawing Miss Miller sketched in my graduation album.

I had never experienced food like she made. After all, my Sicilian mother's only comfort food was chicken soup with pastina. That soup cured every disease known to man. Miss Miller's food consisted of lumpy oatmeal, cream of corn soup, and stewed prunes. I did not behave, and loved to make my friends laugh, so Miss Miller would follow behind me, with her hands behind her back, whistling. Usually I was throwing the food down a drainpipe in the kitchen, or giving my food to someone who was very hungry. Miss Miller changed my life.

One day in class she baked a cake, and that fascinated me. I watched it rise through the glass window in that old stove in the classroom. It was served warm, because we didn't have time to cool it. I remember it was buttery and golden, with a vanilla flavor. Then another new flavor came into my life—she served hot cocoa with the cake. I think she noticed my interest because she gave me an old, ripped-up, public-school paperback cookbook to take home.

I read the book, from cover to cover. I decided to make a chocolate cake for my

I still remember the look on my family's faces when they took the first bite. They were surprised and delighted.

family. The ingredients were cocoa, butter, vanilla, eggs, sugar, and flour. It was moist, a good dark chocolate flavor, not too sweet, and delicious. I sprinkled it with confectioners' sugar when it was cool. I still remember the look on my family's faces when they took the first bite. They were surprised and delighted. I felt enormous affection. You see, my mother didn't like chocolate cake, so she had never made one for us.

That was the moment! My fascination with food was now very important in my life. It was still my mother's kitchen, but with whatever I could find in the ice box, I created sandwiches for my family, and a light bulb went on in their heads. Fifty or so years later, whenever my family came for dinner in my four-star restaurant, Carol's Cafe, they recalled with great fondness how it all started in my mother's kitchen, all those years ago, when I would make sandwiches for the whole family.

Besides making sandwiches for my family, the other opportunity to try my culinary skills would be when my mother would go to Babylon, Long Island, to visit my father's family. I would take out that old cookbook that Miss Miller gave me, and see what mischief I could get into. One day I decided to make caramels. Of course I didn't understand how hot the pot was. I put it into my mother's sink, and burned a black hole the size of the pot, right into the porcelain. I didn't know! I knew my sister Adele would say she had nothing to do with it. As usual, I knew I was going to get it. My mother went crazy! Today they call it child abuse.

Miss Miller signed my graduation album like no other person. She did a black-ink drawing of a little house, a smoking chimney, with trees and bushes surrounding the house, and printed "East or west, Home is best." It was so beautiful and warm that I realized there was so much more to Miss Miller. To this day, that is my favorite doodle.

I did not receive the cooking medal when I graduated grade school, but my adopted English cousin did, because she behaved! I knew then that I wanted to go to cooking school. My mother said I had to go to Lincoln High School because I could walk there. The high school that taught cooking was two stops away on the subway, so my cooking career was on hold until 1972.

Velvet Fudge Cake

4 ounces unsweetened chocolate	½ cup butter, room temperature
½ cup hot water	⅔ cup milk
½ cup sugar	1¼ cups sugar
2 cups cake flour, sifted	3 eggs, unbeaten
1 teaspoon baking soda	1 teaspoon pure vanilla extract
1 teaspoon salt	

Preheat oven to 350 degrees.

Butter or flour three 9×2-inch round cake pans, or use no-stick cooking spray.

Mixing

Heat the chocolate with hot water in the top of a double boiler, or bowl. Cook and stir over boiling water until chocolate is melted, and mixture is thickened.

Add ½ cup sugar, continue cooking and stirring, two minutes longer. Cool to lukewarm while mixing cake.

Combine flour with baking soda, and salt. Sift together three times.

Cream the butter, add 1¼ cups sugar gradually, and cream together until light and fluffy. Add eggs, one at a time, beating thoroughly after each. Then add flour, alternating with the milk, in small amounts, beating after each addition, until smooth, ending with the flour.

Add chocolate mixture and vanilla; blend.

Baking

Pour batter into prepared pans. Bake about 25 minutes, or until a toothpick inserted into the middle of the cake comes out mostly clean.

If you prefer, you can bake this recipe in a 9×13×2 inch cake pan, about 40 minutes.

High School

SO OFF I WENT to Lincoln High School, not interested in anything that it had to offer, except that the boys began to notice me, and I learned how to flirt. I got tired of hand-me-down clothes from my slim sister, Adele. I was built like a brick shit house—an expression that people of the opposite sex liked to say at the time.

My high school graduation photo.

For the first time, clothing stores were offering a credit card and I desperately wanted a poodle skirt with crinoline underneath. The bigger the skirt, the better, similar to the one that I saw this new girl in school wear. She was from South Africa; she was stately, had a great body, but was not pretty, and it didn't seem to matter to her. How I admired her, and wished I had her confidence. She walked naked in the locker rooms, and my cousin and I hid our nakedness from each other in the changing room we shared. I thought it must be that poodle skirt. Having that credit card in my hand was amazing, and I bought that poodle skirt with the crinoline, picking out my own clothes for the first time. I became a shopping junkie. Unfortunately, I had no way of paying for it.

My high school graduation: me, my mother, my Aunt Winnie, and my cousin Terry.

First Jobs

MY MOTHER WAS SHOCKED that I owed the clothing store $100. So I went out and looked for my first job. I was 15 at the time. I became a counter girl in an Italian pastry shop on Avenue U in Brooklyn. The smells of pastries baking made me happy. The customers made me happy. I just couldn't get the knack of tying the strings around the boxes. Opening and closing the cash register and giving change was a problem, too. It looked so easy when the ladies in Ebinger's did it.

One day at work, I dropped a full tray of Rum Babas upside down. I bent down, turned the tray upright, and placed each pastry right side up. I finished picking up the whole tray, looked up, and there was my boss standing in the door. "You're fired!" he yelled. He had been watching me the whole time. That would not be the last time I would hear those words. At least I learned how not to use a credit card. I paid my bill, and have never gotten into this dilemma again, although I'm still a shopping junkie. That poodle skirt did not make me feel stately, or confident, or free enough to walk around naked ... but I make a hell of a Rum Baba!

I became a co-op student, working a week in a law firm as a proofreader, and then going to school for a week. I did that until I graduated from high school, and had no clue what would become of me. From an ugly duckling to a sexy, pretty woman, I didn't know what to do with that either. The teachers said that I was a distraction, and then when I went into the business world, I was told that I was a distraction again. I was very insecure and had to learn about life myself.

My next job was when I went to work for Dominic's Beauty Salon on Kings Highway in Brooklyn, as a receptionist. I really enjoyed dealing with people, and looking pretty. I modeled earrings, gave dandruff treatments to customers, swept floors, and went to shows as a hair model. I worked from 10:00 AM to 10:00 PM. My salary was $50 a week. My hours made it difficult to have a social life, so my high school boyfriend went back to his old girlfriend, who had very large breasts. It hurt me so much that I became involved with an older hairdresser, Phil, who had many love affairs (according to him) with his married clients. He told me that each of those notches on his belt represented a conquest. I did not think he was handsome and wondered why he claimed to have so many girlfriends. He fooled me into thinking he cared about me. He told me he loved me. He even came to my parents' house to meet them. So I had sex for the first time. I learned what his asset was, in a parked car. Out came this enormous, frightening thing. I could not even look at it. Unfortunately that was the only thing that he had. He took about a minute to satisfy himself. I remember thinking, what did I do? I thought

Me at 15. My father cut my bangs.

My Sweet Sixteen. My mother let me borrow the tiara that my father had made for her.

maybe I should feel love. Wasn't he supposed to kiss or hold me first? The sad thing was that I had no one to talk to about what happened. I was 17. He then told everyone at work that we did the dirty deed.

Another male hairdresser who worked in the salon, I met walking in the street one day on my lunch break. He got great pleasure from telling me that Phil had a girlfriend who was a virgin, and that he didn't want to associate with girls like me. I remember the instant shame and pain that I felt; I can't recall how I made it home on that awful day. I stopped working and went into a deep depression, stayed in bed, ate whatever I could, and gained 20 pounds. I never told my parents what was wrong, and kept it to myself. They thought it was because I wasn't seeing Phil anymore. It took me months to lose the weight and get on with my life.

Baba Au Rum

1 package active dry yeast

½ teaspoon sugar

3 tablespoons sugar

1 cup milk (warmed to 100–110 degrees)

2 cups flour

4 large eggs, at room temperature, beaten with a whisk

½ teaspoon salt

12 tablespoons unsalted butter, softened by placing between 2 sheets of parchment paper and beating with a rolling pin

Add the yeast and a ½ teaspoon of the sugar to the warm milk. Set the mixture aside for about eight minutes.

Place the flour, beaten eggs, remaining three tablespoons sugar, salt, and the yeast-milk mixture in a mixing bowl. With a flat beater or wooden spoon, beat the ingredients into a soft batter. Cover bowl and let batter rise until doubled in bulk (about 45 minutes).

With a flat beater or wooden spoon, stir the batter down. Beat in the softened butter, two tablespoons at a time. The batter will gather around the beater and form a silky, smooth dough.

Butter a Savarin mold or 12 small Baba molds. Fill the molds and let the batter rise until almost double.

Place in a 400 degree preheated oven and bake for 10 minutes. Reduce the heat to 350 degrees and continue to bake until golden brown. Savarin molds will take about 30 minutes. Baba molds will take about 12 minutes.

Rum Syrup

2 cups water   ½ cup dark rum (Jamaican rum)

1 cup sugar

Combine sugar and water in a saucepan. Stir over low heat until the sugar is dissolved. Wash down the sides of the pan. Raise heat and boil for five minutes. Remove from heat, cool, and add the rum. If using Grand Marnier instead of Jamaican rum, use ¾ cup of sugar instead.

Do not cook sugar syrup for more than ten minutes or it will thicken. Set cake on a cooling rack over a baking sheet. Douse with rum. Serve with strawberries or summer fruit of your choice. Glaze with apricot preserves. Warm the apricot preserves, until fluid. Strain and brush over the cake warm.

To make individual Babas: Use 2" × 2" tin, seamless molds. Do not put them close together on baking sheet (two inches apart) or they will steam. Individual Babas can be dropped right in rum syrup. You can use Mary Jane Molds so you can fill with whipped cream or pastry cream or fruit. I like to split my Savarin into two layers and fill with pastry cream.

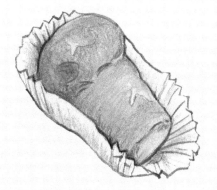

My Brother and Sisters

MY BROTHER, FRANK FRAZZETTA, is considered the most famous fantasy artist in the world. He is known for sketching and painting voluptuous, muscular women, and his works are legendary. Frank was born with this talent, which was recognized at a very young age. Frank's most famous works are *The Death Dealer*, *Conan The Destroyer*, and *Silver Warrior*.

My brother Frank and my father Alfonzo.

Frank would draw cartoons on a blackboard at home. An art teacher came to our house when my brother was a little boy. My brother was drawing Disney characters on the blackboard. The art teacher was amazed by my brother's talent and took my brother under his wing. My brother started studying at the Brooklyn Academy of Fine Arts when he was only eight years old. A famous Italian artist at the Academy, Michael Falanga, discovered Frank's talent, and became his mentor. Mr. Falanga told my brother that he would take him to Italy some day, to study fine art. That never happened, because his teacher died suddenly in 1944, at a very young age. That affected my brother deeply. He always blamed my parents—it was their fault that he wasn't more famous.

Frank affected me, because for some reason, he seemed to enjoy my company. I guess it was because I showed an interest in what he was doing. We all lived in close quarters so watching Frank work was very interesting to me.

Three families shared a one-family house. My brother's studio—I say that ironically because the "studio" on the porch—was a combination bedroom and workspace. The studio consisted of an easel, tubes of paint, black ink, pens, a chair, brushes, and a radio

My brother had a beautiful voice, and he was a great athlete. He could have been a professional baseball player, and was offered a contract to play for the New York Giants.

playing Frank Sinatra. Frank loved Frank Sinatra, and loved to sing like him. My brother had a beautiful voice, and he was a great athlete. He could have been a professional baseball player, and was offered a contract to play for the New York Giants.

During World War II it was difficult for Frank to get supplies. He carved a whole fleet of planes out of wood. They were miniature and hand-painted. I remember the animals he carved out of soap. Especially the black panther. The black panther became one of the characters in his comic strips. It was a woman who turned into a black panther. She had red hair, bangs, and green eyes. So did I.

Frank fell in love with a beautiful red-haired Greek girl named Liz, when they were teenagers. He gave Liz a collection of miniature animals that he had carved out of bars of soap. I remember walking to her house with him. Beautiful Liz came out of the house and told him her parents did not want her to marry a poor Italian artist. Their plans were to find a rich Greek man for her to marry. She was 18 when they found a 50-year-old Greek man, and arranged a marriage. I remember them throwing his sculptures on the street, and the soap breaking. He did not pick them up and walked away crying.

When he was a teenager, Frank got his own comic strip. I don't really remember how he got involved with Al Capp, who did the *Li'l Abner* comic strip. I'm sure that was later on in his life. I remember meeting Al Capp when he was the guest host on the *Tonight Show* starring Steve Allen. My brother took me to see the show. Steve Lawrence and Eydie Gormé were the singers. (They had just fallen in love, and could not keep their hands off each other. When the curtains came down and the applause was so intense, they opened the curtains again and caught them making out. The audience loved it and clapped with pleasure.) Frank soon met his wife, Ellie, and they fell in love. She had a muscular body, and he loved that.

Frank soon met his wife, Ellie, and they fell in love. She had a muscular body, and he loved that.

It did not end well between my brother and Al Capp. Frank was doing all the work and Al was getting all the credit. Frank asked for a raise and Al would not give it to him. My brother quit! It was a difficult time for him and it took awhile for him to get back on his feet. He began drawing book covers for Jack London's novels, and for other writers, which led to drawing movie poster illustrations for movies in Hollywood. Clint Eastwood, Sylvester Stallone, and other celebrities came to my brother's home to meet with him.

My brother married Ellie and they had four children together. He moved to an isolated place in East Stroudsburg, Pennsylvania. His museum is on that property, and my brother was written up in the *New York Times* when he died. I lost touch with him after he married Ellie. She was his manager and handled all business transactions.

Frank and I didn't see much of each other over the years. I only saw him a few times before he died, the last being at our mom's funeral. The last time we had fun together, he came to my restaurant for my mother's 92nd birthday and the whole family came to celebrate. I gave her a birthday party that was spectacular. My business was booming and it was a great time in my life.

MY SISTER ADELE was five years older than me. From the moment she was born, Adele was treated like a princess. She was slim, with black hair and beautiful features, and she was very delicate. I remember my mother giving her a tonic because she would not eat. She also gave Adele chocolates. I did not get chocolates, because I was fat or "chubby," as my family would like to tell me.

Adele and I slept together on a sofa bed in the living room. We would play games in that bed at night, and sometimes I would read in the dark with a flashlight under the covers. Going to the library changed my life. When Adele was a teenager, she suffered from acne and my mother took her to a skin doctor. The doctor gave her a treatment that literally took her old skin off and when she came home, her face was bright red. She could not leave the house for weeks until it healed. I am guessing that it was some kind of acid peel.

I remember when I was 12 years old, she shaved my eyebrows and side-burns. My once-beautiful, full eyebrows never grew back, but my sideburns did! Adele had a beautiful figure and she had a best friend named Josephine, and they liked to walk to Sheepshead Bay past the pool hall. Outside the pool hall, handsome Johnny would stand with his friends. Johnny would whistle at Adele, and soon they became boyfriend and girlfriend, and started "going steady."

Johnny's sister asked them to babysit at her house. I believe that this is when Adele became pregnant. She didn't tell anyone. Johnny had proposed

A family outing upstate with my cousin Frankie, me, my mother, my Aunt Violette, my brother Frank in the background, my cousin Gloria, and my sister Adele with a gun.

to her before she became pregnant and my mother and father planned an engagement party in a hall. The princess was getting married, only no one knew that she was five months pregnant by the time they married. My mother bought Adele a beautiful dress for the party. It was a copy of the white dress that Elizabeth Taylor wore in *Suddenly Last Summer*, except Adele's dress was a light shade of purple, with a fluffy chiffon skirt. It was strapless, and had daisies all over the bodice.

Because she was so slim and didn't "show," I did not know she was pregnant, and neither did anyone else. Her party was a celebration of her and Johnny's love for each other. I still remember her walking into the hall and looking beautiful. I don't remember the moment she told my parents, or when he told his parents that she was pregnant. I remember the discussion in the living room, and how ashamed they made them both feel.

The priest said that they had sinned, and would have to stand in front of the altar, and that they would not be allowed to go into the inner altar, like other married couples. Just the two immediate families were at the wedding ceremony. Adele and Johnny's first apartment was in Brooklyn, not far from my mother's house. When their first child Joann was born, Adele was not prepared for the responsibility. I would go there after school and help her with the cooking, cleaning, and taking care of Joann. My mother did the laundry for them, and also helped with the baby.

When Johnny and Adele separated for a year, she moved in with us. When they went to court to file for a legal separation, my father, mother, and Aunt Grace were there. To everyone's shock, Adele and Johnny left the court together, reconciled, and had two more children over the years (Johnny and Stevie).

Adele and me.

1941

My mother and father bought a house on Crawford Ave in Brooklyn, and Adele and Johnny lived on the top floor in their own apartment. My sister Jeanne and I slept in the kitchen in the middle floor, which they made into a bedroom for us. The basement was now a kitchen, and a television room was off to the side.

I remember how kind Johnny was to me. Johnny is the one who taught me about personal grooming, like shaving the hair on my thighs. One day, we were all at the beach, and I was wearing a sheer, thin, white bathing suit, with my hair growing out of the sides of the bathing suit, and going down my thighs. Johnny

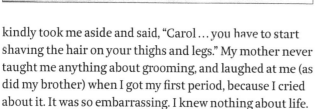

kindly took me aside and said, "Carol…you have to start shaving the hair on your thighs and legs." My mother never taught me anything about grooming, and laughed at me (as did my brother) when I got my first period, because I cried about it. It was so embarrassing. I knew nothing about life.

Johnny once saved me from being beaten up by my brother Frank. One day my brother was watching a baseball game on television, and I walked into the room and changed the channel when Frank stepped out. When Frank came back, he started punching me in the head and face. My face was swollen and red, blood dripping out of my eye, and Johnny came down the stairs and said to him, "What are you doing? Stop! You're going to kill her!" Johnny cared about me, and I will always love him for that.

Adele has been through and survived many illnesses, including thyroid and breast cancer, and at 86 years old, she now lives with her two sons, John Jr. and Stevie. Johnny is 90 now, and he lives near his daughter Joann, in an assisted-living home, where he is very happy.

Left: Sunbathing at Coney Island in the 1950s.
Above: Josephine Vilante and me.

MY YOUNGEST SISTER JEANNE and I became close when we shared a bedroom for a time when we lived with our parents on Crawford Avenue. There was quite an age difference between us, being nine years apart. Jeanne loved to watch me apply my makeup, and style my hair. When I was in my early twenties, I moved out to marry Joe. This is when Jeanne changed.

When Jeanne was a teenager, I remember my mother calling me at my home and telling me of all the trouble that Jeanne was giving her and my father. I was married to Joe and a mother of two young children at the time. Jeanne would jump out of the window at night and run away. My husband would go out to try and find her. Jeanne got pregnant by the time she was 17, and said she knew who the father was. My mother asked me to come to the

A bittersweet memory:
My daughters, Maria and
Terri, with Helene (center).

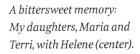

house to meet with his family, and I sat in the living room listening to the mother and father of this handsome young man say that he was not the father, and they wanted nothing to do with the baby.

Jeanne's daughter, Helene, was born and for many years my mother helped raise her before my sister took over the role. Helene was tragically killed in an automobile accident when she was only 17 years old. Jeanne was devastated by her loss.

Jeanne was married to the love of her life, Mickey Faillace, until he passed away at an early age. Even though he wasn't Helene's father, Mickey helped Jeanne raise her as if she was his own. Jeanne and Mickey also had two sons together, Michael and Wayne.

For a time, Jeanne was a matron on a school bus while Mickey was the driver. After his death, she worked in a school cafeteria. Jeanne told me it was a very difficult job. Later in her life, Jeanne picked up a paintbrush and continued the Frazzetta tradition, becoming quite the accomplished painter herself. I stay in touch with Jeanne, and still love her very much, even though we don't get to see each other as much as we both want to. I love when she posts old pictures of our family on the Internet; they bring back such wonderful memories!

Meeting Joe

AROUND MY 18TH BIRTHDAY, I went to work for AT&T as a long-distance phone operator. The training phase was enjoyable, and I did double shifts. I took the subway four times a day, back and forth, from Brooklyn to Canal Street. Once again, being pretty affected my relationships with the other girls I worked with. Eventually, I made friends when they got to know me. One day, I walked into the lunch room and I felt all these eyes on me. I realized I was the only woman there, so I was about to leave.

Me and Joe when we were dating.

Then this young man with lots of black curly hair came over to me and said, "Sit here." Joe said, "My friends bet me that you would not talk to me." I thought he was handsome. I officially met Joe one day on my lunch break, as I was trying to light a cigarette before I went out through the revolving doors; the wind kept blowing out the match. Joe came to my rescue and lit the cigarette for me. In those days we were told that smoking was glamorous, but I quit smoking when I was in my 30s. Joe asked me to meet him the next day in the same place so we could spend some time together. I was very nearsighted from the time I was in the fourth grade, but glasses were not an option for young women in the '50s.

Joe knew how nearsighted I was, so he waited for me in the same spot the next day, but had his friend wait where I was supposed to meet Joe, as a joke. I could not see that I was walking up to a complete stranger, with Joe hiding just out of sight. Joe and his friend had a good laugh about it. I loved Joe's sense of humor, and that's what attracted me to him. That was how our romance began.

I married Joe in 1958, and my whole life changed. My mother-in-law was an excellent cook and seamstress. Of course she made you know that fact, and never let you forget it. It was not a sharing experience. She told everyone that I didn't even know how to peel a potato. She didn't realize that my Mom did not want anyone in her kitchen. The most I could do was watch her, but I could not take away what was most important to her. But it renewed my love for cooking. I also admired Grandma Prince who was Joe's grandmother. She was a fabulous cook. We loved each other immediately. I would sit with her and talk about her recipes. She loved when I made her something special. Then there was Joe's Aunt Rose, who never married, but also loved to cook. She encouraged me as well.

Would you believe that I didn't even own a cookbook at that time, because I never saw my mother or mother-in-law use one. I bought a magazine called *All Beef Recipes*, and I made their meatball stew recipe. That's all I remember. I thought it was very tasty. I asked my mother and mother-in-law

Me and Joe on our wedding day in 1958.

how to make an Italian tomato sauce with meatballs, sausages, bracioles (a braciola is a thin slice of meat, stuffed, rolled, and tied), and neck bones. They did not agree, so I tried to make them happy by combining both of their recipes. My husband arrived home, and the kitchen looked like a disaster. He sat down to my first Sunday Tomato Sauce, tasted it, and announced to me that it was salty. I cried my eyes out. At that moment, I realized how undiplomatic he was. The next time I made the sauce, I did it my way.

The first time I invited my mother- and father-in-law for dinner, it was a nightmare. They were told to arrive at 2:00 PM. They arrived at 10:00 AM. I was so upset that I told her to leave and come back. I should have known, because when I met her the first time, I stepped on dog crap, and walked into her sanitized house. It was an omen.

The affection that I was so hungry for came when people enjoyed my food and acknowledged my cooking abilities.

Instead of being discouraged, I became more and more determined. Not only was I cooking, but I went back to my beloved baking. It was natural for me, and I was happy that my friends and family noticed. I went to the library and took out cookbooks and read them from cover to cover. Julia Child and Simone Beck were my heroines, not realizing that someday I would meet them. I began to collect cookbooks. I would invite people for dinner just to experiment with recipes that I was developing. The affection that I was so hungry for came when people enjoyed my food and acknowledged my cooking abilities.

We wanted to have a baby and it wasn't happening. In those days, if you weren't pregnant right away, something was wrong with you. Finally after my first miscarriage, I became pregnant with my first daughter, Terri. I was thrilled and I remember kicking my feet in the air walking back to the subway after the doctor told me. Joe was so happy and put signs on the cabinets not to stretch. That was the last of his pampering. The delivery was very difficult and I was left alone in the hospital, tied to a bed on Christmas Eve. I heard them partying all night and I heard myself screaming. The doctor my mother-in-law took me to was a drunk, and didn't show up until the next day. A young intern came in and took pity on me and broke my water. Terri was born on Christmas Eve, a seven-pound, four-ounce redhead, with the most beautiful blue eyes, but a little battered. I was practically ripped apart, and could not sit for a month. I developed a 104° fever when I got home, from infection.

My mistake was going to my mother-in-law's house for recovery, thinking that Terri was her first grandchild, and it would make her happy. I attempted to breast-feed but she made me know it disgusted her. She made me sleep on an old couch instead of giving me a bed. She didn't want to disturb my 22-year-old brother-in-law who lived there. I was up all night with the baby and when I finally fell asleep she would vacuum the living room at 6:30 AM. Finally I called my medical doctor and he said, "Even though you have a fever, I want you out of there." He said that because my mother-in-law was his patient, he knew how crazy she was. After that we went to my mother's house, and I cried my eyes out. Of course my mother said, "Don't be a baby," not giving me the comfort that I needed.

My beautiful baby Terri thrived, and I loved being a mother. She loved food as much as I did, and still does! I had five pregnancies by the time I was 27 years old, although I suffered two miscarriages. In the seventh month of my pregnancy with my daughter Maria, I had labor pains, and my new doctor said that I had to stay in bed. I tried to keep myself busy by reading every cookbook I could get my hands on. I could not sleep because Maria never stopped moving, so I read my cookbooks all night long. After my beautiful, very blonde, blue-eyed daughter was born, I resumed my passion for cooking. During the fifth month of my next pregnancy. I suffered my worst miscarriage. I was frying eggplant and felt it happening. I began to cry and knew I was losing another baby. I had to go to the hospital, and all that I remember was how horrible it was to wake up in the maternity room with a girl who had just given birth to healthy twins.

When I moved to Staten Island, I was one month pregnant with my son Joe. It was very difficult to move and leave my family and friends. I had two young children to take care of and I was very lonely. Terri was four years old, and Maria was two at that time. I didn't drive, and I was desperate for my Brooklyn stores. So I developed my own methods of cooking in quantity and freezing not only my stocks and sauces, but also my baked goods.

Joey was born premature and weighed only four pounds, nine ounces. He had to be left in the hospital until he reached five pounds. That took a week. We took him home and I did not sleep for a week. He had trouble drinking enough formula to satisfy him. That did not last long, because soon he looked like a chubby little Italian boy. He was born April 19 and by my birthday, May 11, I knew I was in a deep postpartum depression.

Me with my children,
Terri, Joey, and Maria,
all dressed up.

Of course we didn't know about many things in those days. For the first time in my life, I could not eat and developed ulcerative colitis. My loss of weight was frightening, and I worried about my children. I thought I was going to die. I knew that I was no longer that girl who had this tremendous zest for life. My family problems had taken a toll on my health.

Sunday Sauce

Ingredients for Tomato Sauce

12 cans Redpack Whole Peeled Plum Tomatoes in Puree (1 pound, 12 ounce cans)

12 large cloves of garlic or to taste, minced

8 large onions, chopped fine

½ cup olive oil or more, if needed

1 cup freshly chopped basil

¼ cup freshly chopped oregano

¼ cup freshly chopped marjoram (optional)

1 cup freshly chopped Italian parsley

½ teaspoon sugar per pot of sauce (optional)

1 cup red wine

Salt and freshly ground black pepper

Ingredients for Meatballs

1 pound ground beef (chuck)

¼ loaf Italian bread, soaked in tepid water until soft, and squeezed as dry as possible

3–4 cloves of finely minced garlic

Small onion, chopped fine

4 heaping tablespoons freshly grated Romano cheese

3–4 tablespoons freshly chopped Italian parsley

2 eggs, slightly beaten; if mixture feels dry, add another egg

Salt

Freshly ground pepper to taste

Prep the Meatballs

Mix ingredients thoroughly, make a small test patty.

In a small frying pan, with a tablespoon of olive oil, fry the patty until done and taste for seasoning.

Adjust seasoning and make another patty and taste again. Repeat if necessary.

Make two-inch meatballs and place on wax paper on a cookie sheet. It is easier to fry them, if you chill them for an hour or so.

How to cook Italian Sweet Sausage

1 pound Italian sweet sausage

Place sausage in a cold frying pan and cover with cold water.

Cover and simmer for five minutes. Pour out the water.

Add a teaspoon of olive oil and slowly brown sausage, turning frequently, and set aside.

How to make Braciole

1–2 pounds braciole slices from a piece of fresh pork butt

1–2 pounds braciole slices from a flank steak

Lay out slices on wax paper, season with salt and freshly ground black pepper.

Season each slice with about ¼–½ teaspoon of finely minced garlic, and slices of hard-boiled eggs.

Sprinkle with freshly grated Romano cheese (or Parmesan cheese), freshly chopped parsley, and if you like, some finely chopped onion. Also sprinkle a couple of table-spoons seasoned breadcrumbs, lightly toasted pine nuts, or raisins.

If you prefer, leave out the hard-boiled eggs, but it would break my heart if you do.

Roll up lengthwise, tie with cooking twine, and set aside. Do not tie too tightly.

Note: An Italian butcher can slice beef for the proper braciole. Do not buy braciole already stuffed and prepared. Make your own.

continued

Sunday Sauce, *continued*

Meats for Sauce

You can use any, or all, of the following meats:

2 pounds pork neck bones	1 pound pork (fresh pork butt), cut into 2½ inch chunks
1 pound spareribs	
1 pigs foot split in half, lengthwise	1 pound chuck beef, cut into 2½ inch chunks

Note: If you cannot find pork neck bones, use two pounds of spareribs. The bones give the sauce a wonderful flavor.

Preparing the Sauce

Believe it or not, you are now ready to make the sauce.

You will need several large saucepans, two large frying pans, tongs to turn the meat when frying, and a food processor, or blender.

Prepare tomatoes first by placing them in a food processor or blender, a can or so at a time. Pulse tomatoes briefly and leave chunky. Set aside in large bowl.

In a large saucepan, slowly sauté the onions in ½ cup of olive oil until golden and translucent. This can take about 20–30 minutes; stir occasionally. Do not brown. If they start to burn, add more olive oil.

Add the garlic, stir and sauté, about five minutes. Do not brown.

Divide tomatoes into saucepans, filling up no more than ¾ full.

Divide onions and garlic into saucepans filled with tomatoes.

In a large frying pan, add olive oil, about an ⅛ inch deep.

Heat the oil until hot and add the meatballs, one at a time until each one sizzles. Do not crowd pan, and fry them over a medium heat. Turn them over when nicely browned on the bottom and brown the other side. Do not overcook; remember they will cook again in the sauce.

Add the meatballs to the tomatoes, dividing them among the pots.

Wipe out the frying pan with paper towels. Add a couple of tablespoons of olive oil, and brown the braciole on all sides.

While the braciole are browning, add a couple of tablespoons of olive oil to another large frying pan, and brown the pork bones, spareribs, pigs foot, and any other meat you have chosen.

Do not wash any of the frying pans. Divide your meats into your saucepans filled with tomatoes.

Pour out the fat in the frying pans, if any.

Deglaze each pan with ½ cup of red wine, scraping up any bits, and reduce sauce to half. Add to tomatoes.

Bring to a simmer, and simmer, uncovered, for about two to three hours, stirring occasionally.

Combine fresh herbs and divide among saucepans filled with tomatoes. Add ½ teaspoon sugar to each saucepan. Simmer another 15 minutes or so. Taste for seasoning and season with salt and pepper. Taste again for seasoning, and correct if necessary.

When done, with a slotted spoon remove meats to serving platters.

Add sauce to the pasta of your choice, toss gently, add more sauce on top, and serve with extra sauce and grated Romano cheese on the side.

By making this glorious sauce in quantity, you can now stock your freezer for future dinners. Divide the sauce and meats according to the amount of pasta you need to make for your lifestyle, and family size. Leave a margin of space to allow for expansion, and label and date the contents. Permit the sauce and meat to cool in your containers in the refrigerator before putting them in the freezer.

NOTES:

- It's worth the extra effort to shop for fresh herbs because the finished product will be more delicate and flavorful.
- This recipe can be halved or doubled if you wish.
- The sauce is so delicious that you really should try to make in quantity if you have freezer space.

Jerry Lewis Telethon

ONE OF THE FONDEST MEMORIES that I have with my children was when we decided to hold a carnival in the backyard of our house to raise money for the Jerry Lewis Muscular Dystrophy Telethon. We were all artistic and we made booths, set up games, dressed in costumes, had dancing clowns, and gave prizes which were donated. Everything was set up in the backyard. To get into the carnival, everyone had to first buy a ticket in the garage. It was such a special day! We donated all the money we raised to the Jerry Lewis Telethon.

*Our backyard transformed
into a carnival for Muscular
Dystrophy.*

*One of Terri's classmates,
Paul Bonomo, helped out
as a clown.*

Terri loved Jerry Lewis and was his biggest fan. (How funny is it that her married name is now Terri Lewis!) In 2017, Terri and I went to the St. George Theatre in Staten Island to see Jerry Lewis perform live, when he was 91 years old. He sat in a chair, told stories and jokes, showed films and highlights of his life and career, which of course included Dean Martin. I felt very overwhelmed and sentimental, and tears came into my eyes. Getting old isn't for sissies!

College Years

ONE SUMMER, I DECIDED to register at the College of Staten Island. I wanted to become a nutritionist. That is when I met a fantastic woman named Rosalind Atkinson, who was the dean I needed to speak to. She smiled the minute I walked into her room, and asked me, "What do you do?" I told her that I did nothing, I was just a housewife and mother.

My favorite people:
Anne McAuliffe,
Rosalind Atkinson, and
Edith Susskind.

She asked me to tell her about myself. I told her that I loved to cook and bake, and sew my family's clothes, and that I also studied yoga. She said, "And you do nothing?"

Rosalind told me how she had gone back to school when she was 40 years old, and ultimately became the dean of the college. That was a life-changing moment for me.

That fall, I went back to register for college, and waited on this long, long line. I was so nervous, and when I came up to the window, they told me the classes would cost $75 a credit. I stepped off the line and wondered how I would pay for this. I knew that if I walked away at that moment, I would never go back. So I wrote out a check, and hoped that I would find a way to pay for the courses.

I loved going to college; it made me feel like a person again. I went for two years and passed all my subjects. My husband and his mother made me quit. They tortured me and made me feel guilty about the time l spent going to school.

Starting Carol's Cuisine

I WENT TO THE LIBRARY and took out a book about how to start a business at home. It said to do what you love to do. On a small pad I wrote out my plans to start a cooking school. My first investment was to buy a blackboard. It cost $5.00. On it, I wrote, "Hints of the Day." I did not type yet, so I wrote my recipes out by hand. My plan was to have about eight students in my kitchen, since that was all that I could fit around my round kitchen table. In my dining room, the coffee and cake that I baked were on the table. I would cook on my stovetop, and bake in my wall oven. The first class that I taught was my Sicilian Pizza Class, and it was so frightening, but the ladies loved the class. I charged $8.00 for the lesson, which was three hours long.

Whisking up some egg whites for a soufflé.

With the money I earned from those first cooking lessons in my kitchen, I started to advertise in a local paper. The ad cost $25, and it was a two-inch square. My headline was "Cooking Lessons" in heavy type, and it stated, "Call for information." I also spoke to the other mothers when I went to pick up my children at school, and to my sewing ladies. Whatever I needed to do to get started, I would do. Each step was an adventure and learning experience.

My schedule for the week was: school a couple of nights a week, homework, sewing classes one night a week, yoga one afternoon a week, cooking and taking care of my family, the house, and the dog, and teaching my cooking class on Friday night. I now realize that this is what kept me sane. I didn't have time to think, so I didn't have time to be anxious or depressed. I never wanted to feel like that again.

My new cooking school did not have a name, and I knew nothing about running a business. The only thing that I knew was how to show my students the dishes and desserts I had created. I wondered how long could I possibly do this before I ran out of ideas. I could not afford to go to culinary school at the time. My family came first, and I wanted them to be happy for me. We had no idea where this cooking school would go. My husband and children were creative, and together we thought of artistic ways to let people know that something new and never before seen on Staten Island was about to be born.

> **Whatever I needed to do to get started, I would do. Each step was an adventure and learning experience.**

Sicilian Pizza Dough

5–6 cups Heckers Flour. *Start with 5 cups, then knead. Add ¼–½ cup as needed.*

½ teaspoon of sugar

2 cups of water

2 packages dry yeast

2 teaspoons salt

2 tablespoons olive oil, measured very carefully

Put two cups of water in a one-quart bowl. The water must be 105–115 degrees. Test with a kitchen thermometer. If the water is too hot, the yeast will die.

Add a ½ teaspoon of sugar to the water, and sprinkle yeast on top. Let yeast sit for a minute. Stir to dissolve and let sit for 8–10 minutes, until it foams.

Place five cups of flour into a large mixing bowl. Make a well.

Add olive oil, salt, and dissolved yeast. Stir with a wooden spoon or flat beater of electric mixer.

Start kneading by hand, or with dough hook of electric mixer. Add the rest of the flour, or more if needed, until dough is smooth and elastic. If kneading by hand, it will take about 8–10 minutes. If kneading with a dough hook, it will take about eight minutes on speed 2.

Do not add flour until you have kneaded properly.

Test by sticking your finger into the dough, and counting 10 seconds. Slowly withdraw finger. If the dough rolls off your finger and is slightly sticky, do not add more flour.

Very lightly oil an eight-quart bowl. Place dough in the bowl, turning once to grease all sides of the dough.

Tightly cover bowl with plastic wrap. Let dough rise at room temperature until double in volume, about 1½ hours. Punch down the dough, and let rise again; about one hour.

Punch down dough, and shape into two balls.

Cover with kitchen towels, or plastic wrap, and let rest for 10 minutes.

Now you are ready to roll out dough.

Sicilian Pizza

Pizza Sauce

4 cans Redpack Whole Peeled Plum Tomatoes in Puree (1 pound, 12 ounce cans)

12 cloves garlic, chopped fine

1 tablespoon dry oregano, or to taste

⅔ cup extra virgin olive oil

1 teaspoon sugar or to taste

½ cup fresh basil leaves, ripped

½ cup fresh flat leave parsley, chopped

Fresh oregano sprigs, just the leaves, to taste

Freshly ground black pepper to taste

Kosher salt to taste

Put tomatoes in a food processor or blender and pulse briefly. Tomatoes should be very chunky.

In a large pot, add the tomatoes and rest of ingredients.

Stir to blend and bring to a boil, quickly. Lower flame to medium and cook uncovered for 20 minutes. Stir occasionally! Taste for seasoning and correct if necessary.

You will have extra sauce. It freezes very well.

Pizza

Lightly oil two 18-inch cookie sheets. Roll dough out with a rolling pin or press dough out with the palms of your hands to a ¾-inch thickness. Preheat your oven to 400 degrees for a ½ hour.

If you have a bread stone, be sure it is in the oven while you preheat.

Cover dough with towels and let rise again until double.

Place dough on the cookie sheet in the oven for one to two minutes to form a skin. Remove.

Spoon about a cup or so of pizza sauce on the dough. Do not spread it out. Place in oven for 20 minutes. Remove from oven and let cool if you are not finishing pizza right away. This shell can be frozen. Double wrap in foil.

Pizza Toppings, with Mozzarella and Pizza Sauce

Fresh-Roasted Peppers, dressed with extra virgin olive oil, touch of red-wine vinegar, crushed garlic, fresh herbs, parsley, basil, fresh oregano, pinch of sugar, salt and freshly ground black pepper, and a pinch or red pepper flakes.

Blanched Broccoli Florets, blanched about one minute and shocked in ice water to stop the cooking. Dress with extra virgin olive oil, Parmesan cheese, freshly grated nutmeg, and season with salt and pepper.

Caramelized Onions, cooked in a large cast-iron frying pan. Use at least six large onions, sliced thin. Start in a cold pan, add olive oil and butter, add onions, sprinkle with salt and a little sugar. Add fresh herbs of your choice. Slowly cook until onions turn golden, stirring occasionally. Cover pan and watch carefully, stirring frequently, until golden brown (can take 30–45 minutes). Season with salt and pepper. Set aside.

Mushrooms of any kind that you like. Slice the mushrooms thinly. In a very hot pan, add butter and olive oil and mushrooms and cook quickly, stirring frequently. Cook until all the liquid is gone and mushrooms are a deep color. If you like, add some shallots and garlic and cook five minutes more. If you like, flambé with dry Madeira. Add fresh-chopped parsley, fresh sage, and season with salt and pepper.

White Clam Pizza

You can also make a White Clam Pizza, just as you would make a sauce for linguini.

To make pizza: Spoon a little more pizza sauce on pizza shell. Cover with chopped fresh mozzarella. Sprinkle with Parmesan cheese. Drizzle with more sauce, here and there. Sprinkle with dry oregano and fresh chiffonade of fresh basil. If you are making this pizza without other toppings, drizzle with extra virgin oil and place in oven. It will take about 10–15 minutes until mozzarella starts bubbling. Don't let it brown.

If adding other toppings: After placing mozzarella on top, add the toppings of your choice, drizzle with extra virgin olive oil, and bake as above.

I like to quarter the different toppings on a very large pizza that fits in a commercial oven.

For a home oven, you can put two toppings on an 18-inch pizza. Use your imagination. You can also put the toppings on, and place in the refrigerator until you are ready to bake in a very hot oven for the final baking.

For appetizers, cut into two-inch squares. Otherwise, cut it the way you like.

Charlotte Russe

I TAUGHT MY Charlotte Russe Cake for my second lesson. For my family, I would bake it in a 15-inch roasting pan, cool it upside down, propped up on two Redpack tomato cans, so the air would circulate all around the pan. I did not have the proper baking pans or cooking equipment at that time.

My famous Charlotte Russe Cake.

When I was growing up in Brooklyn, a Charlotte Russe was a small round piece of sponge cake, placed on a round white cardboard, and cut into the shape of a king's crown. The sponge was covered with a big swirl of whipped cream with a cherry on top. I still remember how it tasted, and what a special Sunday treat it was. This was the inspiration for what would become my most famous cake.

It is an American sponge cake, sliced into two layers, filled with sweetened whipped cream, seasoned with vanilla extract, and covered with sliced fresh strawberries. The top of the cake is decorated with whipped cream, and whole strawberries are placed on the top.

The Charlotte Russe Cake became the most requested cake in my catering business. It was also the birthday and wedding cake that most people asked for at Carol's Cafe. The cake was no longer that simple sponge cake that I made for my family. The cake itself was now lighter, with lots more vanilla. The cream

This cake established my style of baking, and my belief that a cake has to be delicious first.

was now seasoned with liquors and pure extracts, like strawberry, raspberry, almond, and then even more vanilla, and sifted confectioners' sugar. This cake established my style of baking, and my belief that a cake has to be delicious first. The cake was made in all different sized pans, from six-inch up to fifteen-inch rounds. It was used for birthdays, weddings, anniversaries, and as a dessert at Carol's Cafe.

Julia Child and Simone Beck inspired me in every way. Their book *Mastering the Art of French Cooking* enabled housewives like me, using American ingredients, to actually try a cuisine that was unfamiliar to us. There was so much to read and understand. Words that I've never heard of like Pain Français, Brioche, and Classic French Puff Pastry, were explained in detail, with step-by-step ink drawings. This gave me the courage to try and make these things that I had never made before. There were phrases like "We urge you to give it another try, and you will understand why it has long been so popular with great chefs." These words were very encouraging to me.

In their cookbook, they discussed how Beef Wellington had lost its reputation. My first Fillet of Beef Wellington (Whole Tenderloin of Beef Baked in Pastry) was prepared in my house kitchen the day I was to show my students how to make it that evening in the cooking school downstairs. I could not afford to buy more than two tenderloins. It was the most expensive

One of my students, Joe Perlstein, presenting my Sicilian Pizza at one of our anniversary parties.

part of the beef. I had to make one ahead and demonstrate one in front of the students.

When it came out of the oven, I knew it had to rest for at least 20 minutes. I was so excited about it. The 20-minute rest time gave me a chance to call all of my neighbors to come over and admire my very first Beef Wellington. It was a masterpiece, and I did not want to cut into it at all. I did not think to take a picture so I would always be able to look at it, and remember that day.

CAROL'S MOST FAMOUS CAKE
Charlotte Russe Cake

For one 9×2 inch round layer cake

6 jumbo eggs, cold from the refrigerator

¾ cup sugar

¼ cup cold water

1–2 teaspoons of pure vanilla extract, or to taste

½ teaspoon cream of tartar

¼ teaspoon salt

1 ¼ cups sifted cake flour (do not use self-rising cake flour)

Separate eggs, using three bowls: one for the whites, one for the yolks, and one for the bowl to separate the eggs, just in case some yolk gets into the whites. Use that egg for something else. There must not be a speck of yolk in the whites or the whites will not whip properly. It is easier to separate the eggs when they are cold, then bring them to room temperature.

For this cake, I like the egg yolks and whites to sit at room temperature for a couple of hours. Cover the whites with plastic wrap and press the plastic wrap lightly into the yolks, so they do not get rubbery and dry. Let sit at room temperature for a couple of hours.

Preheat oven to 325 degrees.

Have ready an absolutely spotless and dry pan, to bake your cake.

You can use a 10×4 tube pan, or a 12×2 inch round pan, or two 9×2 inch round pans or square pans.

Place egg yolks in the large bowl of your electric mixer and with flat beater, beat until they are thick, lemon-colored and form a ribbon. Use a medium-to-high speed. This can take 10–15 minutes.

Continue beating, add sugar gradually, sprinkling around the bowl, and scrape down occasionally with rubber spatula. It should take about 10 minutes or until very creamy.

Add ¼ cup cold water, and vanilla, and beat on low just to blend. Set aside.

Gently fold 1¼ cups sifted cake flour into egg yolk mixture. Do not over fold but be sure that all of the flour is incorporated. Set aside.

In a clean mixing bowl, beat the egg whites with whisk attachment of electric mixer, until frothy.

Add ½ teaspoon cream of tartar.

*A holiday version of my
Charlotte Russe Cake.*

Add ¼ teaspoon salt and beat until egg whites stand up in a stiff, wet peak. The peaks are soft, not dry.

Gently fold egg whites into egg yolk mixture. Do not stir.

Fold until almost completely blended.

Pour batter into ungreased, clean pans almost to the top. Gently smooth the top with a metal spatula. Do not bang the pan. While pouring, check to see if clumps of egg whites are not blended. If so, blend gently with rubber spatula.

Place pan on middle rack in preheated 325 degree oven for about 30–35 minutes. Cooking time depends on size of cake. Do not open the oven until ½ hour has gone by.

Test for doneness with a wooden toothpick. The cake should be a light golden brown.

To cool cake: Place on a cooling rack upside down for at least an hour or until completely cooled.

This cake freezes very well. Double wrap in plastic wrap and then in foil. It will keep for months.

NOTE:

· See next page on how to decorate cake.

continued

HOW TO DECORATE A CHARLOTTE RUSSE CAKE

Chantilly Cream for 9×2 inch cake

4 cups heavy cream

12 tablespoons confectioners' sugar, or to taste

12 tablespoons pure vanilla extract

1 teaspoon pure raspberry or strawberry extract (optional)

If you like, you can add liquor to the Chantilly Cream. The liquor must be clear or the cream will become discolored. Framboise or Kirschwasser are good choices. Add two tablespoons, and taste for seasoning.

Chill the cream in the mixing bowl that you will whip it in. Chill the whisk separately. The cream should chill in the refrigerator for several hours or up to a week. Be sure to tightly cover the cream with plastic wrap or it may pick up odors in the refrigerator.

Taste the cream before using, and correct seasoning if needed.

Filling

1½ cups strawberries, ripe peaches, or nectarines cut into ½-inch pieces; blueberries, blackberries or raspberries.

Cut berries or fruit into ½-inch pieces, no need to cut blueberries, blackberries or raspberries.

After whipping your prepared Chantilly Cream, reserve about ⅓. Fold in your fruit of choice, and fill layers. You may use any combination or just strawberries. The amount of fruit needed for the filling is about 1½ cups in total. Brush or spray sugar syrup on each layer before filling.

Decorate top of cake with whipped cream and, if you can, make stars and rosettes and top with whole strawberries or use your imagination.

Dessert Syrup: ⅔ cup water, ½ cup sugar, three tablespoons Kirschwasser liquor (cherry brandy)

Place the water and sugar in a saucepan, bring to a boil, stirring the sugar until it is dissolved. Remove from heat and cool, add Kirschwasser. Brush cooled syrup on cake layers to keep them moist.

Keeps very well in the refrigerator. I would make it in quantity for restaurant desserts.

Brioche Dough

Sponge

2 envelopes active dry yeast   8 ounces flour

8 ounces milk

Dissolve yeast in warm milk (105–115 degrees), and add the flour, mixing thoroughly.

Allow to rise, loosely covered, at room temperature, for 45 minutes.

Dough

6 ounces unsalted butter   3 large eggs

3 ounces sugar   1 egg yolk

1 teaspoon salt   12 ounces flour

Cream butter with sugar and salt. Add eggs, and the egg yolk, one at a time. Beat in flour until dough is smooth.

Add sponge and beat again, until smooth.

Knead dough in bowl, or on a lightly floured board, about 15 minutes, until dough is smooth and elastic. Or you can knead the dough in your mixer, using a dough hook, about seven minutes at medium speed.

Put dough into a greased bowl, turning over once, so all sides of dough are lightly greased. Cover bowl with plastic wrap.

Allow dough to rise (at room temperature) until doubled in size. This can take up to two hours.

Punch down dough, and return to the bowl, and cover tightly, using new plastic wrap.

Allow dough to rise in the refrigerator at least four hours, or overnight.

continued

BRIOCHE VARIATIONS:

Brioche à Tête

Divide the dough into 1–1½ ounce pieces, and round each piece.

Form head and place each in a greased brioche mold.

Allow to rise until doubled in size.

Brush with a glaze of one egg yolk and one tablespoon cream, beaten together.

Bake at 375 degrees for about 15 minutes.

Brioche à Sucre

Round one-ounce pieces of brioche dough, place on lightly greased cookie sheets, and paint with egg glaze.

Sprinkle with coarse sugar, then loosely cover with kitchen towels, and allow to rise until double in volume.

Bake at 375 degrees for about 15 minutes.

Large Brioche à Tête

Divide brioche dough into two portions, roughly ¼ and ¾ in size. Round both pieces.

In the larger of the two pieces, pierce a hole in the center of the dough using two fingers. Revolve the dough around your fingers until you make a two-inch diameter hole in the middle.

Shape the smaller piece of dough into a pear shape, and insert the pointed end of the smaller piece into the center of the larger piece of dough.

Turn the dough over, and pinch the point of the smaller piece of dough to the larger piece, to ensure adhesion.

Turn back over, and place the dough in a large greased brioche mold.

Allow the dough to rise, about one hour, or until double in volume.

Paint with egg glaze, and bake in a preheated 325 degree oven for about 45 minutes.

The New York Times Review

THE FIRST TIME MY COOKING SCHOOL was reviewed was when I was teaching in the basement of my house on Scranton Street. They came to review our Tuesday class at 11:30 AM–2:30 PM. Patricia Wells, food critic from the *New York Times*, came down the basement stairs and into the class. I was so nervous about her reviewing me that I felt my colitis coming back. The cooking students were regulars by now, and they knew how important this was, and how much it meant to me. I do not remember what we made. When the review came out, it was great. Patricia Wells was lovely, and she admired the way I cooked. Patricia then asked the *New York Times* to feature me. They answered, "No one knows who she is." Patricia became a well-known cooking teacher and author in Paris.

A family backyard barbecue on Scranton Street in 1974 with Terri, my mother, Joe, me, Jeanne, and Mickey (left to right).

The next time the *New York Times* reviewed me, it was by Florence Fabricant, a well-known food critic and author. Once again, I was critiqued during my morning class. Patricia Wells mentioned to me that we needed to have more participation in class, so that is what I tried to do. My students were not familiar with participation, as my classes were mainly demonstrations. They enjoyed it, and that was the beginning of a change in the way that I taught. Florence was different than Patricia Wells, and was all business. When she walked into the wrong room (behind my fish tank where my furnace was), it was very comical. We still got a good review even though she was embarrassed. I think traveling to Staten Island from Manhattan was not something the food critics relished. I began to realize that being a Staten Islander was a detriment, and felt that the New York Association of Cooking Teachers looked down on me.

Connecting with New York Chefs

EVENTUALLY I JOINED THE New York Association of Cooking Teachers, where I met Peter Kump, Ann Amendolara Nurse, Nick Malgieri, Jerry Huven, Anne Casale, Carole Walter, and Richard Grausman and many other cooking teachers. I soon learned how important it was to be involved in the New York City scene. I learned about the politics of the association, and this new phenomenon of cooking schools. When I began to teach cooking in my home in 1972, none of this was happening.

In 1975, Peter Kump (an educator and entrepreneur, with a great love of food) taught five students the basic techniques of cooking in the small kitchen of his Upper West Side New York City apartment. Not long after, the *New York Times* wrote favorably of his fledgling school. As a result of the public interest inspired by that article, Peter Kump's New York Cooking School was born. Within five years, the school was flourishing.

In 1983, Kump inaugurated the culinary career-training program, to train aspiring chefs. He himself had learned from the best, and former teachers of his, such as James Beard, Simone Beck, Marcella Hazan, and Diana Kennedy all came to teach classes at the school. Illustrious food leaders such as Julia Child, James Peterson, and David Bouley were frequently guest instructors. Peter was the first of my peers to ask me to be a guest teacher. I was so busy teaching, catering, running the store, and taking care of my family that I never gave him a date, and that was a mistake.

When James Beard passed away in 1985, Peter Kump, along with Julia Child, and another cooking icon, Jacques Pépin, went on to establish the James Beard Foundation. The organization has inspired and showcased American chefs through dinners at the Beard Foundation's Greenwich Village townhouse ever since.

Peter taught his Classic French Cooking Class at my cooking school in Staten Island. He was charming and intelligent but there were more dirty pots and pans in the sink that night than I had ever seen for a class. He passed away in 1995. An obituary in the *New York Times* proclaimed him "one of the most influential figures on the American food scene." To me, he was a dear friend.

In 1986, Chef Nick Malgieri's association with my cooking school began. He was a former executive pastry chef at Windows on the World, and the James Beard award-winning author of five books. Nick taught many baking classes at my cooking school, and before the first class he was to teach, he went into my office to change into his chef clothes, and did not lock the door. I walked in, and there he was standing in his white Jockey underwear, and I said, "Don't worry, I didn't see anything!"

Nick charged $400 a class. In Staten Island, we could not charge the same price for classes that they did in the city. Staten Islanders are hard-working middle-class people. My cooking classes were $30 to $40 for guest teachers. Eventually my highest-priced classes were $65 for regular classes and $75 for speciality ones that had expensive ingredients or included wine or cocktails. I didn't raise my prices for the next 20 years. When a class did not book, we would cancel the class. Nick's last class had seven students and

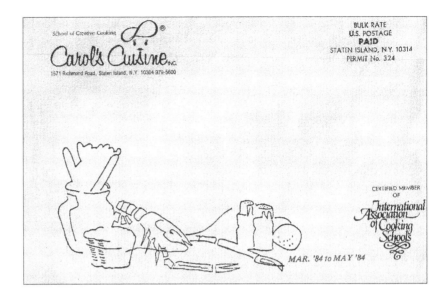

The first brochure for my cooking school at the new location.

that did not cover our costs. We did not cancel his classes, but after a couple of years things changed. Guest teachers were not booking so I did not hire guest teachers anymore. I taught all the classes along with with my daughter Terri. Nick did not understand, and I was too embarrassed to tell him that I couldn't afford him any longer. I know he was never my friend again. When I asked him to write something on the back of my first cookbook, *Carol's Cafe Pasta Sauces,* he turned me down.

Ann Amendolara Nurse was bigger than life. She had a booming voice. I believe she sang professionally when she was a young woman. She spoke with authority and was a great cook, although not professionally trained. She learned her recipes from her family. We met during a meeting for the New York Association of Cooking Teachers. Since it was the second meeting and there were just a few people there, I thought I was a charter member of the association. Ann told me that I could not be a charter member because I was not at the first meeting, even though I did not know about it.

We spoke on the phone and had great conversations about food. I am Sicilian, and she was not. I think her family was from northern Italy, and to some that meant she was classier than me. She invited me to come to her home in Brooklyn. The world-famous chef Edna Lewis was her guest. Edna Lewis was an African-American chef and author best known for her books on traditional Southern cuisine. She was doing her part to bring Southern cuisine into focus for the modern culinary world, and to elevate its status among the younger generations, so they could appreciate Southern culture.

Edna's cookbook, *The Taste of Country Cooking,* had a white-cake recipe in it. The day that I met her, I had no idea what an icon she was in the industry. I asked her about white cake, because I had a problem with it whenever I made it at home. I found it heavy, and I love white cake, so I wanted to know how to improve it. She looked down at me because she was quite tall. I saw Ann's face, and knew then that I should not have asked the question about improving the recipe. I didn't think I was being rude. After all, my students asked me all kinds of questions, and if I could help them, it made me happy. But it was a lesson learned!

Ann Nurse taught a class at my cooking school where she demonstrated baccala (a salt cod dish), and her class was filled with students. It takes two days to soak baccala in cold water, and the water has to be changed several times. You have to taste the fish for saltiness. If it is still salty, it needs to be covered with fresh water and soaked again. The skin and bones are removed and the fish is drained and rinsed.

The reason I tell you this is because Ann arrived at my school with baccala that she just purchased from the supermarket. She was not prepared, and washed the baccala in the sink in my kitchen. It simply was not soaked enough. She explained this to the students but her dish was very salty. This was Staten Island, not Manhattan, and in Staten Island it is special to be able to afford a cooking class. I felt she was unprofessional so I never asked her to do a class again.

A reporter for the *Daily News* called me around the holidays one year. She asked me for a Christmas Ham recipe. Ann is famous for her Christmas Baked Ham. It is delicious and I have made it many times with her lima beans. Even when I made it in a class, I always called it Ann Nurse's Christmas Baked Ham. So for the *Daily News,* I knew I had to create a totally new recipe, and that is what I did.

Somehow Ann heard that I was submitting a ham recipe, and got very angry. She called me very early in the morning, knowing I go to bed very, very late. She accused me of giving the reporter her recipe. I told her I was sleeping and the only thing that was the same in the recipe was the ham. Somehow, the recipe was not printed in the article. The *Daily News* has used other recipes that I have given them over the years. I think that was the last time I spoke to Ann, but it was not the end of the story. She was friends with Arthur Schwartz, host of the WOR radio show *Food Talk*, and best friends with Nick Malgieri. Arthur Schwartz tried to end my career with his Saturday morning show. I think this made all three of them very happy. Some time after that, Schwartz was fired from his radio job, which made me very happy.

Jerry Huven was a very dear man, my friend, and a cooking teacher who specialized in eclectic cooking and African cuisine. He planned to write a cookbook about that subject. I was invited to his house in Connecticut where he lived with his partner. It was beautiful, warm, and the grounds were sprawling. I was so impressed with his collection of copper pots and bowls that hung proudly in his kitchen.

I walked the grounds with Anne Casale, another Italian-American cooking teacher. She was a smart, funny, down-to-earth cooking teacher and author and we became friends instantly. She wrote on the back of my first cookbook, "Easy-to-read, easy-to-follow directions, delightful anecdotes and preparation tips galore. Carol Frazzetta's recipes are straightforward, sure-fire, and most important, unfailingly delicious. This book is a delight to read as well as to cook from." When I read an article in the newsletter from the NYACT (cooking school association) that she had died of cancer, my heart sank. She was so full of life and had so much more to give.

I walked the grounds with Annie Casale, another Italian American cooking teacher.... She was so full of life and had so much more to give.

Jerry Huven came to my wedding party at Carol's Cafe after I eloped in New Orleans, and married Les Prigerson. I had no idea how sick Jerry was at that time. He bought me an antique bread-dough kneader. On the cover it says, "Put in all liquids first, then flour, turn three minutes, rise in pail. After rising, turn until dough forms a ball, take off gross piece, and lift out dough with kneader." His wedding card is still inside the pail. I was so busy greeting guests, that I did not have time to spend with him. He stayed a little while. When he came over to me, I noticed he didn't look well, and a bit sad. What I didn't know was that he had AIDS. He died two weeks later. My heart was broken! For him to come, I knew he loved me.

When I saw Ann Nurse at the James Beard house, she said she was so angry that Jerry had donated his beautiful copper pots and bowls to the James Beard house. She said, "I asked him for those copper pots." She thought he would leave them to her. I remember when I went to her house, her basement was filled with china and cookery. People gave her gifts because she had an infectious personality. I smiled and looked up to the sky. Jerry was a very smart man!

I have lost many talented cooking teachers, students, and chefs to AIDS. It was during the AIDS epidemic when my hairdresser Tommy was one of the first people I loved to have died from this horrible plague. I was told Tommy contracted the disease when he was in Nicaragua. It was just the beginning of this horrible infection that there was no cure for.

A Catered Affair

Catering

I BEGAN MY CATERING career in my house on Scranton Street. Many of my students and customers lived on Todt Hill (the richest neighborhood on Staten Island). These wealthy students were married to successful doctors, lawyers, and businessmen. Some were mob wives. A few of my clients were married to the biggest Mafia men in Staten Island, Brooklyn, and Manhattan. The mob wives, along with the other rich students, came to the Tuesday morning classes. That was how my catering business began.

Charlotte Russe Wedding Cake decorated with fresh flowers.

It all started with rich wives and girlfriends buying my frozen breads and cakes out of my freezer in the basement. Their favorites were my holiday breads—like my panettone (an Italian sweet bread originally from Milan). The original recipe for my panettone was from Joe's Grandma Prince. You were supposed to use a special panettone tin, which I didn't have. So I would make the breads in coffee cans, and miscellaneous shapes, including soufflé dishes. The panettones were a ton of work, and I would make them in quantity. I adjusted the recipe to make them lighter in texture. I sold them by weight. Years later my recipe appeared in *Italian Cooking and Living Magazine* magazine in a three-page full-color article.

I was just beginning to learn about the retail business. Fruitcakes, pound cakes, marble cakes, Swedish rye, white, challah, honey whole wheat braided loaves, and whatever I was teaching, all made in many sizes. Whatever I finished after the students left, I would freeze, and they would look in my freezer each week and buy whatever

Catering for Thanksgiving was the hardest work.... I would not go to bed for two days before Thanksgiving, working nonstop through the night to cater all these turkeys.

they liked. Cakes for special occasions had to be made to order. Soon the word was out, and my freezer would be cleaned out.

Catering for Thanksgiving was the hardest work. In addition to the catering, I would teach my traditional turkey dinner class every November, and then have to make dinner for my family. I catered countless full Thanksgiving dinners for the families on Todt Hill. I used one oven in my kitchen, and one oven in the basement. I had to use my garage as a refrigerator when it was cold enough to do so. I would not go to bed for two days before Thanksgiving, working nonstop through the night to cater all these turkeys. My husband would take pictures of the kitchen, so he could show me what a mess I made. Joe was a cleaning fanatic (just like his mother, "Felix Unger"), but he never helped me cook, or clean, at all.

I would have to carry 35-pound cooked turkeys up the stairs from my basement when the customers would arrive at 1:00 PM, to pick up their complete "homemade" turkey dinners, with all the trimmings. When all the cooking was finally over, and the turkeys were picked up, I would have to make my family's Thanksgiving dinner. I will never forget when my

Teaching my recipe, Blue Crabs in Red Sauce, to my students in my home on Scranton Street.

mother-in-law made a comment one Thanksgiving that "I've never heard of eating at 3:00 PM." I could not even keep my eyes open. I was falling asleep at the table, but my family had their gourmet Thanksgiving dinner.

In December one year, I catered for the Gambino family (a notorious Mafia family here on Staten Island). I remember this because we had a heatwave (it was 72 degrees outside at the end of December!), so my garage was no longer my refrigerator. It was a real problem, and we had to improvise and pack things into the two refrigerators that we had. We had a regular size fridge in my kitchen, and a smaller one in the basement.

Mr. Gambino came to my house to pay me in advance, and he pulled into my driveway in an old car. He apologized and said his Jaguar was being repaired. He did not come in the front entrance, he said he didn't want to, so he came into my basement through the garage. He had a long coat on, reached into his back pants pocket, and took out a very large roll of bills to pay me. Terri's boyfriend at the time was in the basement, and his eyes popped out when he saw that large roll of hundreds. At first, my catering was only pickup; eventually, customers would let me come into their homes and cook for them in their kitchens.

Once I catered a party in a beautiful home on Todt Hill. The owner was a young, stunning, blonde student who came to my classes every Tuesday morning. She asked me to come to her house and cater a buffet. We arrived at this amazing house with marble floors, an enormous commercial kitchen, and Picassos on the wall. What I didn't know was that this was a test for the Staten Island Academy Auction that was coming up. Her husband was going to run it that year and he wanted to taste my food. We set everything up in their dining room, with all of the china and silverware we had rented. I had to learn about finding the best place to rent tableware, linens, buy flowers, and hire dependable service people. I had no idea what I was getting into. I was in the kitchen cooking, and his wife came in and said, "If only I could cook like you," and I said, "If only I had your necklace!" Thank God, she laughed! Everything we served was delicious, and they were very pleased.

We did get the Staten Island Academy Auction and it was the biggest job that we ever catered. It was for about 700 people. I hired extra prep people and cooks; some were excellent, and others were just entertaining. For example, "Gene" liked to tell us dirty jokes, which kept up the staff's energy. One day, Gene was very late (or should I say, as usual!), and showed up with two black eyes. This is the story he told: "I was at a bar, minding my own business, I looked out an open window and BAM!, I got punched in both eyes." Gene spent a lot of time in the bathroom at work, and I can only imagine what he was doing. I did not go home while working on this job, except to sleep a little, shower, and change clothes. I had a broken-down sofa bed in the office where my workers would take naps. The men spent more time in the office than I did.

Preparing sheet cakes for 600 guests.

Cakes I prepared for a wedding, including my Charlotte Russe Cake and a Gâteau au Chocolat.

I don't remember the whole menu for the S.I. Academy event, but I do remember the hundreds of Sicilian rice balls that we made. They were cursed! I remember these two young women who graduated from the Culinary Institute in Hyde Park. One of them worked for me for at least a year and she asked her friend to come in and help for the event. My recipe for the rice balls said, "Do not cover the pot, when cooking the rice"—which was underlined. They not only covered the many pots when cooking the rice, which made the rice mushy, they added pounds of butter and Parmesan cheese, additional to what is called for in the recipe, before showing me what they did. I was so furious that the whole thing was wasted, I asked them to leave.

That is not the end of the story. Gene piled the trays of rice balls, one on top of the other, when we were leaving for the affair. All of the rice balls were squashed! We prepared many appetizers, pastas, entrées, salads, and homemade breads but the array of pastries and cookies I made took me a month to do. We served it buffet-style with the service people we hired. The guests were the elite of Staten Island: rich, politicians, and mafioso.

When it became time to present my beautiful pastries, that I had slaved over for many weeks, a terrible thing happened—the power went out! My client did an expensive light show in the gym. The show lasted two minutes or so and the fuses blew. It was black in the room. When the lights came back on, all my pastries were gone. Crumbs and a couple of pastries were left on the table, scattered.

They did not get to see and appreciate all the work and dedication I put in to making these beautiful desserts. I could have put store-bought pastries on the tables, for all they knew, or cared. The next morning, when I got out of bed, I was so exhausted that I fell on the floor and all of the blood vessels in my legs had broken.

I remember another party we did where Maria's friend Joe, the bartender, showed up to the party without a tie. He was lucky he didn't get shot that day. We had to get him a tie, and somehow, we did. Our menu consisted of Mahogany Chicken Wings, Mini Quiches with White Wine and Shallots, Mini Quiche Lorraine, Christmas Baked Ham, Asparagus with Strawberry Vinaigrette, Homemade Potato Rolls, Pignoli Cookies, Neapolitan Rainbow Cookies, and Jelly Butter Cookies.

The only thing that the client had to do was get the paper plates, silverware, and to have proper lighting over the serving table. It was a disaster! The plates she bought were too small and limp, and the buffet table was set up in the darkest corner of the room. I remember this very important congressman coming up to the table many times, taking my Mahogany Chicken Wings. Over and over, and he would ask me, "Are they burnt?" I said that they were called "Mahogany Chicken Wings" because they had a deep, rich color. I felt indignant because it was so dark in the corner, you really could not see the beautiful food that was being served. I believe I charged only $15 a person for that party.

Her husband insisted we come back to his house to get paid. I was so exhausted, I just wanted to go home. I remember getting to his house, and sitting on this expensive couch that my whole body sunk into. He said he wanted to show me his orchid greenhouse. I was so impressed and it was something I will never forget.

I think if I wasn't a chef, I would have liked to be a horticulturist. I have a green thumb and a beautiful garden in my backyard, where I grow herbs, vegetables, tomatoes, and flowers.

> ## I think if I wasn't a chef, I would have liked to be a horticulturist. I have a green thumb and a beautiful garden in my backyard.

In my house I have many green, healthy plants. We went back into the living room where other guests had arrived. One was a local real estate agent, Otto Vitale, with his wife. Little did I know that this would be the man I would buy my building on Richmond Road from, years later. That building would become my cooking school and restaurant, and where I would eventually live. When he asked me about my future plans, I told him I was looking for a building to expand my business. He never forgot that, and called me when a building was available.

I once did a costly First Communion party for a Staten Island "Family." The little girl's dress was made to order. The backyard was decorated with summer flowers. The menu included handmade appetizers, a homemade pasta course, and entrées: eggplant Parmesan, fillet of beef, veal, and fish. Caesar salad was tossed to order.

My Chocolate Cloud Wedding Cake with fresh flowers for Arnold and Lucy Simon's wedding.

For dessert I made a Charlotte Russe Cake decorated with Chantilly Cream and fresh strawberries, topped with summer flowers. Of course, they wanted all my Italian specialties: Pignoli Cookies, tiny cream puffs and eclairs, and my Sicilian mother's Anisette Biscotti, which I made much smaller than my mother's. In fact, my mother's biscotti got so big, that I could no longer dunk them in my cold milk. As my mother got older, her biscotti got bigger (as did her meatballs and braciole)!

At one point during the party, I was in the kitchen, carving fruits and vegetables to decorate the dining room table—apple swans, lemon pigs, olive rabbits and carrot lilies—and in walks one of the most important heads of the Mafia. He was fascinated and wanted to learn how I did that.

My short, chubby, Jewish husband Les put his hands on his hips and told him to get out of the kitchen. He said, "Can't you see she is busy?" This time he went too far, and I thought the man was going to shoot him. To my amazement, the man laughed because Les had the gumption to stand up to him. Thank goodness we were a success! The word went out and we became one of the top caterers. We not only catered in Staten Island, we began catering in Manhattan, Brooklyn, and Long Island.

Once we opened Carol's Cafe, our catering became mostly on-premises. We hosted private parties on Sundays, when the restaurant was closed. We were limited because we could seat no more than 50 guests in the main dining room. We had the pub which could seat an additional 20 guests, but people did not want to be separated. There were exceptions though, when we would use the cafe for the adults, and the pub for the kids. We had a special menu for the kids and had coloring books and a staff member supervising them. Our menu was eclectic and interesting when I planned it with the clients. Then a decision was made by Terri to have a set menu with choices, so that we could be competitive with other restaurants.

Our success was limited because there were so many places opening on Staten Island. One opened a few doors down from us that was a lot bigger and had outdoor seating. What we had was delicious food made fresh, my famous cakes and desserts, and upon request, live jazz music. Having parties only on Sunday also limited us.

I remember a lovely young couple who were married under our arch in the dining room, the arch covered with fresh flowers. The wedding cake was decorated with flowers that matched her bouquet, and the arch. That couple enjoyed their wedding in the cafe so much, that they came back every year to celebrate their anniversary.

Many of our customers had all their special parties at the restaurant, right up until we closed. I have so many fond memories of the great customers who chose us for all their special occasions. We attracted a different crowd than the typical Italian restaurants on Staten Island. We had the intellectuals, the politicians, show-business celebrities, musicians, and just regular, great family people.

We did not have ambulances and police cars in front of our restaurant. We did not attract the same crowd as the Mafia restaurants. We hosted birthdays, anniversaries, christenings, First Communions, and special events like wine dinners, pharmaceutical company dinners, Red Hat Society Christmas parties, reunions, and more.

One of my biggest clients was Dan Tomai. He owned a construction company that was based in Manhattan. I worked for him in the mid-nineties. The first job I did for him was a surprise birthday party for his wife Sonya in his home on Staten Island. He asked me to make steak tartare but I had never made it before. I researched it and decided the best place to buy the meat was from my German butcher, Walter, who owned the Karl Ehmer's meat market on New Dorp Lane.

Walter had a crush on me, and went out of his way to talk to me about food whenever I went into his store. He would take me in the back and into the walk-in refrigerator, showing me how he aged the beef. My favorite thing that he prepared was German Beef Rouladen. The meat was seasoned with salt and pepper, spread with mustard and one piece of bacon, one pickle spear, raw sliced onion and rolled up like a braciole and tied with cooking twine.

Walter had a crush on me, and went out of his way to talk to me about food whenever I went into his store.

My handsome friend Walter stopped being my friend when I married Les. He would not talk to me anymore. I broke his heart. The problem was that he was married even though he was attracted to me. The store closed when Walter could no longer afford the rent (after a new owner bought the building), so he went to work for one of the other Karl Ehmer's franchises in Brooklyn. Getting back to the steak tartare: I can sum up why people are intimidated by making this at home in just two words: raw beef. When you're not cooking it, the quality of the beef you buy matters more than ever, so you have to buy the highest-quality beef possible.

I got to the the Tomai house on a hot summer's day, and placed my beautiful beef tartare on the kitchen table. I told the guests that this had to be eaten immediately, but no one did. Mr. Tomai didn't cook, or care one bit about my beef tartare. I watched the meat turn gray where it sat on the kitchen table. You can't serve it in the refrigerator! I can't remember if he put his hand into the meat and tasted it that way. He just didn't understand what I went through to make the tartare perfect, and that I am a chef, and what he did broke my heart.

That was just the beginning of my association with the Tomais. After that, I catered all his big parties in the city. I had to meet with his wife, Sonya, to plan the menus. Because there was little seating at his office, and he

My Anisette Biscotti, Pignoli cookies, and struffoli.

invited a lot of guests, they wanted cocktail parties. I had to come up with new and exciting choices every year. It was very difficult because Sonya was not easy to please. She also never smiled.

For the events, I'd send a full staff of service people while I stayed in the restaurant and cooked for my customers. He would get permission to have the party on Broome Street where his office was located and the guests would stroll, eat, and drink. It was a very tough job for my bartenders and servers.

The food was heated in convection ovens inside a rented bus that was parked on the street. We used silver trays to pass the appetizers which had been prepared in advance at the cafe. The equipment needed was rented, as well as the linens, china, silverware, glasses, and barware.

After the stock market crashed and the recession began, everything changed for Mr. Tomai, both in his business, and personally. The Tomais divorced, and I did not see him for a long time, until he came into Carol's Cafe to have dinner several times with a new woman. I believe this was his third wife. I see Sonya in the hair salon from time to time, and she still doesn't smile.

I once got a call from a cooking student of mine, telling me that she needed to talk to me about planning a last-minute wedding. The wedding was originally going to take place the following year, but a terrible health emergency came up, and they needed to plan it immediately. I met with this beautiful young couple in the kitchen of the restaurant. They told me that her fiancé was terminally ill; he looked thin and gray and all his hair was gone.

The couple informed me that we only had a week to plan, cook, and make the wedding cake for them. The wedding would be held in the backyard of her mother's house. There also was a heat wave that week, and it was over a hundred degrees. I had to prepare everything to serve in the small kitchen of her mother's house. There was a small air conditioner in the window of the kitchen, but I did have to heat the food in the oven. I asked permission for the first time if I could wear white shorts and a sleeveless blouse instead of a warm chef's jacket.

The backyard was beautiful and it would be where the wedding cake would be presented. The priest came and the ceremony took place in the backyard under an arch covered with flowers. I watched and cried; as tears flowed down my face, I began to realize that I had a tremendous responsibility to make this an unforgettable day.

I watched and cried; as tears flowed down my face, I began to realize that I had a tremendous responsibility to make this an unforgettable day.

I wanted the wedding to be a day that this lovely family would never forget. I was alone in the kitchen and it was up to me to coordinate the dishes served.

The appetizers were a combination of hot and cold. They included: Shrimp Cocktail, Spicy Italian Sausage Stuffed Mushrooms, Fresh Salmon Mousse served with Toast Points, French Country Paté served with Cornichons, and Asparagus Vinaigrette. I remember serving fresh homemade manicotti filled with ricotta, fresh mozzarella, prosciutto, and Parmesan cheese, topped with my Sunday Sauce. The entrée was Veal Galantine with a Sicilian Spinach Stuffing, and a pan gravy. I cooked and Brian served, and it was perfect. The family came into the kitchen to tell me how they were enjoying the food and hugged me.

The menu was eclectic, and the desserts they chose were fantastic: Italian wedding cookies, Triple Chocolate Brownies, Hazelnut Biscotti, and Pignoli Cookies, which were placed on the banquet table before the presentation of the wedding cake. The wedding cake was placed on a separate round white pedestal table, and when the bride and groom cut the cake, the tears were flowing for this beautiful moment. Brian and I felt so good that we created a beautiful wedding for the couple. It was a day that we would never forget. Sadly, the groom died a month later.

Panettone

Grandma Prince made a similar holiday bread for Easter and Christmas.
I've adjusted her recipes for today's tastes and ingredients. This panettone is
unusually tasty.

12–14 cups unbleached all-purpose flour	1 teaspoon sugar
1 teaspoon salt	½ cup warm water, 105–115 degrees
1 pound dark raisins	1 pound unsalted butter, melted, then cooled until it's just warm
1 pound light brown sugar	2 cups scalded milk, cooled until warm
½ pound pignoli nuts	
½ pound citron, sliced into very thin layers and chopped fine	6 large eggs, room temperature, beaten
4 ounces fresh yeast, or 4 packages active dry yeast	Milk Wash: ½ cup lukewarm milk to brush the breads before baking

Sprinkle the yeast into a half cup of warm water, add a teaspoon of sugar, and mix
well. Let the yeast proof for 10 minutes.

In a 12-quart bowl, or a large pot (like Grandma used), sift the flour and salt together.
Start with 12 cups of flour. Add all dry ingredients: raisins, brown sugar, pignoli
nuts, and citron. Mix and knead very well, about 15 minutes, or until smooth and
elastic. If the dough is too wet, gradually add more of the remaining flour, up to
two cups, kneading to combine.

Add all liquids: dissolved yeast, melted butter, milk, and beaten eggs. Mix and
knead very well, about 15 minutes, or until smooth and elastic. In a lightly buttered
12-quart bowl (or you can divide dough in half, and use two smaller buttered bowls),
place the dough in the bowl, turning once. Cover the bowl tightly with plastic wrap
and let rise until double in volume. It may take two to four hours.

When fully doubled, punch down. The panettone can be made in various sizes.
Containers can consist of disposable baking pans, coffee cans, soufflé dishes, and
various size baking pans. Just be sure to butter them very well.

Fill them no more than halfway full. Divide the dough into sizes needed for the
pans. Shape and pinch the bottoms tightly and place in buttered pans. Cover with
tea towels and let rise to double. It may take about two hours. When risen, brush
with warm milk. Cut top with scissors, making little X's in a decorative way.

Brush with warm milk again. Bake in the middle of a preheated 300 degree oven for about 1 hour and 10 minutes, or until deep golden brown. Remove carefully from baking pans immediately and cool completely on a cooling rack, before wrapping.

Serve them the next day with sweet butter. Panettones freeze very well. Double wrap, defrost wrapped. To serve warm, wrap in foil and place in a 350 degree oven for about 10 minutes or until warm.

NOTE:

- If you prefer, you may make half the recipe.

Italian Meatballs in Tomato Sauce

*Makes about
53 meatballs*

3 pounds ground chuck (beef-to-fat ratio of 70/30 or 80/20)

9–12 large eggs, depending on the ground beef

About 1½ loaves of day-old seedless Italian bread, cut into 3- or 4-inch slices

Tepid water to soak the bread in, enough to cover

3 cups finely chopped onion, or more if desired

12 cloves minced garlic, more if desired

1 cup flat leaf parsley, chopped

18 heaping tablespoons, grated Romano cheese

9 heaping tablespoons, grated Parmesan cheese

Kosher salt and freshly ground black pepper, to taste

In a large bowl, soak the bread—crust and all—in the tepid water until soft, about 10 minutes. Squeeze all of the water out of the bread.

Place the ground chuck into a large 13-quart stainless steel bowl. Slightly beat the eggs in another bowl.

With your hands, quarter the ground chuck by making a mark. The size of that quarter (even a bit larger) will be the amount of bread that will be used in the meatball mixture.

The proportion of meat to bread is ¾ meat to ¼ bread. Now add all the rest of the ingredients. Mix well with your hands.

Heat a small frying pan until hot, add a teaspoon of olive oil. Make a tiny, one-inch patty and brown on both sides. Drain on paper towel. Taste for seasoning. Repeat this until the seasoning of the meatballs is very delicious.

Now you are ready to make the Meatballs. Roll into two-inch balls and place them on a waxed-paper lined sheet pan, and refrigerate while you prepare the Tomato Sauce.

Tomato Sauce for the Meatballs

12 (1 pound, 12 ounce) cans of Italian style plum tomatoes

Olive oil as needed

Unsalted butter if you like

12 cups finely chopped onions

30 cloves of minced garlic, or 30 teaspoons

½ cup minced shallots (optional)

Fresh basil to taste

Fresh oregano to taste (optional)

Dry oregano to taste, rubbed through your fingers. *Be careful, start with 2 teaspoons and then taste.*

Fresh chopped flat leaf parsley, to taste

Kosher salt and freshly ground black pepper, to taste

Large pinches of sugar to correct the acidity

About 2 cups dry red wine (not cooking wine)

Now you are ready to fry the Meatballs.

Heat a large heavy frying pan, until hot, add enough olive oil to a depth of ¼ of an inch, no more. When hot (not smoking) add your first meatball, lower the heat to a medium flame, spacing the meatballs at least an inch apart. Add one meatball at a time.

Turn the first meatball quickly as you finish adding all the meatballs that fit in the frying pan. Turn them when they are golden brown to the other side and cook that side until it is golden brown. Remove from pan and set aside on a sheet pan; do not pile or they will become soggy, or break.

When you are finished frying the Meatballs, add the onions to the same frying pan, so the onions will pick up all the flavors and bits left in the pan. If needed, add olive oil and butter. Season the onions with salt, pepper, and a large pinch of sugar.

Simmer slowly until golden brown, about 20 minutes; add garlic and simmer another eight minutes or so. If you like, you may add a half cup of shallots when you are adding the garlic.

Put tomatoes in a blender or food processor and pulse on and off until the tomatoes are very finely chopped. You can push the chopped tomatoes through a food mill if you want to remove the seeds. We removed the seeds and so did my mom.

Place the tomatoes in a large stock pot that conducts heat well. Add the red wine and reduce the wine to half. Add the onion, garlic, and red wine mixture to the tomatoes. Add the Meatballs and bring to a boil, then lower to a simmer. Add fresh and dry herbs, salt, and freshly ground black pepper and pinches of sugar to taste. You will add fresh and dry herbs and season again when the sauce is done.

Simmer uncovered for about three hours. Taste again and correct seasoning.

Sicilian Stuffed Rice Balls

You will need about six of Italian Meatballs in Tomato Sauce (page 102).
When you make your Meatballs, reserve them in lots of tomato sauce and freeze them for the rice balls. This saves lots of time.

Rice Mixture

2 cups Uncle Ben's Converted Rice (not instant)

1 quart boiling water

A sprig of Italian parsley and a few basil leaves. A sprig of fresh oregano, if available

Kosher salt to taste. *Start with a teaspoon.*

Black pepper to taste

¼ pounds unsalted butter

¼ pounds Romano cheese

¼ lbpounds Parmesan cheese

1 cup of finely chopped fresh mozzarella

4 egg yolks

Bring water, herbs, salt and pepper to a boil in a six-quart saucepan. Stir rice into boiling water, lower flame to a simmer. Cook, slowly, uncovered, I repeat, <u>uncovered</u>, until all water is absorbed. There should be a little dry crust on the bottom. Watch carefully, stirring occasionally. Remove sprigs of herbs and discard.

Add: ¼ pound unsalted butter, ¼ pound Romano cheese, ¼ pound Parmesan cheese and a cup of finely chopped fresh mozzarella. Fold into cooked rice.

Add four egg yolks to rice mixture. Taste for seasoning and adjust. Spread out on a platter. Reserve egg whites. Chill rice mixture for a couple of hours or overnight. Do not cover till cool. Place in freezer if you must for 10 minutes or so.

Assembly:

Italian unseasoned bread crumbs for coating

Reserved egg whites

About a cup of petite peas

Fresh mozzarella cut into ¼-inch pieces, about 2 cups

Reserved Meatballs in lots of tomato sauce, cooled and mashed with a fork

Parchment or tin foil on large sheet pan

Canola oil or vegetable oil of your choice for frying

In a small bowl, add the Meatballs with the tomato sauce. Gently stir in a small amount of petite peas. Set aside.

Arrange your ingredients in order for making the rice balls. You should make the rice balls about three inches round. Shape a portion of rice mixture in the palm of your hand. Make a cavity in the center. Fill with a portion of the meatball and pea mixture. Sprinkle with pieces of mozzarella. Cover with more of the rice mixture to form a three-inch ball.

Squeeze tightly! Your hands should turn red from the tomato sauce.

If they do not, then add more tomato sauce to the Meatballs. Wash hands occasionally. Dip each ball into a slightly beaten egg whites and roll in Italian unseasoned bread crumbs. Repeat until all rice mixture is done. Place on parchment paper and chill for an hour or so before frying. Do not cover!

Place oil in large frying pan over medium flame. The oil should come halfway up the side of the rice ball, no more or less. Bring the oil to 350 degrees. Sprinkle some bread crumbs in oil and when they sizzle and rise to the top the oil is ready. The oil must not be too hot or the rice balls will brown on the outside and be cold on the inside.

Place the rice balls, one at a time in the oil; wait for the previous one to sizzle. Slowly cook the first side until golden brown and turn over. The mozzarella should start to melt and come out of the sides a little. Do not crowd the pan. Repeat as necessary. You might have to change the oil if making more than one recipe.

I like to serve the rice balls with a little fresh tomato sauce around the rice balls. Garnish with fresh basil leaves. Serve immediately. You can reheat if you must in a 350 oven for 10 minutes or until hot.

You can freeze them, if you must. Wrap in tin foil. Thaw out in refrigerator and bake in a preheated 350-degree oven, until hot. Uncover the last five minutes.

Mahogany Chicken Wings

20 servings

1½ cups soy sauce

¾ cup dry sherry

¾ cup hoisin sauce

¾ cup Chinese plum sauce

18 scallions, finely chopped

6 large garlic cloves, minced

¾ cup cider vinegar

½ cup honey

7 pounds chicken wings

Parchment paper, cooking spray

In three-quart saucepan, combine all ingredients except wings. Bring to a boil and simmer for five minutes. Cool. While sauce is cooling, cut off wing tips and set aside for stockpot. Disjoint wings and place in large storage container. Pour cooled sauce over wings, cover, and refrigerate overnight.

Place oven racks in upper and lower thirds of oven and preheat to 375 degrees. Oil two large shallow roasting pans, or line with parchment paper, then spray with cooking spray.

Drain wings but do not discard sauce. Divide between prepared pans and bake uncovered for 1 to 1½ hours, basting about every 20 minutes with remaining sauce and turning to brown evenly. Be sure to switch the position of the pans halfway through cooking.

Remove wings from pans and allow to cool on cooling racks sprayed with cooking spray, or in disposable pans. When cool, wrap and store for up to three days. Serve at room temperature.

NOTE:

- Mahogany Chicken Wings freeze very well. If you prefer, you may make half a recipe.

Chocolate Roulade

Anisette-Vanilla Biscotti

Yield: Not enough

6 extra large eggs, room temperature

2 cups sugar

1 cup of vegetable shortening, packed, melted and cooled

2 tablespoons of pure vanilla extract

6 drops of anise oil, not extract. (You can purchase anise oil in an Italian grocery store or at a bakery or even a drugstore.)

4½ cups of all-purpose sifted flour (Heckers is recommended.)

2 big heaping teaspoons of baking powder, or a packed ⅛ of a cup

1 teaspoon of salt

Colored sprinkles

Preheat oven to 350 degrees.

Melt shortening in a small pan or a two-cup glass measuring cup in the microwave, just until melted. Check the measure carefully, it must come right to the one-cup line of the glass cup.

Beat eggs for 10 minutes at high speed.

Gradually add sugar, and beat another 10 minutes until thick and creamy.

Add the cooled, melted vegetable shortening.

Add the vanilla extract and anise oil. You can also decide to flavor the biscotti with just vanilla. Mix just to blend.

Carefully measure the flour by lightly spooning the sifted flour into the dry measuring cups and leveling off with a metal spatula. Set aside on wax paper. Use the wax paper to pour the flour into the egg mixture.

Add the flour with the salt and stir in on low speed. Scrape down with a rubber spatula.

Taste the batter for seasoning. It should be very tasty. Add whatever is needed and taste again.

Lightly grease three 18-inch cookie sheets.

With a large serving spoon drop batter in mounds, three inches apart. Sprinkle with colored sprinkles, lightly.

Bake about 15–20 minutes or until golden brown.

Remove cookie sheets from oven and cut mounds into one-inch slices with a sharp knife. Carefully lift with a metal spatula, and separate them to toast.

Retum to oven for five minutes, turn the cookies to one side and toast for another five minutes.

Turn to the other side and toast for another five minutes. If you prefer them softer, then toast for just 10 minutes. Watch that they do not get too dark. They should just be toasted lightly. Remove from pan carefully.

Cool completely on a rack and enjoy. Serve and store at room temperature in a tin or cover with plastic wrap. They will keep for days. Do not refrigerate or freeze.

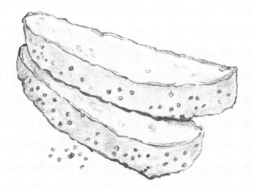

Manicotti Crepes

Crepe Batter

2 cups flour	2 cups water
1 teaspoon salt	Butter for skillet
4 eggs	

Preparation

In a bowl, sift the flour and salt together. Set aside.

Beat the eggs in a blender or with a portable electric beater until very well beaten (yellow and foamy). I use a Kitchen Aid mixer with a whisk attachment to beat the eggs.

Add the two cups of water to the eggs and beat in the blender or with a portable beater.

Pour the egg and water mixture into a bowl with the flour and stir until blended. Beat with portable mixer until smooth.

To make crepes: I recommend you purchase a seven-inch French crepe pan, or you can use a shallow, small skillet.

Heat pan and grease lightly with a little butter. With left hand, wearing a potholder mitt, hold skillet handle. With your right hand, pour a scant ¼ cup of the batter mixture into skillet while tipping pan with left hand to spread batter as thin and evenly as possible. Cook until dry on top and very lightly brown on bottom. (Do not turn over.)

Remove from pan to plate. Grease skillet only if necessary for the rest of crepes. Place crepes on cooling rack. You may place crepes in a pile after they have cooled off; they will not stick.

Cooking time for each crepe is about a minute. Refrigerate or freeze if you are not going to fill them right away.

Cheese Filling

2 lbs. ricotta cheese	1 whole egg
¾ lb. mozzarella cheese (chopped in small cubes)	2 egg yolks
¾ cup grated Parmesan and Locatelli cheese, combined, *or you may use just one of the cheeses.*	2 tablespoons chopped fresh parsley
	⅛ teaspoon black pepper
	¼ teaspoon salt, or to taste
	½ cup chopped ham or prosciutto

Blend all ingredients together.

In a large shallow baking dish, assemble crepes (example: cookie sheet).

Spread two tablespoons of filling on each crepe in the center and overlap each edge.

Press edges gently together to prevent the filling from falling out. Place filled manicotti (which resemble little muffs) side by side in a baking dish in which you have spread a little tomato sauce.

Cover crepes with tomato sauce of your choice. Sprinkle with grated cheese.

Bake uncovered in a preheated 375–400 degree oven for 10–15 minutes.

Serve hot.

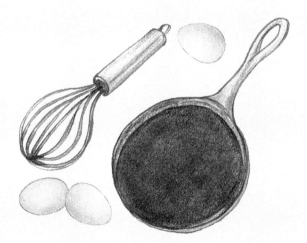

I was thrilled to have
a conversation with
James Beard.

James Beard

WHEN JAMES BEARD WAS still alive, I was a guest in his home, and sat with him in his kitchen. I chatted with him as he sat on a high stool, holding court. His pug dog, Percy, was always at his feet. Whenever James placed his champagne glass on the floor, Percy lapped up the champagne. Eventually, Percy fell over drunk. I loved that we cooked food for the special diet that James' doctor had put him on, but he just pushed it aside, and ate the food that all the chefs had prepared. James especially liked my Sicilian Pizza that I made into sections with different toppings, such as White Clam Sauce, Fresh Roasted Red Peppers, Broccoli Rabe and Wild Mushrooms with Homemade Mozzarella, and a garlicky Plum Tomato Sauce.

My Sicilian Pizza with all the toppings that James Beard enjoyed.

There was an Italian cooking teacher there named Anna Teresa Callen. She did not like the attention my pizza was getting, so she went around telling everyone, "That isn't Italian." I was born in Brooklyn, not Italy, and was not married to a CBS television producer like she was. When *Bon Appétit* magazine called me and said that they were going to feature me in the magazine with my Italian recipes, she found out about it. They called me and canceled my opportunity because she complained, and said that I was not really Italian. She was quoted as saying, "Americans do terrible things to Italian food." She was featured instead of me. I cried my eyes out! I was beginning to realize that it was very important who you knew. Even though I wasn't born in Italy, I was very proud that everyone loved my Pignoli Cookies when I brought them to the meetings of the New York Association of Cooking Teachers.

My Pignoli Cookies.

Pignoli Cookies

1 pound of good quality almond paste *(Note: Solo or Odense brands are not recommended, they are poor quality, and will yield a flatter cookie)*

1¾ cups sugar

4 extra large egg whites, slightly beaten

½ teaspoon almond extract

About ¾ cup pignoli nuts (pine nuts)

Preheat oven to 350 degrees.

Line two 18-inch cookie sheets with parchment paper.

Glue the parchment paper down with a few drops of the lightly beaten egg whites.

Place almond paste in a large bowl of an electric mixer, and beat for a few minutes to smooth it out. Do not overbeat, or the almond paste will dry out.

Add sugar and slightly beaten egg whites, and beat on medium speed for about five minutes, or until creamy.

Drop batter by rounded teaspoon onto the lined cookie sheets, one inch apart. Or you can use a small ice cream scoop so the cookies will be the same size.

Place about 8–10 pignoli nuts on the top of each cookie. Lightly press pignoli nuts into the cookies.

Bake about 10 minutes, and carefully turn the cookie sheet around in the oven, and bake another few minutes, until the cookies are golden brown on the bottom, but very lightly colored on top. Do not over bake or under bake.

Cool completely on the parchment paper. Remove carefully with a thin metal spatula.

Store in an airtight container in the refrigerator.

Serve at room temperature, after sifting confectioners' sugar on top of the cookies.

NOTES:

- Almond paste is available for purchase in Italian specialty markets, such as Pastosa Ravioli's.

- Amazon sells almond paste. Check reviews and buy the best.

The James Beard House

I WAS ASKED TO do a private dinner at the James Beard House for 70 guests in October 2003. It ended up being 90 guests. I had no idea what an honor it was to be the first woman chef to do that. I also had no idea how difficult and exhausting it would be. I wanted to create a new entrée for the dinner. I created an original recipe: Sautéed Medallions of Venison with Caramelized Onions and Oyster Mushrooms in a Port Wine Sauce. Len Pickell told me that if the meat was changed to filet mignon, the New York Beef Council would provide the meat free of charge. That filet mignon entrée became a classic dish at Carol's Cafe, and one that I would teach many times over the years at my cooking school.

James Beard in his home celebrating his birthday.

Julia Child and James Beard sitting together at his birthday party.

The menu for the James Beard House began with appetizers: Maple-Roasted Stuffed Bacon Rolls, Spicy Italian Sausage Stuffed Mushrooms, Miniature Crab Cakes with Sherry Wine Sauce, Homemade Sicilian Pizza with Caramelized Onions, Barbecued Duck with Ginger and Sesame Seeds, and one of my signature dishes, Mussels in White Wine.

The salad I chose was Savory Autumn Salad with Poached Pears, Blue Cheese, and Candied Walnuts. The Brioche Rolls took three days of preparation. I made what is still to this day my most famous pasta dish: Penne with Seared Shrimp and Broccoli Rabe, with many cloves of garlic slowly roasted in a cast-iron pan, and Potato Torte, that is delicious but so time-consuming to make.

How did I do that in James Beard's kitchen? The kitchen was small, with only two commercial stoves. One of the stoves did not have an exhaust. I had to sear filet mignon for 90 guests. The smoke traveled through the three floors into the dining rooms. The wait staff was complaining about the smoke. Of course there was smoke, but there wasn't a thing I could do about it. The maître d' said, with a sneer on his face, "Would you hurry this up?" We had just served six appetizers, and my famous mussels, having the use of only two ovens.

I finished making my Filet of Beef in a Port Wine Sauce, with the Potato Torte as the side dish. I had my daughter Terri, and chefs Sal and Benny to help me. It was time for dessert, and we had to portion the Apple Crumb Pies, whip the Chantilly Cream, and then decorate the plates with Vanilla Bean Crème Anglaise. The finale was the assorted pastries. These included Triple Chocolate Brownies, Italian Sesame Cookies and my famous Pignoli Cookies, all served with a dessert wine selected by Len Pickell. He had chosen all the wines that were served with the dinner that night. Len asked me to go to each floor and take a bow. I was so exhausted, and I don't know or even remember what I said, I just heard the applause.

When I got back to the restaurant, I recall that I said, "I will be back." I climbed up the 38-step stairway to my apartment, and walked into my bedroom. I fell on my bed and that's all I remember.

After the event, I received a beautiful acknowledgement from the James Beard House, with a pencil drawing of James Beard, thanking me for my outstanding contribution to the Foundation. I hung that plaque proudly at Carol's Cafe until I retired.

Potato Torte

Serves 12

4 cups heavy cream

1 large egg

2 large egg yolks

Kosher salt and freshly ground pepper, to taste

Ancho chile powder to taste

8 large Idaho baking potatoes, peeled and sliced very thin

1 large onion minced. *Sprinkle with a big pinch of sugar and salt and slowly sauté in a couple of tablespoon of butter and olive oil, add a couple of sprigs of herbs if you like.*

1 teaspoon garlic, minced

1 teaspoon fresh-squeezed, strained lemon juice

Freshly ground nutmeg to taste

½ cup Parmesan cheese

1 tablespoon Dijon mustard or to taste

1 10-ounce package frozen whole leaf spinach. *Defrost, follow instructions on package. Cool, squeeze dry and chop fine in food processor or by hand. Or use about one pound of fresh spinach, washed and dried very well. Chop fine and reserve.*

½ pound Gruyère or imported Swiss, grated or to taste

1 cup freshly grated Parmesan cheese, or to taste

¾ pound baked ham or Boar's Head ham, sliced very thin

4 large roasted red peppers, *covered for 30 minutes with plastic wrap to steam. It makes it much easier to remove the black skin. Never wash, it removes flavor. When cool, peel and remove the seeds and cut into one-inch slices.*

6 cloves of garlic, smashed

In a large bowl, combine egg, egg yolks, cream, salt and pepper. Rinse the potato in cold water and pat dry with towels or paper towels. Add the potatoes to the seasoned cream mixture, stirring until they are well-coated. Taste the potato for seasoning, to see if it needs salt and pepper.

In a frying pan, cook the onion with a little sugar, ancho, salt, butter, and olive oil. Cook until sweet and golden, about 10 minutes or until golden brown. Add the one teaspoon of minced garlic and cook another few minutes. Add the defrosted spinach, nutmeg, lemon juice, salt and pepper. Taste for seasoning. If using fresh spinach, cook just until wilted. Add the Parmesan cheese, and mustard to taste. Taste and adjust the seasoning. Set aside. This can be done the night before.

Dress the roasted peppers with olive oil, balsamic vinegar, six cloves of smashed garlic, fresh basil, parsley, fresh oregano or dried oregano, salt, pepper, a pinch of sugar; set aside at least an hour. Taste for seasoning. Refrigerate, covered, overnight, if you have the time.

Butter a 9×13×2 inch pan. Drain the potatoes. Place a layer of potatoes and grated cheese and a grinding of black pepper in the bottom of the pan. Drizzle some of the cream mixture over this layer and top with ham.

Repeat the potato, cheese, and cream layer. Top with the spinach mixture.

Repeat the potato and cheese layer of potatoes and cheese and cream; add a layer of roasted peppers and a layer of potatoes, cheese, and cream.

Top with additional grated cheese.

Preheat the oven to 325 degrees.

Bake the torte on a baking sheet for two hours. Check after one hour and if it is getting too dark, loosely cover with a piece of tin foil. The torte should be quite firm when pressed with a spatula. It is very important to eat a slice of potato from the middle to see if the potatoes are cooked thoroughly. They should not be hard. The top will be very well browned.

The dish is served hot as a main course or at room temperature and sliced thin. It is better the second day, reheats perfectly, and freezes well.

NOTE:

- I like to roast my peppers right on the burners, turning frequently until the skin turns black. Then cover the peppers in a bowl with plastic wrap for at least 30 minutes. Do not wash the pepper, just peel the black skin. Remove the seeds and slice.

- For my customers who do not eat ham or pork products, we use thinly sliced turkey breasts as a substitute.

Sautéed Medallions of Filet Mignon

This is the entrée recipe I developed for the dinner at the James Beard House. I wanted to use wild game but the Beef Council that paid for the filet mignon wanted us to use beef. It became a classic entrée at Carol's Cafe.

Sautéed Medallions of Filet Mignon with Caramelized Onions, Oyster Mushrooms in a Port Wine Sauce

Serves one

6–8 ounce filet mignon, cut crosswise into two steaks

Kosher salt and freshly ground black pepper, to taste

Ancho chile to season beef

Extra virgin olive oil

1 tablespoon unsalted butter, or more if needed

1 cup sliced onions

Pinch of sugar

1 sage leaf, ripped

1 cup oyster mushrooms

2 tablespoon minced shallots

1 teaspoon minced garlic

½ cup fine port, to flame

1 cup of beef stock, or whatever is needed

Beef glaze, about ½ tablespoon

Fresh herbs: sprig of fresh tarragon, 2 tablespoons chopped chives, and fresh parsley to taste

½ tablespoon Dijon mustard

½ cup heavy cream

Preheat cast-iron frying pan. For individual portions, I used a 7- or 8-inch pan. Season beef with salt, pepper, and ancho chile on both sides. Drizzle both sides with olive oil. Place beef medallions in pan and sear over very high heat; when nicely browned turn to the other side and repeat. I recommend medium rare, never more. We knew by touch what the temperature of the beef was. Use an instant chef's thermometer, if you have to. Set aside on a rack with a dish underneath to catch the precious juices. Reserve pan!

To the same pan, add olive oil and butter, enough to cook the onions. Add the onions, sprinkle with pinch of salt and sugar. Cook until onions are caramelized, stirring continuously. They should be golden brown. Add oyster mushrooms, cook until colored. Add shallots, garlic, and fresh herbs. Cook another few minutes. Flame with port. Reduce until the port is a glaze. Season with salt and pepper. Add heavy cream, and reduce. Taste for seasoning and correct. Add fresh parsley.

Place beef and juices back in pan and bring to a simmer. Place sauce on plate and place beef medallions askew. Garnish with sprigs of fresh herbs.

This is what I came up with for customers who wanted something healthier.

Grilled Filet Mignon with Caramelized Onions, Wild Mushrooms, Red Bell Peppers and Cherry Peppers

Serves one

6–8 ounce filet mignon, cut crosswise into two steaks

Kosher salt and freshly ground black pepper, to taste

Ancho chile (optional)

1 cup red onions, sliced ¼ inch thick

1 cup wild mushrooms, sliced

1 red bell pepper, sliced

Extra virgin olive oil

Balsamic vinegar, reduced

Fresh herbs: rosemary, thyme, sage, and oregano to taste

Pinch of sugar

Freshly ground black pepper

Hot or sweet cherry peppers, to taste

Preheat the oven to 400 degrees.

Season beef on both sides and drizzle generously with olive oil. Set aside for 10 minutes.

Prepare vegetables: Slice red onions ¼ inch thick, slice mushrooms, slice red bell pepper lengthwise about ¼ inch thick and marinate with extra virgin olive oil, reduced balsamic vinegar, sprigs of fresh herbs (rosemary, thyme, sage, and fresh oregano). Season with salt, sugar, and freshly ground black pepper. Set aside. Add cherry peppers to taste after the vegetables are caramelized.

The amounts are determined by how many pieces of beef you are going to grill. For each piece, slice one-half onion, pepper, and a cup of mushrooms. Sprigs of herbs or what you like.

Preheat grill pan. It must be hot. Hold your hand over the pan. If you have to remove it after four seconds, it is hot enough. Spray with organic Pam. Place beef on grill, one at a time. Cook until marks form. Quarter turn to make perfect marks. Turn over and repeat.

Place beef in oven to finish cooking to desired temperature. It will take eight minutes for medium. Check temperature with chef's thermometer: 120 degrees for rare, 127 degrees for medium rare, 130–135 degrees for medium, 140 for medium well, and 150–160 for well and very well.

While the meat is finishing in oven, cook vegetables in the same pan the meat was grilled on. Add the marinated vegetables and toss and turn until golden brown. Add the cherry peppers and toss for one minute or so. Serve grilled meat with vegetables on top. At the restaurant, I would garnish with a flaming sprig of rosemary.

Sesame Cookies

Makes about six dozen cookies

8 cups sifted all-purpose flour

1¾ cups granulated sugar

3 teaspoons baking powder

1 teaspoon salt

1½ sticks unsalted butter

6 ounces vegetable shortening

2 large eggs, slightly beaten

1 cup milk, plus a little extra in a bowl

3 teaspoons pure vanilla extract

1 to 1½ pounds toasted sesame seeds, rinsed in a fine strainer and kept damp *(Note: toasted sesame seeds may be found at some Italian specialty stores.)*

Preheat oven to 325 degrees. Sift together flour, sugar, baking powder, and salt into a large bowl. With a pastry blender or two knives, cut in the butter and shortening until mixture is like lumpy cornmeal. Add eggs, milk, and vanilla, and stir together with a large spoon.

With your hands, work the dough just until it comes together into a ball. Take a handful of dough, squeeze it together with your hands, and roll it out with your fingers to make a sausage shape, about ½-inch thick. Cut dough into two-inch logs.

Dip logs in bowl of milk and then roll in the damp sesame seeds. Place on cookie sheets, allowing enough space in between the cookies for expansion. Bake in the center of the oven for about 45 minutes, or until golden brown. Remove from oven and cool on a wire rack. When completely cooled, place in an airtight container. They keep in the refrigerator for a few weeks, or in the freezer for even longer.

The James Beard Tribute at Rockefeller Center

I WAS INVITED BY Borough President Guy V. Molinari's office to participate in the American Chef's Tribute to James Beard. This was to benefit Citymeals on Wheels. A total of 28 chefs joined efforts in the "movable feast," a tasting buffet celebrating "100 Years of New York Eating" in the gardens of Rockefeller Plaza.

*Me and Craig at Rockefeller
Center with my Ode To
Ebinger's Cakes*

I was inspired by my childhood memories and since I am also a pastry chef, I chose to treat the 1,200 New Yorkers attending the gala with my interpretation of one of my "Ode to Ebinger's" cakes.

I was quoted in the newspaper as saying, "I thought of Ebinger's right away because of its significance to me.... When you mention Ebinger's to guests, their faces light up. From the moment I was born, I remember my mother went almost every single day to buy cake at Ebinger's. I always remember the variety of cakes, one more delicious than another."

Everyone mentions Ebinger's Blackout Cake, but there is another Ebinger's favorite that I loved! A yellow butter layer cake filled with chocolate buttercream and a hard chocolate glaze that was sold as an eight-inch layer cake. For the hordes of the gala guests, I prepared 30 sheet cakes. The cake had to be served at room temperature, so transporting the cakes by van to Manhattan did no harm.

Les drove the van to Rockefeller Center and when we got to where we had to make the turn, the police stopped us. President Clinton was in town and streets were blocked. I will never forget Les storming out of the van and demanding we turn into that street. After all, he was a parole officer. He explained to the police that we had cakes in the van and they were for a benefit for Citymeals on Wheels, which provides weekly meals for the city's homebound elderly. The police allowed the van to get through.

I cut the cakes into squares, and was concerned about serving the cakes outdoors, but they held up beautifully. I was particularly proud of the fact that all the most famous chefs there tasted and enjoyed the cakes—chefs like Wolfgang Puck, Jean-Georges Vongerichten, and Marc Forgione.

Unfortunately, when Les loaded my camera with film to take pictures of the event, he put it in backwards and so all the photos taken with the great chefs were lost. Craig Olsen, a young cook who was part of our kitchen staff, was there to help, and did send me a couple of pictures of our table, and the three of us: Les, Craig, and myself.

Ode to Ebinger's Yellow Layer Cake with Chocolate Buttercream and Regal Chocolate Glaze

Yellow Butter Cake

*Yield: One 9-inch
2-layer cake*

Prep Time: 25 minutes

Cooking Time: 30 minutes

3 cups sifted all-purpose flour, *lightly spoon sifted flour into a stainless steel measuring cup, level off with edge of metal spatula*

1 tablespoon baking powder

¾ teaspoon salt

¾ cup (1½ sticks) unsalted butter, at room temperature

2 cups granulated sugar, sifted

4 large eggs, at room temperature

1 cup whole milk

2 full teaspoons pure vanilla extract

Preheat the oven to 350 degrees.

Spray two 9×2 round cake pans with baking spray or grease, and flour them. I like to line them with rounds of parchment, and spray again.

In a medium bowl, whisk together the flour, baking powder, and salt.

In a larger bowl, cream the butter for five minutes. Beat in the sugar and mix until fluffy, about 10 minutes. Beat in the eggs, one at a time.

Add the dry ingredients in two parts. Mix in half of the dry ingredients, then half of the milk, then the rest of the dry ingredients, and then the rest of the milk and the vanilla. Be sure to scrape the sides of the bowl as you are mixing to incorporate all the ingredients. Do it quickly, do not over mix. Taste for seasoning and add more vanilla if needed, carefully.

Divide the batter between the two prepared cake pans. Bake for about 30 minutes, or until a toothpick inserted into the center comes out clean. Let cool for 20 to 25 minutes, then run a spatula along the edge of each pan and invert onto a rack to cool completely. Be sure to peel off the parchment paper.

If you are going to freeze the cakes, leave the parchment paper on, but remember to peel it off and discard.

Your cakes are ready to frost, or you can wrap them and keep them overnight until you are ready to frost your cake.

continued

Ode to Ebinger's Yellow Layer Cake, *continued*

Chocolate Buttercream Filling

1 cup unsalted butter (room temperature)	5 ounces good quality, unsweetened chocolate, *melted over a double boiler, and left to cool after you shut off the flame.*
1 cup plus 2 tablespoon sugar, or to taste	2 teaspoons pure vanilla extract, or to taste
	6 large eggs at room temperature

Cream butter and sugar until light and fluffy, about 10 minutes. Beat in chocolate and vanilla, then add eggs, one at a time, beating two minutes after each egg. Continue to beat until sugar is thoroughly dissolved; taste for seasoning and adjust if necessary. Chill at least an hour or overnight, or, if you like, freeze for later use.

Regal Chocolate Glaze

Makes about 2¼ cups

18 ounces of semisweet or bittersweet fine quality chocolate, chopped (or use tablets)	9 ounces (18 tablespoons) unsalted butter of good quality
	18 tablespoons water (the water should be 120 degrees)

Chop the chocolate into small pieces. Place the butter in the top of a double boiler and add the chocolate. Fill the bottom of the double boiler with about three inches of hot water, about 140 degrees.

Place the top over the bottom and melt the chocolate and butter until melted. Stir once to combine. Add water, which should be about 120 degrees, and stir until smooth.

Pour the mixture over the surface you wish to glaze while the glaze is warm and liquid. Place the cake on a rack with a cookie sheet underneath to catch the drippings. For this cake, I like to pour it over the cake two or three times to glaze the cake completely. Let sit and dry, before refrigerating.

Do not cover with plastic wrap. Use a dome not touching the glaze.

If you have leftover glaze in the refrigerator, place it in a bowl over hot tap water and bring it to a pouring consistency. Can be frozen.

To finish the cake

I like to cut each yellow layer cake into two layers. It is easier if you freeze the cakes for at least an hour.

Trim the outside of the yellow cakes after filling them with chocolate buttercream. They should line up perfectly. This is so the chocolate glaze will cover the cake perfectly. Chill before covering the cake with glaze. Be sure to brush off any excess crumbs. You should have three layers of buttercream. This is a high cake, so serve small wedges. Clean your sharp knife each time you make a cut.

Gracie Mansion

I WAS ASKED TO COOK for a dinner to benefit the Gracie Mansion Conservancy on Monday, February 28, 2011. Gracie Mansion was built in 1799, but since 1942, the house has served as the official residence of the mayor of New York.

The kitchen in Gracie Mansion. You can see some of the Maple-Roasted Bacon-Wrapped Chicken Liver Rolls that I prepared for the event.

The participating chefs and purveyors were asked to come for breakfast at Gracie Mansion at 8:00 AM after a big snowstorm in New York City, to meet Mayor Bloomberg, and take group pictures with him. I went with my daughter Terri and Carol Ann.

When we were asked our names, our location, and the name of our restaurant, the mayor began to tell a story about his last visit to Staten Island. He said the borough president took him to a restaurant on Bay Street called Vida's. Vida is a lovely, talented woman chef, who had opened a restaurant from scratch. In his whiney voice, he mocked the restaurant by describing it as having linoleum floors and tables. He said the food was okay. I thought to myself, how nervous she must have been to have him there, and as usual, Staten Island is being put down. I don't think anyone understands what it is like to start a business with nothing. Mayor Bloomberg is very short and so am I. All the short people stood next to him in the group photo. I suppose it was to make him appear taller.

For the event, I made my Maple-Roasted Bacon-Wrapped Chicken Liver Rolls, which are quite complicated. You are kind of making a chicken liver paté meatball, and wrapping each small hors d'oeuvre in bacon, then roasting them until the bacon is crisp. The night before, at Carol's Cafe, I worked all through the night by myself to prepare them. My staff went home and left me there. This was not their job! When I got to Gracie Mansion with all my many trays, we were directed to a pretty green kitchen with two commercial ovens. All the chefs were crowded into the kitchen, waiting their turn to use the oven.

I was in the kitchen with Alex Guarnaschelli (executive chef-owner of Butter, and an Iron Chef on the Food Network). She brought two very nice chefs with her to cook her appetizer. Husband-and-wife team Anna Klinger and Emiliano Coppa, owners of Al Di La in Brooklyn were also in the kitchen. Anna was so nice to me. I told her how much I wanted to go to her restaurant, but on the night I wanted to go, she wasn't there. All of the chefs were told that Mayor Bloomberg was going to come into the kitchen to thank us, but of course he never did.

I did receive this note of thanks from the Gracie Mansion Conservancy on behalf of Mayor Bloomberg:

Dear Carol,

We cannot thank you enough for your generosity and participation in our benefit, the Mayor and his staff at City Hall are equally appreciative of your invaluable support.

All of our guests enjoyed the celebration enormously. The combination of a unique and historic setting and an exceptional menu—your maple-roasted bacon wrapped chicken liver rolls were absolutely delicious—provided for a truly memorable evening. The dinner was a resounding financial success as well, raising much-needed money for the restoration and upkeep of one of our City's most beloved landmark treasures.

Please know that we would be delighted to offer a special tour of Gracie Mansion to members of your family, friends, or colleagues as another way of saying thank you for all your help with our dinner. We look forward to hearing from you and to welcoming you back to the house sometime soon.

With gratitude and all warmest regards,

Susan Danilow, Director
Diana Toole, Curator

You are so inspiring!

Joe's Health

DURING THE TIME I WAS taking John Clancy's cooking classes in Manhattan, my husband Joe had triple bypass surgery. It was the first of his many heart procedures. When I asked John Clancy if I could make up the class because my husband was having a triple bypass, he said, "Absolutely not." I could not believe it, but I learned that day that John Clancy was strictly a businessman. It taught me a valuable lesson. I had to make strict business rules, stick to them, and print them in my cooking-school brochures.

Joe and me celebrating our 25th wedding anniversary at Il Cortile in Little Italy.

Joe's father had had a heart attack in his fifties, later dying of a stroke at only 57 years old. I adored my father-in-law, and was frightened when he suffered his stroke at my kitchen table while having dinner with us. I was pregnant with my son Joey at the time, and while bending over to serve him dinner, I saw his face become all distorted, and I was horrified. When I went to see him in the hospital, he was delirious and was talking to his dead mother, asking her to help him. I was so sad to see this sweet man suffering. When he died, I was heartbroken, and he never got a chance to meet his first grandson.

Joe realized something was wrong when he had an angina attack in the city, and was told by the telephone company doctor (where he worked) to see a heart specialist. Joe was 47 years old and did not want anyone at work to know about his health problems. When he could not even carry his attaché case, he decided the bypass surgery was his only option.

Joe's cardiologist in Staten Island wouldn't even speak to me. He felt that he didn't even need to tell Joe's wife about the seriousness of what was about to happen to him. I remember the feeling of how this male chauvinist pig of a heart doctor treated me, as if I was of no concern to him. Years later, this doctor's wife took afternoon cooking lessons with me, and she could only take them if she had permission from him. I remember how meek she was, and how later on, he left her for another woman.

Because Joe's heart operation was a new procedure at the time, he decided to have his surgery done at NYU in New York City, one of New York's leading heart hospitals. Thankfully the surgeon that performed the operation on Joe was not the same doctor from Staten Island. Joe's surgeon told me that his surgery would last many hours, and I should not wait at the hospital. He told me to keep busy by going to the cooking class that I was scheduled to take, which I did.

I could not see Joe after his procedure until the next day, because he was in intensive care, all hooked up to monitors and machines. I drove to the city in the snow, terrified, with my neighbor, Ann Starace, who had a better sense of direction than I did. When I saw Joe, I was shocked. He was all hooked up to these monitors, and was intubated. He was unconscious, and did not know we were there. I did not know how serious Joe's surgery was, because I was not informed.

When they removed the tube from his mouth, Joe cried, and I was so relieved. Three weeks later, Joe came home. Uncle John (who was my favorite of Joe's uncles) went and picked Joe up from the hospital. When they came home, they sat in the kitchen while I made them lunch. Joe watched

Terri, Joe, and Maria at my parents' house in Brooklyn in 1979.

Terri's wedding at the Alice Austen house on November 15, 1985, with my son Joe, my daughter Maria, Terri, and Joe.

as I grilled him a Genoa salami, imported Swiss cheese and sliced tomato sandwich. When they began to eat, Joe cried and said that it was the most delicious thing he had ever eaten. I was so shocked that he actually complimented me, and showed affection, that my eyes filled with tears. In those days, no one told us about how bad smoking was for you, or that you should watch what you ate. Joe had no idea how worried I was about him.

For at least a month, Joe sat in the recliner and was terrified about his health, having anxiety attacks. I became so nervous that I got hives all over my body worrying about him. I think when he went back to work, he began to feel like his old self. He began to travel a lot, go out with the "boys," and drink a lot for his job. I had to resume all the responsibilities for my family. Joe never went to open school week, and never saw them perform in dance recitals or school plays. I think some of the best times I had with my children was when Joe was away. But you can never make up for those lost times. The kids and I laughed a lot, and it was more relaxing.

I treasure those moments, and I can still see Maria dressed in a pink ballerina costume, lying in the box that we made, her head coming out on one side, and her feet coming out of the other, with my son Joe dressed as a magician wearing a black top hat, and sawing her in half. The audience was enthralled and it made everyone laugh. It was a wonderful day!

Photo taken by the Staten Island Advance *when I first opened my retail store.*

Moving to Richmond Road

AS MY BUSINESS BECAME more successful, my neighbors started to complain about the parking situation on our block. The students were taking up all the parking spots. I realized that it was time to take my cooking school to the next level. I had outgrown my home and I needed to find a bigger space.

The front of Carol's Cuisine at our new location on Richmond Road.

*Another view of my
gourmet shop.*

Once I knew that I had to expand my business, my husband Joe and I
started looking at several properties, one of them being a building on Clove
Road. I was not thinking of a restaurant! I just wanted a building that could
house my cooking school, and a retail store for cooking equipment and
gourmet food items.

One of my Tuesday morning cooking students, Noreen Ropas, wanted
to become involved in my business and work in the store. I was so busy
working that I left it up to Joe. I was on my way to the airport (where I was
going to San Francisco to attend the annual meeting of the International
Association Cooking Professionals) and Joe told me that the deal was off. He
didn't tell me what happened and I never asked him why. Many years later,
Noreen came to dinner at the restaurant, and she informed me that Joe was a
terrible man. She was with a group of her friends, and didn't want to discuss
it in detail. All Noreen would say was that my husband was a philanderer.
I told her that we were divorced, and he never told me the reason the deal
didn't go through. I am still troubled by this, and still wonder to this day
what happened.

That building we looked at became Mauro Graphics where my daughter
Terri ended up working years later, framing works of art. I wound up buying
my building on Richmond Road from Otto Vitale, and once again, Joe was
very involved in every aspect of my business.

When I bought the building, I didn't get the backyard, but I got the
crumbling staircase going up to the backyard, and the crumbling cement
wall holding up the backyard. According to Joe, I would not get the building
unless I agreed to these terms. I got four apartments in great need of repair.
One apartment had a fire and one apartment had an alcoholic woman living
there with her daughter who was mentally challenged from all of the alcohol

Terri and me teaching a class before we opened the restaurant.

her mother consumed while she was pregnant. She stuccoed the whole apartment instead of painting it. The apartment was in horrible disrepair. Jeff, my son-in-law, became gravely ill renovating that apartment (without getting paid, as he was helping me out because I didn't have the money to pay someone at the time). He developed a severe lung infection that turned into bilateral bacterial pneumonia, permanently damaging his heart, and resulting in congestive heart failure.

Otto Vitale promised me that he was going to make the two apartments on the Four Corners Road side of the building, into offices. Otto Vitale ended up leaving Staten Island because of an issue with his real-estate partner. He moved to Florida and the never-ending nightmares of those apartments continued until I sold my building. I never had the money to fix the building. I had to pay Joe $580 a month in the divorce settlement for five years because he hid his income and pension from me in the divorce proceedings. I still don't know what the truth is about that building, but I know that I was never given what I was promised.

In 1989, my dream for my cooking school was to offer degree programs to students. In order to do that , the school had to be licensed by the state of New York. Obtaining a license was a complex procedure. An application form had to be accompanied by the company's certificate of incorporation, recent profit and loss statement, and balance sheet, diagrams of the school, certificate of occupancy, and a surety bond in the amount of $20,000 forwarded to the Department of Education for review and approval. If all went well, the entire process would take six months.

The license application fee was $500, made payable to the state, along with a $100 licensing fee for each teacher, and a $100 fee for an agent for the

*Joe and me sitting
in the back yard in
happier times..*

school. Obtaining the required surety bond also involved an expense, but my lawyer, Linda M. Ryan, was one of my cooking students and bartered with me for cooking lessons. Surety companies consider such bonds a risk and therefore required cash collateral in the amount of $20,000. After these items had been approved by the state, the second part of the process started. They required that a detailed description of the school's curriculum be prepared and submitted for approval.

I did not have the money I needed because I was going through a divorce. After 30 years of marriage, I left Joe without leaving a note because of his infidelity, and because he had become even more mentally and physically abusive towards me than before. When I decided my marriage was over, I slept in Maria's bed that summer while she was backpacking in Europe. My view from her bed was a large picture of Prince that hung on her closet door. I would come out of her room when Joe went to work. Then I would go to work at the building, and I would come home when Joe was sleeping. One morning, he shouted, "When are you coming out!"

I chose this sleeping routine after Joe threw a portable television at me because he said it was too loud. It hit the hall wall, just missing my head. He threw it so hard that it smashed apart. One day, Joe Jr. had just finished mowing the lawn, and instead of thanking him and complimenting Joey about what a good job he had done, Joe as usual just started putting Joey down. I asked him why he would do that, and in response, he threw a can opener at me that just missed my eye, and made a dent on the front of the refrigerator.

Joe had hired a private eye to check on me during this time. I suspected it was a man in my "Tech and Theory I" class, who looked like he came out of central casting for a retired police officer. At the end of the three-hour

The new Carol's Cuisine.

class, he said he needed to speak to me. I knew he wasn't interested in learning how to cook. He said my husband hired him to spy on me to see if I was fooling around. He had been following me around for weeks. He said he told Joe I wasn't doing anything but working. Joe was so angry that he didn't find anything, that he refused to pay him. I could not believe it, but it was true.

Joe wanted his girlfriend, and not a divorce. He was drinking heavily, and one day he drove me to work. The car swerved back and forth on Richmond Road so much that I was shaking when I got out. The most shocking incident was when one of my tenants (who confessed to me that she was a confirmed alcoholic) walked into my kitchen. She said, "I have to tell you something. Your husband spends his time drinking with me in my kitchen." She wanted me to know that Joe wanted to sleep with her. I was so shocked that he needed to do that! He picked a woman who was beneath my dignity. He should have gone for help, but he did not believe in going to a psychiatrist.

Another incident with Joe that really upset me, was the way he treated me after I had catered an off-premises wedding. When I got home from the wedding, I was drenched to the bone from the extreme summer heat. Joe was sitting on the recliner and would not talk to me. He was very angry that I did not get home sooner.

All of a sudden, I felt sick to my stomach. I knew that Joe couldn't even understand how important this wedding was to the bride and groom. The groom had come down with a terminal illness, and had only months to live. It was a last-minute wedding, and I felt I had to do it for them. Joe and I were supposed to go out for dinner that night, after I got home from the wedding. I didn't know I would get home late, which made me late for dinner.

I told Joe that I would shower, get dressed, and be ready to go in 15 minutes. When I got out of the shower, the front and side doors to the house were wide open, and I was the only one home. He was gone. I kept calling his name, and got really frightened that he deliberately left the doors open, and left me home alone. I couldn't believe how cold he was, and that he didn't care that anyone could have walked in on me. I couldn't take it anymore.

I knew I had to leave, so early one morning, I packed my bags quickly (because I was scared) and left. My neighbors and family were shocked, but I never told anyone that I had to leave the house for my safety. It was a very

Piping rosettes of Chantilly Whipped Cream for my students.

difficult decision that I made in haste, and it hurt my children especially. I knew everyone would think that I was the villain, and even though I knew my children loved Joe, I had no choice.

I left the house and slept in my office on a broken-down sofa bed and without a window for fresh air. The lawyer I hired worked for my business lawyer in Manhattan. I gave her $3500 as a retainer and in the middle of everything, she quit the firm and that money was lost. Next I hired a woman lawyer in Staten Island who showed up in court wearing sweatpants.

The person who really helped me was my son-in-law Jeff's uncle, a very rich businessman who lived on Todt Hill. I knew he had feelings for me (or should I say lusted after me), but I told him I was not interested, period. His wife was Jeff's aunt and I knew what a womanizer he was. He disgusted me mentally and physically, but he helped me, and with his lawyer, I worked out my divorce agreement.

I had to pay Joe about $580 a month for five years because the building was community property even though he was not listed on the mortgage. He did not want to be responsible in case my business failed. He did not contribute a dollar to the business. He was there physically to help guide the construction that needed to be done, but no more than that. I was working at the house, teaching classes every night, and catering. I was taking care of running my business.

Sadly, my dream to have a professional school in Staten Island, licensed by the state of New York, ended. Financially and emotionally, I wasn't able to achieve my goal. I was not able to focus on all that it would take to run my school, with everything else that was happening in my personal life at the time.

My cookware store in the front section of the cooking school was a first on Staten Island.

My cookware store in the front section of the cooking school was a first on Staten Island. I learned how to sell kitchenwares in my house, and continued selling them at the new location. I learned the retail business and went to all the trade shows at the Javits Center in Manhattan. I had kitchen and housewares, knives, expensive pots and pans, food processors, thermometers, and cast-iron pans, which later on became all the rage. This was all new to Staten Island. The Lodge cast-iron pans that I cook with were not something people used before I introduced them to my customers.

I had a refrigerated showcase where I displayed my homemade breads, cakes and pies. I made soups, tomato sauces, casseroles, holiday specialties, and entrées. People would get off the bus from work and buy food to eat at home. The first year went great and my first Christmas, I was cleaned out. My friend and student, Diane Razzano, made gift baskets for me and even taught a class on how to do that.

We had a beautiful young girl working the cash register for about a year. We noticed how well dressed she was, but didn't know that she was stealing money from the business. We did notice the expensive stockings she wore. One day I had an appointment with a catering client at 1:00 PM. The client arrived early, and was sitting at the table speaking to this girl when I got there. When I sat down to begin going over the client's menu with her, this girl kept interrupting me with suggestions of her own. I asked her to go into the office, that I was capable of handling this myself. She left in a huff, mumbling something under her breath as she left. After the appointment was over around 2:00 PM, the client left me a $300 cash deposit, which I placed in a cigar box in the office for Terri to deposit in the bank later that day. I called the girl into the kitchen and told her that she should have not interrupted me, that it was rude, and unprofessional. She got angry and started mouthing off to me, so I told

Interior of the Cafe.

her if she didn't like it, she could leave. She went into the office, grabbed her purse and the $300 out of the cigar box, and left.

Around 3:00 PM Terri was going to go to the bank to deposit the money, and saw that it was missing. We knew immediately that this girl had stolen the cash. Jeff got on the phone, spoke with her brother, and threatened that if he didn't drop off the money within an hour, Jeff was going to call the police and have her arrested. By 4:00 PM, her mother, and her brother were in the store with the three $100 bills in hand, apologizing for his sister stealing the money. She came from an old-fashioned, religious, Italian family, and her mother was crying and begging me not to press charges. The mother did not want the father to know. I don't know how much money she had been stealing all along, because I was busy in the kitchen and trusted her. She now has a public relations business and is respected on Staten Island. Of course she called me a monster and bad-mouthed me all over Staten Island after the incident. She even opened a fancy French restaurant and hired a talented chef who had worked for me for a little while. He had to leave to help out a friend who had lost her chef and was in a panic. The restaurant lasted a year. Running a restaurant looks so easy but it is one of the most difficult things to do in life.

Another look inside the Cafe.

Years later, I was honored as a Power Woman in Business by the Star Network and guess who else was honored? The woman who stole from me! They had us sitting at the same table. The woman who nominated me and I were looking at the food on the tables. Who walks over to say hello to my friend, but the same girl, 20 or so years later. Her face turned white when my friend tried to introduce us. I just said I know her. I told my friend the story and did not sit at the table with her.

The stock market crashed and my beautiful store that I loved had to close. That room became a waiting room for the students before they came into the kitchen for the cooking classes.

For two years I looked at that empty room. It was a beautiful room from the 1800s, with its brick walls, tin ceilings, and wooden floors. One day I said, "I think I will open a restaurant." I knew nothing about the business end and did not have the money to go to restaurant school. I bought the tables and chairs, china and stemware, rented tablecloths, and put fresh flowers on the tables. I opened on a snowy day in December. My whole Italian family came from Brooklyn as our guests, and we were filled to capacity. Of course, we did not have a proper restaurant kitchen. It was my cooking school with Formica cabinets and two stoves, and we did not buy a heating lamp to keep the food warm. It was terrifying and we could not keep up with the orders. Terri was the waitress, and she began to cry. I hugged her and said, "Everything is going to be all right." My son said, "Mom, you need to buy a heat lamp."

One day I said, "I think I will open a restaurant."

Marriage to Les

I FIRST MET MY second husband Les, when he was a student at my cooking school. We became friends and I found him easy to talk to. He really loved to cook, and after taking lessons with me, he became so good at it that he eventually assisted me in the classes. My students loved that we taught together. It was brilliant and humorous. He was the hardest worker with an intelligent personality. We could have never catered all the parties and events without his cooking talents.

Our wedding photo.

For years he worked for the restaurant on the salad, appetizer, and pasta station. He was a force of nature. Les was very generous, and lavished me with gifts and affection. I was overwhelmed with his kindness and sweetness. My first husband, Joe, was the total opposite of that. I loved traveling with Les to many places.

A few years after he retired from his job as a parole officer, Les wanted me to move to Florida and leave my family. He wanted me to give up the restaurant, and give up my career as a chef and cooking teacher, so that we could live near his daughters in Florida. Our marriage was over when he chose them over me. I know that was his choice, but it wasn't mine. I felt so hurt when he packed his belongings and moved, that it was unbearable. Before he left, he made sure I had the apartment set up above the cafe, and bought me furniture. Les also needed a place to stay when he visited his mother in Manhattan. I could not afford to rent my own apartment or house, because of my investments in the building and business, so I moved into one of the apartments in my building.

I went to Florida a few times to visit Les, and it was a horror. His daughters and his ex-wife, who was remarried, did not want me there. I also hated Florida because of the heat, the bugs, and his damp, smelly house. Mostly it was a farce because he was on one end of the bed, and I was on the other. I never went back. He came to Staten Island and stayed in my apartment a few times. It was then, after a few visits, that I told him that I no longer felt the same about him. He had gone back to being a heavy smoker; he smelled of cigarettes, his beard was yellow, and he no longer took care of himself.

We decided not to divorce, and kept in touch by writing letters on the computer.

When Les's mother Dorothy died, I gave the eulogy at her funeral, because he and his sister Jill refused to do it. Les did not have a suit with him to wear, and had to get one for the service. It was ill-fitting. He looked awful, and when he came over to kiss me on the cheek, I turned my face away. I used to tell a story in my classes about when I met Dorothy for the first time, and how this little Italian woman from Brooklyn walked into her apartment, and she told me how pretty I was. We loved each other immediately. She died at the age of 92. It was after Les had moved to Florida. Even though she had been very ill, Les only came to New York to visit her the day before she died.

Les and my granddaughter Amanda at the circus at Madison Square Garden.

Les and his sister did not stay in her apartment the night she died, and left her with an aide to die alone. It was only a matter of hours so they could have been with her. I always felt the coldness in the apartment when I visited her. He and his sister played cards while I talked to her. She was very generous to them, and when Les's children got in trouble, she bailed them out financially. Les's father died when he was two years old and he resented his mother for not ever talking about him. I still miss Dorothy, this independent woman, who gave me such affection and love.

In 2016 his daughter Melissa called Terri and said that Les needed a divorce, because he was in ill health and would have better health benefits if he were single. I was hurt, and felt stupid that I had agreed to not getting a divorce for all those years.

In July of 2018, Terri received the sad news that Les had passed away from colon cancer.

Higher Education

THERE WERE MANY SCHOOLS that I attended over the years in order to improve my cooking and baking skills, and to become a better teacher to my students. Because my interests were so diverse, I was lucky to have studied in France, Italy, and England, as well as different parts of the U.S.

Some of the schools and courses that I've attended include:

    The Wilton School of Cake Decorating in Chicago

    New York Community College

    The Culinary Institute of America in Hyde Park

    John Clancy School of Baking in New York City

    Norman Weinstein in New York City for Chinese Cooking

    École de Cuisine La Varenne in Paris

    Advanced Certificate from Le Cordon Bleu in London

    L'Academie de Cuisine in Bethesda, Maryland

    Marcella Hazan's school in Northern Italy

    The New School in New York City

    The College of Staten Island, attended two years

    Windows on the World Wine and Wine Service in New York City

John Clancy

John Clancy's School of Baking was a six-session, hands-on baking course. It was one of my first experiences in seeing how other cooking teachers taught. John Clancy began his career as a head chef at a successful restaurant in Cape Cod, and eventually moved on to become the head chef at The Coach House in Greenwich Village. He found further success with the support and guidance of his friends and mentors, Julia Child and James Beard.

John established himself as a culinary arts teacher, opening his own cooking and baking school, John Clancy's Kitchen Workshop. The *New York Times* hailed the school as one offering "New York City's Best Baking Course." That is how I found out about the course.

I was very nervous and found John Clancy to be very stern and serious. What I learned from him was how to do a baking class with participation. I modeled my Baking Workshop Class after his. He had about five to eight students in his townhouse, and his assistant prepped the ingredients for us to participate with. That young man was a very talented baker who later opened his own bakery. I remember how sad I was when I learned that he died in his twenties during the AIDS epidemic.

John would serve his finished bread or cake to us to taste. I remember once when the bread he made did not taste right. He had left the salt out of

*Left: My classmates and me
at the Cordon Bleu.
Right: This was our tiny
workstation.*

the dough. He did not apologize or make excuses. He simply used that as a lesson, telling us how important measuring correctly, was. He taught us a delicious Dresdner Stollen, Danish pastries, puff pastry, braiding breads in unique ways, and Genoise—a French sponge cake that is leavened naturally with eggs. The class that I enjoyed the most was when John taught us how to make apple strudel.

I remember after a brioche class, I had to travel back home to Staten Island by bus. We would take our dough home from class, to raise and finish at home. On my way home after the class, the bus never came, and a nice person showed me where we could take take another bus. The dough was in my large shoulder bag, in a plastic bag. Standing there at the next bus stop on a nice warm summer evening, my pocketbook began to grow as the dough began to rise. There was a comment from the group of people standing there that my pocketbook was growing. We all had a good laugh, as I explained to them what was happening.

When John Clancy said he had a guest chef coming to teach fruit and vegetable carving, I eagerly told him I wanted to take that class. I think to this day, it was one of the funniest classes I've ever taken. There was this middle-aged woman chef standing in front of the class, all dressed in chef whites with medals hanging around her neck. She told us that she brought all her fruit in from California, because New York fruit and vegetables would not do.

She stood behind the counter and I watched intently as she proceeded to cut herself. She did not want us to know what she did, so she dropped her arm down behind the counter, as the blood dripped down to the floor. I was helping out because I was there for two classes that day. Her evening class came, and as the students watched intently she cut herself again, dropping her arm to her side the way she did earlier, dripping blood all over the floor. This time I got her a towel. The thing was, no one would say anything because of her medals, and because she was very proud of what she did. I thought to myself, "I could do this." I developed my own Fruit and Vegetable Carving Class, and it became very popular with my students.

The World Trade Center

The World Trade Center restaurant, "Windows on The World," offered a Wine Appreciation Class, called "Windows on the World Complete Wine Course" with Kevin Zraly, who has been described as America's most famous and entertaining wine teacher. In May 2011, Zraly was awarded the prestigious James Beard Lifetime Achievement Award.

Kevin Zraly was the wine director of Windows on the World from 1976 until 2001. Located on the top floors of 1 World Trade Center, Windows on the World once held the title of America's top-grossing restaurant.

I arrived at the World Trade Center, and took the elevator to the top floor. It took my breath away. The view was just incredible, and the room was filled with sophisticated wine drinkers and people who owned some of the best liquor and wine stores in Manhattan.

"Where's my Barberone?" Kevin Zraly was a ball of fire! He spoke fast, he walked fast, and was so fascinating.

"Here I am!" I yelled, and I heard my daughter laughing as I ran into her arms.

I tried to keep up but I was tipsy every week, even though I spit the wine out into a bucket after tasting it, as I was instructed to do. After each class, I had to go home to Staten Island, and one night I knew I wasn't able to find my way back. I called my daughter Maria who was in Manhattan at the time, and she and her best friend Vinessa came to take me home. I remember calling to her in the front entrance courtyard, and swaying while walking to meet them. "Here I am!" I yelled, and I heard my daughter laughing as I ran into her arms. At the end of the course, there was a fabulous dinner ceremony with matching wines. I had no one to go with, because it was an expensive dinner, so I made the wrong decision of not attending the ceremony, but at least I had my diploma!

I love wine and was introduced to it by my maternal grandfather Stefano Prinzi. My grandfather made a hearty red wine every September. He had a grapevine growing in the backyard but there were not enough grapes. He bought grapes and they arrived in wooden boxes. He had a grape press, and wooden barrels on the side of the house where we lived in Brooklyn. I was just a little girl but I was fascinated as the barrels rolled in. The wine was stored in the dark, damp cellar where I used to hide from my mother. I was a curious child and was always in trouble.

My grandfather's wine was delicious! I say this because I have tasted homemade wine that was terrible. I remember sitting on a couch with my sister Adele in Long Island, where my father's family lived. I was a child, drinking wine that was left on the coffee table. I learned that I absolutely loved red wine, along with laughter. That was my introduction to the rest of my life. When I married Joe, he did not buy bottles of wine, it was not in our budget. Instead, he bought jugs of Barberone—a red blend that is full in flavor and body, with pleasantly sweet aromas of dark fruit. Joe could drink a lot of wine, but I couldn't. I have a low tolerance for alcohol. I think that saved my life!

L'Academie de Cuisine

Going to L'Academie de Cuisine near Washington, D.C., was the first time I took a plane by myself. I wanted to learn more about catering, buffets, ice carving, and fruit and vegetable carving. The Classic French Cuisine class was made up of professionals, and it was full participation! The kitchen layout was professional, expensive, and had all the finest equipment. The teachers were top notch. I thought of my school back in Staten Island, and what little I had to work with.

The most difficult thing we did in those classes was to learn how to bone a duck to make a galantine. A galantine is a French dish of deboned stuffed meat, most commonly poultry or fish, that is poached and served cold, coated with aspic.

We made a ballotine, which is traditionally a boned thigh of chicken, duck, or other type of poultry, that is stuffed with mixed lean meats and other ingredients. It is tied to hold its shape and sometimes stitched up with a trussing needle. A ballotine is often shaped like a sausage or re-formed to look like the leg, often with a cleaned piece of bone left in the end.

Fruit and vegetable carving that I made at L'Academie de Cuisine.

The watermelon carvings we made were spectacular edible summer centerpieces. Baby carriages, treasure chests, and kitty cat watermelon carvings decorated the table. They were all brimming with freshly carved fruits, which looked absolutely beautiful. We worked in teams creating these baskets, sometimes it was pleasant, but sometimes the students did not get along.

The first time I saw an ice carving was at the Culinary Institute in Hyde Park. We were taken outdoors on a balcony and watched this artistic chef carve an eagle out of ice. It was spectacular! We also watched a small ice carving in a large sink at the C.I.A. I knew that many of the things I was learning at this school were interesting but they were not something I could use at Carol's Cafe. I did offer both an individual, and a six-session, catering course at my cooking school.

While I was there, I stayed in a small hotel near the school. It had a restaurant on the bottom floor. The owner of the hotel was an attractive, middle-aged man, who introduced himself to me as I sat in the restaurant by myself. He sat at my table and we talked about what I was doing there. I finished my dinner and said goodnight. I went up to my room and was lying down in bed. I heard a knock on my door and saw the doorknob turning. I was frightened to death and told him to go away. Of course, I knew what he wanted. He was out there for quite a while. I heard him pacing. It was my last night there. The next day I left for the airport to begin another nightmare.

It was a stormy day; my flight home was only one hour, but the plane was delayed eight hours. When we finally boarded, we had to walk out on the field and climb the steps to get into the plane. I sat next to a colonel's wife who was a very experienced traveler. It began to thunder, and lightning flashed outside our window, over and over, as we swayed from side to side. I was terrified, and thought I was going to die. She said to me that this was the worst flight she had ever been on. She said she'd been to Africa, China, Japan, and traveled all over the world with her Army husband and never had an experience like that. When I got off the plane, Joe was waiting for me at the airport. I ran into his arms and he said he knew it was a terrible flight. I believe this event made me afraid to fly for the rest of my life and has held me back.

New Orleans Cooking School

One of my favorite classes that I've ever taken was at The New Orleans School of Cooking. It was a demo class: watch, learn, and eat. We learned how to make a gumbo, jambalaya, bread pudding, and pralines. It was Louisiana cooking in a way you'd never forget. The cooking instructor was a middle-aged guy named Joe. In his kitchen, he had shelves covered with trophies. They looked like bowling trophies! I thought he was a little intoxicated and relaxed, but he was funny and his dishes were delicious. He gave us recipes but he truly did not follow them. I so wanted to know him better. I knew he was a very talented man.

At the end of the lesson, he presented himself with a trophy and walked off and left the kitchen. I ran after him, down the street, asking him cooking questions, but I knew he had personal problems and teaching this class was a way for him to make a living. His heart was not in it. He impressed me so much that I began to study on my own and experiment with Cajun dishes and spices. I put a class together and it was so new to Staten island, that it was an instant success. It was called "The Fabulous Cooking of New Orleans." I wrote it this way: "Experience the New Orleans taste which leaves a terrific 'pow' in your mouth and a song in your heart. Cajun popcorn (Crawfish) with Sherry Wine Sauce, Shrimp Étoufée, Cajun Seafood Gumbo, with Andouille Sausage, Jalapeno-Jack Corn Muffins and New Orlean's Bread Pudding with Whiskey Sauce and Chantilly Whipped Cream." The Bread Pudding became a classic at Carol's Cafe and was never taken off the dessert menu.

New Orleans Bread Pudding with Whiskey Sauce and Whipped Cream

Serves 10–12

8 cups day-old French or Italian bread, cut into 1½ inch cubes

4 cups milk

2 cups sugar

8 tablespoons unsalted butter (1 stick), melted, cooled slightly

3 large eggs

3½ tablespoons pure vanilla extract

¾ cups black raisins

¾ cup shredded coconut

1 cup pecans, coarsely chopped

2 teaspoons ground cinnamon

1 teaspoon freshly ground nutmeg

2–3 tablespoons brandy

In a large bowl whisk all ingredients together, add bread cubes and soak for one hour before baking.

Pour into a well buttered 9×13 Pyrex baking dish.

Place into oven. Do not preheat oven. Bake at 350 degrees for 1 hour and 15 minutes, or until top is crusty and golden brown. Serve warm with Whiskey Sauce and Whipped Cream.

Whiskey Sauce

8 tablespoons unsalted butter, room temperature

1½ cups confectioners' sugar

3 large egg yolks

½ cup bourbon

Place butter and sugar in a medium saucepan, and stir over medium heat until combined and creamy.

Remove from heat and blend in egg yolks, one at a time. Pour in bourbon, gradually, stirring constantly.

Strain sauce. Sauce will thicken as it cools. If you prefer not to use liquor, substitute your favorite fruit juice. Sauce must be warmed to thin out before serving with bread pudding.

Whipped Cream

2 cups heavy cream	4–6 teaspoons pure vanilla extract
6 tablespoons confectioners' sugar, strained	Confectioners' sugar to garnish
	Fresh mint sprigs

Place in stainless steel mixing bowl, cover, and chill for at least an hour.

When ready to serve bread pudding:

Warm bread pudding servings in a 350 degree oven, covered with foil lightly, just until warm.

Warm whiskey sauce to thin out.

Whip cream until soft peaks form.

To serve: Place a portion of the whiskey sauce on dessert dish, top with a portion of bread pudding, and top with whipped cream. Garnish with confectioners' sugar, and a sprig of fresh mint.

Variations: walnuts or almonds, toasted; two cups semisweet chocolate chips

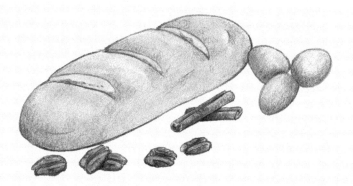

CAROL FRAZZETTA

Carol's Cafe

PASTA SAUCES

Writing My Cookbook

"GET OUT THE BIBS, lots of crusty Italian bread for dunking, a bottle or two of good red wine—you're in for a glorious meal." This quote sums up the set of family recipes that I compiled for my first cookbook, *Carol's Cafe Pasta Sauces*. I also offered recipes that I developed as a cooking school teacher, and later as a caterer and executive chef of my restaurant.

The cover of my first cookbook,
Carol's Cafe Pasta Sauces,
designed by my daughter Maria.

When I finally saw my efforts in print, I was happy with the result. It was something I wanted to do for a long time; it was a dream come true. I actually had thought about a cookbook years earlier. But when I bought the building on Richmond Road, everything changed; the book was put on the back burner. When I had the time to review my first attempts at writing, I didn't recognize the person who had written it. It wasn't the same kind of book that I wanted to do originally. I am an eclectic cook and baker, so at first I didn't have a clear direction. Then my daughter Terri suggested I do a pasta book because I love pasta. A single-subject book was perfect for me, and that's what I did—write a collection of my favorite pasta sauce recipes.

The book was edited, designed, and produced by my daughter Maria Giudice, and her business partner, Lynne Stiles, by their company, YO, in San Francisco. It was important to me that the book had a spiral binding so it would lie flat when open, for the cook. That turned out to be a big mistake because Barnes and Noble wanted me to add a strip to the binder so that you could see the book's title, and see the author's name on the shelf in the store. I simply could not afford to do that at the time, so it went out as is.

During the two years I took to assemble the cookbook, I discovered that many of today's cooks needed more descriptive terms and explanations than previous generations of home cooks. As a result,

My mother never had formal recipes and she didn't know about seasoning and techniques, but she was a wonderful cook and baker.

I had to spend more time on details. Being a cooking teacher, this helped me understand that sometimes people did not have the cooking knowledge that you would expect them to have.

Each chapter starts with the simplest recipe and goes to the most difficult. Also, if the recipe had a large quantity of ingredients, I wanted to make it understood that you could halve or quarter it. Writing the book was the most difficult thing I've ever done in my life. Recipes that were passed down by my mother were not handwritten, but are scattered throughout my 72-page book. The book is dedicated to my parents, my mother Mary Frazzetta, who loved to cook, and my father Alfonzo Frazzetta, who loved to eat.

My mother never had formal recipes and she didn't know about seasoning and techniques, but she was a wonderful cook and baker. I adapted her recipes for my classes. Two of my mother's recipes are among my longtime

Prudence Caprice at my book signing in the Staten Island Mall.

favorites and are included in my book. "When my mother made the Chicken Cacciatore as a child, I was in heaven." At Carol's Cafe, I often made Rabbit Cacciatore with Sweet Sausages and hard-boiled eggs. Equally appealing was her Spaghetti with Shoulder Lamb Chops, Rosemary, and Petite Peas. I changed the lamb recipe a great deal, and reinterpreted it for the book by incorporating modern techniques. I browned the lamb chops slowly in a cast-iron pot, setting them aside when they were done. Then I add lots of onions and cooked them for a long time with fresh herbs, adding the minced garlic and shallots and cooking it until soft, about 10 minutes. After adding the white wine, I reduced it until it is gone. You then add the lamb back into the pot, and add homemade chicken stock, covering the meat by about three inches. Season and cook for about three hours, until the meat is falling off the bone. The peas are added at the end and heated through. My mother would just throw everything in an aluminum pot. Wine was not added! It was served over cooked spaghetti. This became a classic at Carol's Cafe, and was not taken off the menu. I tried to do that, especially in the summer, and my customers would get very upset.

I enjoyed the first book signing in March 1997, where a table was set up in front of B. Dalton's Bookstore in the Staten Island Mall. Many of my students (old and new) came out, some using walkers, which brought tears to my eyes. I autographed many books, and being new at this, I laid them out on the table as I signed them. Many senior students of mine took other people's books with the wrong name in the book. I was so happy and proud that I just signed another book for them.

The most meaningful moment of my book signing happened when I saw my former student and neighbor, 80-year-old Prudence Caprice coming toward me using her walker. She was in the very first class that I ever taught in my home. Prudence lived across the street from our house on Scranton Street. In the worst of times—when I was suffering from postpartum depression and bleeding from ulcerative colitis, I was not eating and lost twenty pounds—Prudence was there for me. One day, I was in such pain, she came and made me take a shallow sitz bath with Epsom salts to create a soothing solution. She knew how unhappy I was, and she helped me get through it.

Years later, I became an author! Prudence's face lit up when she came to purchase a copy of my book, and I knew she was very proud. We reminisced about the past, and how that I overcame so many obstacles in life because of people like her.

A reunion of me and Joe in the backyard at Scranton Street.

Apple Cranberry Pecan Crisp

6 servings

1 cup pecans (about 4 ounces)

¼ cup plus 2 tablespoons all-purpose flour

¼ cup plus 2 tablespoons light brown sugar

½ cup plus 2 tablespoons granulated sugar

6 tablespoons cold unsalted butter, cut into ½-inch dice

½ cup old-fashioned rolled oats

½ teaspoon cinnamon, or to taste

Freshly ground nutmeg, to taste

2½ pounds Granny Smith, Cortland, or other tart cooking apples, peeled and quartered, cored and sliced crosswise ¼ inch thick

½ cup fresh or dried cranberries or dried cherries (about 2½ ounces)
It really is a matter of taste, add more if you like.

Calvados (apple brandy) about 2 tablespoons (optional)

1 teaspoon fresh lemon juice, strained, or to taste

Add granulated sugar to season the apples, to taste. I like the apples to sit for awhile, drizzled with a teaspoon of fresh lemon juice, tossed, and then sugared. Taste the apples several times for sweetness and add as much sugar as you like, tossing frequently.

Preheat oven to 350 degrees. Spread the pecans on a baking sheet and bake for 6–8 minutes, or until lightly toasted. Let the pecans cool and then coarsely chop them. Leave the oven on.

In a food processor, pulse the flour with the brown sugar and ¼ cup of the granulated sugar until combined. Add the cold butter and pulse until the mixture resembles coarse meal. Transfer the crumbs to a bowl and stir in the toasted pecans, oats, cinnamon, and nutmeg. Taste for seasoning. If needed, add more sugar, cinnamon and nutmeg.

Generously butter a medium baking dish or disposable aluminum 12-inch rectangle pans (available in the supermarket) or six individual baking dishes; they should be six inches wide and one inch deep, In a medium bowl, toss the apples with the cranberries and the remaining sugar (add as much sugar as the way you like your apples to taste), cinnamon, nutmeg (careful with the nutmeg, it is very strong), apple brandy, and lemon juice. Pile the apples high to allow for reduction.

Divide the apple mixture among the prepared baking dishes or use the medium baking dish and cover loosely, with the crumb topping. Set the dishes on a large baking sheet and bake in the bottom third of the oven. For individual dishes, bake for 35 to 45 minutes or until bubbly, golden brown, and caramelized. For medium baking dish, it can take as long as an hour, up to an hour and a half.

To test for doneness, pierce an apple or very carefully taste to see if it is very tender. Serve warm with vanilla ice cream or sweetened whipped cream.

Inspirations

I BECAME OVERWHELMED WITH my life, caring for my children and my home, with no help from Joe who traveled for his job, leaving me alone for weeks at a time. I suffered with terrible anxiety and depression. I sought the advice of the same medical doctor who helped me after the birth of my first child. I went for help, and learned so much about myself. It took a year to slowly recover. The first thing I did was to develop an interest, and get out of the house for one night a week.

Anne McAuliffe

I DECIDED TO TAKE sewing lessons. That is when I met this great lady named Anne McAuliffe. I remember the day I walked into her sewing school. I was so frightened, but knew I had to take the first step. That was the beginning of a lifelong friendship. Anne became my inspiration. I made wonderful friends in her classes, and began to bring my baked goods, cakes, pies, and cookies with me to her lessons. The other sewing students began asking me for my recipes.

I decided to make Anne a Paris-Brest for her annual Christmas party. A Paris-Brest is made up of choux pastry that is piped into the shape of a two rings, one on top of the other. After it is baked and cooled, it is filled with either pastry cream, or chantilly whipped cream and fresh berries.

Every year all of Anne's sewing students were invited to her house. Each student had to make something or buy a gift. She decorated her house and Christmas tree with handmade ornaments. Her enormous dining room table was filled with homemade dishes, cookies, and cakes. She would put all our names in a chef's hat and whoever's name was chosen would get a handmade apron, which said Queen of whatever year it was.

One of the students, Rose, came to my house because we were going to drive to Anne's party together. I was so excited to bring the Paris-Brest because it looked beautiful. Rose offered to carry it to the car. It was a very windy December day. I was too embarrassed to say no. She came down the stairs and got to the sidewalk. I watched in slow motion as she tripped on the sidewalk that was lifted up from the roots of our tree. The Paris-Brest went up in the air and flew onto the car windshield. There was my beautiful dessert smeared across the car window. She was not really hurt but her son told her that she should sue me because I had homeowner's insurance. Rose was also one of my cooking students. I was hurt by her decision so that pretty much ended our relationship. I was also very upset that my masterpiece was destroyed after I worked so hard preparing it.

Anne suggested I teach cooking at the adult education courses at a local high school. When I went to the high school to inquire about teaching there, the gentlemen in charge would not even give me a chance. He dismissed me, but I followed him down the hall, and asked, "What do I need to do?" He did not stop walking, but turned for a moment and said to me, "Go to college for eight years," in a mocking way.

Anne McAuliffe and Maria helping Terri get ready to "walk down the aisle." Anne gave Terri the gown she is wearing which she had inherited from her mother.

Julia Child

Meeting Julia Child for the first time. She was saying, "Fromage!" for the camera.

THE FIRST TIME I SAW Julia Child in person was in a large dining room in a hotel in San Francisco and she was at the podium. The question posed was where we should have our next meeting for the International Association of Cooking Professionals. The question was answered by Julia Child in a loud, resounding voice heard over the microphone. "Hawaii!" Immediately the room burst into a roar of laughter. If only they would have had chosen Hawaii. But none of them were like Julia.

I attended a meeting for the International Association of Cooking Professionals in Chicago. Joe came with me. I remember the gathering in a large, basement room in the hotel, filled with well-known cooking teachers who were drinking cocktails and wine. I walked in with Joe and saw Julia Child at the front of the room. I remember someone pushing me towards her. I believe that if it wasn't for me watching every episode of Julia Child's *The French Chef* on PBS Channel 13, I would never have become a cooking teacher. I had taken out all of her books that were available at the public library and tried to duplicate her recipes. The most famous was her beef wellington, a few pages long. My biggest regret was that I did not own a camera to take a picture of my first beef wellington sitting on top of the four burners of my stove in my kitchen on Scranton Street.

I was pushed towards Julia Child and my heart was beating with excitement. When I reached her, she looked down and rubbed the top of my head and said, "You're so cute." I relaxed a little and she asked me to tell her about myself. She was six feet two inches tall and I was five feet tall. I told her I was Sicilian and so she named me "The Little Sicilian." I so wanted to become her friend, but my life changed, and she moved to California. I left the Association when I went through my divorce because I could no longer afford it. I could no longer associate with my cooking teacher friends and Julia. It was a terrible detriment to my career.

The last time I saw her was at a celebration honoring James Beard at the James Beard House. I was a bit more sophisticated then and was dressed beautifully. I looked pretty and felt confident. When she saw me walk in, she called me over and said, "Have an oyster." There was a whole table filled with platters of raw oysters. Julia Child and James Beard loved oysters. I had never tasted raw oysters. My Sicilian mother hated fish. How could I tell her that oysters reminded me of the raw eggs my father forced me to gulp down?

When my father was being brought up in the Catholic home, he would gather fresh eggs in the morning, laid by the chickens. The priests in charge made him eat eggs that way. Of course, I did not tell her. The oyster went down my throat and it was one of the most difficult things I have ever done. I made it a point to work on recipes at Carol's Cafe with oysters and made them many ways. My customers in the restaurant loved them. I made Oysters Rockefeller, Oysters with an Asian Mignonette and Hot Sauce, Grilled Oysters in the Shell, Southern Fried Oysters, and my favorite, Baked Oysters with Mushroom, Garlic, Breadcrumbs, and Romano Cheese. People often ask me what I do not like to eat. Simple—raw clams and raw oysters. Of course, it is my father's fault! Never force your children to eat something that they do not like. Let them experience and taste for themselves and learn what great food is.

Edith Susskind

I MET EDITH SUSSKIND when l shopped in her gift shop. Now I was very successful and could afford to shop there. For years I knew what it was like not to be independent and to live on what my husband gave me.

Edith Susskind with her friend, Dr. Jodi Smith. They often dined together at the cafe..

Joe was not generous but l managed because of the way I cooked and baked. I did not have a credit card or checking account. Everything changed when Carol's Cuisine took off. I was free!

I walked into her wonderland. She had the most beautiful and unusual jewelry and accessories l had ever seen. She was there with her husband and we had an instant connection. I was taken with her and she with me. Her blonde hair was a lacquered bouffant. It did not move. Her husband was devoted to her and told me how it was her vision to have a store like this. He believed in her and helped her financially. It was beautiful, and l wished that l had a husband like that. I told her my story, and it turned out that my mentor Rosalind Atkinson, the dean at the College of Staten Island, was her sister. I was so proud that these intelligent Jewish women took an interest in me.

When Edith came to eat in my restaurant, I always cooked her food to her specifications. Her favorite dish was grilled lamb chops with mint jelly. We made sure to always have the jelly on hand just for her. The lamb had to be medium rare, and she had this notion that herbs like rosemary would upset her stomach so no herbs were allowed. Her mashed potatoes had no caramelized onions on top. Our famous rum-glazed carrots were never on her plate. She loved dessert, and her favorite was chocolate cake or apple pie. I always made her feel special, because she was a special person.

Edith usually came to dinner with her friend, Dr. Jodi Smith, a professor from Wagner College, and he always ordered a medium-cooked beef wellington. He was not well, and was seriously ill. They knew how much I loved them both. Edith inspired me. She was a successful businesswoman who was ahead of her time. Two days before she died, she came to Carol's Cafe with her caretaker. She whispered in my ear she wasn't going to make it. She was 94 years old when she passed away. I was very honored to be mentioned in her eulogy.

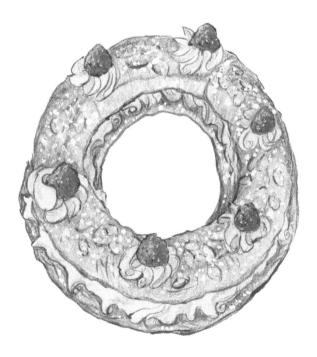

Paris-Brest

Ingredients for Pâte à Choux:

1 cup water

6 tablespoons butter, cut into small pieces

1 cup all-purpose flour, sifted after measuring

1 teaspoon sugar

5 eggs, large (4 eggs for the pâte à choux; 1 egg mixed with ½ teaspoon water for egg wash)

⅛ teaspoon salt

3 tablespoons almonds, slivered

Ingredients for Chantilly Cream:

2 cups heavy cream

4 tablespoons confectioners' sugar

2 teaspoons pure vanilla extract

¼ teaspoon almond extract

Preparing the Pâte à Choux:

In a heavy two- to three-quart saucepan, bring the one cup of water and butter to a boil over moderate heat, stirring occasionally. As soon as the butter has completely melted, remove the pan from the heat and pour in the flour and sugar all at once. Beat the mixture vigorously with a wooden spoon for a few seconds until it is well blended. Then return it to moderate heat and cook, still beating vigorously, for one or two minutes, or until the mixture forms a mass that leaves the sides of the pan and moves freely with the spoon.

Immediately remove the saucepan from the heat and use the spoon to make a well in the center of the paste. Break an egg into the well and beat it into the paste very quickly, to avoid the egg cooking. When the first egg has been absorbed, add three more eggs, one at a time, beating well after each addition. The finished paste should be thick, smooth, and shiny.

continued

Paris-Brest, *continued*

Preparation for the pastry crown:

Preheat oven to 400 degrees. Line a cookie sheet with parchment paper. Using a bowl or cake pan with a 10-inch diameter, mark a line onto the parchment paper around the mold. Make sure the line is dark enough to see through the paper, then flip paper over.

After the pâte à choux has been prepared, fit a pastry bag with a one-inch round tip and pipe the dough into a one-inch-wide round, following your line through the parchment paper. Squeeze another ring inside or outside the first, depending upon how large you want the Paris-Brest to be. Then, squeeze one more ring on top of the first two you have piped. Brush the pâte à choux with the egg wash and sprinkle one tablespoon of the slivered almonds on the top.

Allow the cake to dry for about 20 minutes. Bake at 400 degrees for 45 minutes, then shut off the oven and open the door to allow some of the steam to escape. Leave the cake in the oven for one hour so it cools and dries. Remove from the oven once cooled, and using a long serrated knife, cut a lid off the cake.

Fill the cake generously with Chantilly whipped cream (recipe to follow), crème praline, or pastry cream of your choosing. After making your filling, use a pastry bag with a decorative tip to fill the bottom part of the crown. The cream should rise well above the rim of the pastry. If using Chantilly cream, you may top the cream with sliced strawberries for a nicer presentation. After filling the cake, replace the crown so that it floats on the cream, and sprinkle the top with confectioners' sugar. Keep in a cool, dry place. To serve, cut into small wedges using a serrated knife.

Preparation for Chantilly Cream:

Using a mixer fitted with a whisk attachment, whip the cream in a large, chilled mixing bowl until it begins to thicken. Add the sugar, vanilla, and almond extracts, and continue beating until the cream holds its shape firmly. It may now be piped or spooned into the cooled Paris-Brest.

Colleagues

Len Pickell

LEONARD PICKELL WAS CHAPTER Director of Les Amis du Vin, an instructor at Les Amis du Vin, an instructor on best buys for Club Cuisine, retail store manager, restaurant consultant, wine instructor at the New School, professional member and consultant to the James Beard Foundation, and then became the president of the James Beard House in New York City.

My favorite students enjoying their wine in the cafe.

When I met Len, he said that wine does not always have to be expensive to be delicious. The problem, however, is in knowing how to select less costly wines, and in knowing which of them are the best value.

The first wine class I did with my friend Len was called "Introduction to Wine." The course was designed to provide the student with all the basics for understanding wine. Participants learned how to taste wine and understand the different varietals in today's marketplace. At least 10 wines were tasted and analyzed. We served a variety of imported cheeses and French bread.

We then decided to have special wine dinners at least twice a year that we called Food and Wine Galas. We would usually choose a cuisine, and I would plan the menu. Then Len would select the wines to accompany each course.

The Wine Gala that stands out in my mind was the night we did a French-themed dinner for 50 guests. The entrée was cassoulet. It is a White Bean Casserole with Duck, Pork, Rabbit, Lamb, and Sausage. The night before the class, I prepared it in an enormous copper pot that I borrowed. I cooked it on the antique stove in the back of the kitchen. When I was done at 5:00 AM, I realized I could not lift the pot. I just sat there and decided not to cry, but to wait until my dishwasher arrived in the morning.

We started the Gala with foie gras terrine that we purchased from D'Artagnan which we served with crusty French bread. This began my over 20-year relationship with this amazing wild game company. I still buy wild game from D'Artagnan for my house freezer.

The cassoulet turned out as good as I had hoped, and the students loved it.

For dessert, I made Tarte Tatin with Chantilly Whipped Cream (Upside-Down Caramelized Apple Tart).

Len and I worked as a team throughout the evening. I would cook in the kitchen where I taught all my classes, and Len would be in the dining room serving the wines. I would come out when dessert was served and answer any questions about the food I cooked. It was the beginning of great times until it came to a tragic end.

We served foie gras, caviar, wild game, cassoulet, and the finest wines.

There was a big scandal at the James Beard House when my dear friend Len Pickell was arrested for stealing funds and foodstuffs. He lost all of his friends, but not me. I knew his wife lost her big position on Wall Street and their finances changed. It took a year for the trial to begin. He received a five-year prison sentence, but never actually served more than a year, and that was spent entirely in the prison hospital.

Len told me that the shoes that they fitted him with were too small and he developed a severe infection in his feet. He was released after one year on compassionate release, due to his medical condition. He wrote me shortly after his release, telling me that I was his only friend. I told him that when he was feeling better we would do a new food and wine gala just like the good old days.

A week later, his daughter called me and told me he died of a blood clot to the brain. Our classes were so special. We served foie gras, caviar, wild game, cassoulet, and the finest wines. My customers and students would ask when we were going to do it again. I had to tell them that it would never happen again because Len Pickell died. I will never know another person like Len.

Cassoulet

The Beans

An 8-quart pot containing 5 quarts of boiling water

5 cups (2 pounds) dry white beans (Great Northern or small white beans)

½ pound fresh or salt pork rind

1 pound lean salt pork simmered for 10 minutes in 2 quarts water

A heavy saucepan

1 cup sliced onions

A large herb bouquet, all tied in washed cheesecloth: parsley sprigs, 4 unpeeled cloves garlic, 2 cloves, ½ teaspoon thyme, and 2 bay leaves

Salt

Drop beans into the boiling water. Bring rapidly back to the boil for two minutes. Remove from heat and let beans soak for one hour. Meanwhile, place pork rind in a saucepan with one quart water, bring to a boil and boil for one minute. Drain, rinse in cold water, and repeat the process. Then, with a sharp knife, cut rind into strips ¼ inch wide; cut strips into small triangles. Place again into saucepan, add one quart water, and simmer very slowly for 30 minutes; set aside.

As soon as beans have soaked for one hour, add the salt pork, onions, herb packet, and pork rind with its cooking liquid to the eight-quart pot. Bring to simmer, skim off scum, and simmer slowly, uncovered, for about one and a half hours or until beans are just tender. Add boiling water, if necessary, during cooking, to keep beans covered. Season to taste with salt, near the end of cooking. Leave beans in cooking liquid until ready to use.

The Pork

2½ pounds, boned pork roast (loin or shoulder) excess fat removed

Roast the pork to an internal temperature of 155 degrees using an instant-read chef thermometer.

Set aside, reserving cooking juices.

The Lamb

2½ pounds, boned shoulder of lamb	½ teaspoon thyme
3 to 4 tablespoons olive oil	2 bay leaves
A heavy flameproof casserole or large frying pan. I like cast iron.	2 cups dry white vermouth or white wine of your choice
1 pound cracked lamb bones	3 cups beef stock
2–3 cups finely chopped onions	1 cup water
4 cloves smashed garlic	Salt and pepper
6 tablespoons tomato paste	

Cut lamb into two-inch chunks, dry thoroughly, and brown a few pieces at a time in very hot cooking oil in the casserole or frying pan. Remove meat to a side dish. Brown the bones, remove them, and lightly brown the onions in the same pan.

Drain out browning fat, return meat and bones, and stir in the garlic, tomato paste, thyme, bay leaves, wine, and beef stock.

Bring to a simmer, season lightly, cover, and simmer slowly for 1½ hours.

Discard bones and bay leaves, skim off fat, and season cooking juices to taste with salt and pepper.

Homemade Sausage Cakes

1 pound lean ground pork	2 teaspoons salt or to taste
⅛ teaspoon finely chopped, fresh bay leaf (optional)	⅛ teaspoon fresh ground black pepper or to taste
⅓ pound (⅔ cup) fresh ground pork fat	Big pinch of allspice, or to taste
1 to 2 cloves smashed garlic	Optional: ¼ cup brandy

Mix all ingredients together. Make a tiny test patty and brown on both sides until done and taste it for seasoning. Adjust seasoning if needed.

Form mixture into cakes, two inches in diameter and ½-inch thick.

Brown lightly in a skillet and drain on paper towels.

continued

Cassoulet, *continued*

Final Assembly

Drain the beans, discard herb packet, and cut the salt pork into ¼-inch serving slices.

Cut the roast pork into 1½–2 inch serving chunks.

Arrange a layer of beans in the bottom of the casserole or baking dish.

Cover with a layer of lamb, pork, salt pork, and sausage cakes.

Repeat with layers of beans and meat, ending with a layer of sausage cakes.

Pour in the lamb cooking juices, pork roasting juices, and bean cooking liquid to barely cover the top layer of beans.

Mix bread crumbs and parsley together, spread over the beans and sausage cakes, and dribble on the fat or butter.

Set aside or refrigerate until ready for final cooking.

Baking

Preheat oven to 400 degrees.

Bring casserole to simmer on top of the stove, then set it in upper third of preheated oven.

When top has crusted lightly (about 20 minutes), turn oven down to 350 degrees.

Break the crust into the beans with the back of a spoon and baste with the liquid in the casserole. Repeat several times as the crust forms again but leave a final crust intact for servings.

If liquid becomes too thick, add a few spoonsful of bean cooking juice. Cassoulet should bake for about an hour.

NOTES:

- Feel free to use other meat choices: roast or braised goose, rabbit, duck, turkey, or ham hock or veal shank; or Polish or Italian sausage. Any of these may be added to or substituted for these meats in the recipe, but if the cassoulet is to be delicious, you must have some excellent flavoring juices to give it the right taste. You can purchase these meats online from D'Artagnan, a wild game company that I've been a customer of for over 25 years.

- This dish is best served in the winter on a cold day. Bon Appetit!

French Tarte Tatin
Upside-Down Apple Tart

Pastry Dough

Yields enough dough for a 10" pie

Serves 8–10

2 cups all-purpose flour (Pillsbury or Gold Medal)

1½ sticks (6 ounces) cold unsalted butter cut into ¼" cubes

¼ teaspoon salt without iodine

1 tablespoon sugar

About ⅓ cup very cold water

Place the flour, butter, salt, and sugar into a medium bowl. Mix ingredients together until the butter cubes are coated with the dry ingredients. Cut into the butter with a pastry blender. Don't worry if little pieces of butter remain.

Add the cold water gradually, one tablespoon at a time and stir with a fork. This will give the dough some flakiness. This process can be done in the food processor if you prefer. Gather into a ball and form into a hamburger shape. If overworked, it will become elastic. Wrap with plastic wrap and chill in the refrigerator for a least one hour before using.

When you are ready to make the tart, place the dough on a floured board or Silpat™ baking mat and roll uniformly, turning the pastry to prevent sticking and to form a circle. The dough should be about ⅛" thick and at least 12" in diameter. Rolling the dough back on the rolling pin, lift up, and roll onto the cooked apples.

Filling

8 Golden Delicious apples or Rome Beauties

⅓ cup sugar or more if apples are tart

Zest of one lemon

1 teaspoon ground cinnamon or more

½ teaspoon freshly ground nutmeg

½ stick (4 tablespoons) unsalted butter

1 pinch of salt

For the caramel

⅔ cup sugar

½ cup water

continued

French Tarte Tatin Upside-Down Apple Tart, *continued*

Peel, core, and slice eight apples. Cut into ¼" thick slices. You should have six cups of sliced apples.

To make the caramel for a 10" pie pan, place ⅔ cup of sugar with ½ cup water in a saucepan. Bring to a boil and keep boiling until it turns a nice caramel color. Be sure not to stir or agitate the caramel as it cooks or it will crystallize. Do not let it burn; if the caramel gets too dark, make a new one.

Pour the caramel into the pie pan. Tilt it so that the whole bottom and half of the sides are coated. Do this quickly before the caramel hardens. Set aside.

Place the ½ stick of butter in a large sauté pan and melt until foaming. Add the apples, ⅓ cup sugar or more, the lemon zest, cinnamon, nutmeg, and pinch of salt.

Sauté apples for five to six minutes gently, tossing with a wooden spoon. Flambé, if desired, with Calvados (apple brandy). Taste for seasoning, adding more sugar and spices if needed. Pour out onto cookie sheet to cool.

When cool enough to handle, start arranging the nicest slices out in a circular pattern, from the middle of the pie pan. Overlap the slices so the rounded sides are hidden. The nicest side shows after the pan is inverted. Continue to arrange in layers until the bottom and part of the sides are covered. Fill the cavity with the remaining apples.

Take the rolled-out pastry dough, and place it on top of the arranged apples. Trim the dough so that it comes to the edge of the pan. Brush the top with an egg wash consisting of one beaten egg. Prick with a fork.

Place on a cookie sheet in a preheated 400 degree oven for 45 minutes or until golden brown. Then run a knife or an offset spatula around the perimeter of the pan to loosen the crust.

Let the tart rest for five minutes to set. Place a platter on top of the pie pan and quickly (and very carefully) turn upside down. The pan should release easily. If some of the apples stick to the bottom, rearrange them back into the design.

NOTE:

- You must allow the tart to set before inverting or it might collapse. However, if left to cool too long, the caramel will harden and half the apples will stick to the pan. If this happens, heat the pie pan on the stovetop for a few seconds and then unmold.

Decorating the tart

1 cup Smucker's apricot preserves   **½ cup sliced almonds**

Heat preserves in a small saucepan or microwave until fluid. Using a fine strainer, remove large pieces of fruit from the preserves. Toast the almonds in a small sauté pan over low heat until golden, stirring occasionally.

Brush the strained preserves on the top of the tart and garnish with the toasted almonds.

Friends

Dr. Lou

WHO IS DR. LOU, as I call him?

One night Dr. Louis Gianvito came to the restaurant with his friend, John Scalia, who I became involved with later on as a business partner. John owned The Historic Old Bermuda Inn and was a funeral director. Dr. Lou, a renowned Staten Island doctor, who people loved, was 75 years old at the time and had just become a widower the year before we met.

The students in one of my advanced techniques of cooking classes are sharing a laugh with Terri and Dr. Lou Gianvito (pictured in the center).

Dr. Lou loved our food, and decided to learn how to cook. He took all the Italian, ethnic, bread baking, and Techniques & Theory classes. He became a dear friend and my personal doctor. He was the kind of doctor who made a house call, walking up three flights of stairs to my apartment when I didn't feel well. He knew how busy I was, and took time out of his busy life to make time for me.

One night, right before I was going to teach an Italian class, I was eating and sucking on lobster bodies left over from our famous lobster bisque. I felt something happen to the side of my face. My face swelled up and when he arrived for the class he came up to my apartment and said, "You look like hell," as a joke. Terri postponed the class to another day. He then drove me to an oral surgeon a half hour away, because my salivary duct had closed up and the doctor needed to cut it open. It took a while for my face to return to normal. That was the kind of man Dr. Lou was. We really cared about each other, but he had a girlfriend who was a nurse at a local hospital.

One night Dr. Lou came to the restaurant and described to me what he felt like having for dinner. I made him a filet of fish poached in plum tomatoes and fish stock, with extra virgin olive oil, shallots, garlic, hot cherry peppers (in vinegar), fresh basil, and Italian parsley. Lou loved a medium spice and I named it Dr. Lou Gianvito's fish of the day. It became one of the most popular fish dishes on my menu.

Bonnie Marchese

BONNIE MARCHESE IS A BEAUTIFUL Jewish redhead, who came into my classes about 20 years ago. Her whole family were my customers in the restaurant and came for all their family holidays.

Bonnie's two daughters became my students, and her son-in-law attended classes with his two sons, for my Parent and Child Classes. Her daughters were so different from each other.

Bonnie's oldest daughter is an attractive, intelligent woman, who I really like. She was a whiner and always complained so I found a plaque on one of my vacation trips that expressed the whining issue with a sense of humor. When she would begin to whine, I would just point to the plaque. She loved that, because it was subtly done and it prevented me from yelling at her. I had that plaque for many years, until one day, my dishwasher who had been with me for over 20 years, threw it away. Why? I still don't know! Many of the cooking items that I loved would disappear or break over the years. Bonnie's daughter was very upset that the plaque was gone. She ended up being a schoolteacher who opened up a gluten-free baking business.

Bonnie's other daughter, Mara, was quiet and intelligent, and would always take cooking classes by herself. When I did a television show for ABC, she and Bonnie came, and they were so attractive sitting there quietly in the audience.

> **Bonnie became my dear friend, and her new Italian husband was a talented, funny musician, who entertained in the cafe a few times.**

Bonnie was a serious student and really wanted to become a fine cook. She did it right! She took Techniques & Theory I and II, and Advanced Cooking. She also studied Baking I and II and Advanced Baking. She also brought in many new cooking students, which helped book my assorted classes. She loved to chatter and sometimes, because I wanted her to learn, I would yell at her for not focusing. I found that the students who really came to learn, I was tougher on.

It was so difficult to keep my personal life separated from my work. During this time period, after 30 years of marriage, there was my divorce, no money, and menopause. Bonnie became my dear friend, and her new Italian husband was a talented, funny musician, who entertained in the cafe a few times. He had a doo wop group. I asked him and his group to perform in the restaurant, and I planned a whole dinner that would be set in the 1950s.

What I remember about that night was Caesar Salad, Potato Torte, Beef Stroganoff, and frying 200 yeast doughnuts. It was a fun night for everyone, except I was exhausted from all the cooking and baking that I did. My kitchen staff did not understand this food, and they did not like to come in on their night off to help with special occasions. Sal would come in when I really needed him. Terri and Carol Ann were the servers.

I was proud of Bonnie because she became a fine cook and hostess. I know because she was kind enough to invite me to her beautiful home in Grymes Hill in Staten Island a couple of times. When she came to the restaurant with her friends for dinner, she always had my signature dish, Mussels in a Plum Tomato Sauce, with a touch of spice, and she would share it with her friends. She would always say that her mussels never tasted like mine. Her favorite entrée was my Vienna Schnitzel with Spaetzle.

Bonnie and her husband sold their beautiful home and retired to Florida, where she has a group of friends who love to cook and entertains regularly. We keep in touch, but I am not a Florida person and even though she has invited me, I probably will never visit. We'll see. Never say never!

Tony Gula

TONY GULA WAS A COOKING STUDENT of mine who came into Tech and Theory I, and is the sweetest man I know. He was the only man enrolled in that particular class and it didn't bother him a bit. Some of the women in the class would tease him, but he had a good sense of humor. He recently wrote to me and said, "You might have instilled a love of cooking within another." He is talking about his only son who now is enrolled in the culinary program in the University of South Florida.

Tony is retired now, living in Florida with his wife and son. He also enrolled himself in the culinary program in the University of South Florida. He wants me to come and visit him there, because he thinks I would enjoy Florida and to have something to look forward to after I finish my book. Yet another student who wants me to go there!

Kathy Guzzo

KATHY WAS MY STUDENT for 10 years and a faithful customer at Carol's Cafe. She loved to cook and eat and was my dear friend. Her favorite class was when we taught her my Crispy Braised Pork Belly with Mixed Greens.

She loved to bring me presents. I particularly remember when she bought me persimmons and I put them in my car to take home but forgot about them. They became very ripe in my Honda and the next day I got in the driver's seat and sat on them. My black mink jacket was totally stained with squashed persimmons and the seat in my car was saturated. I laugh about it now with fondness for my friend. I did not laugh when I had to get my coat cleaned.

Kathy brought me fresh herbs and vegetables from the garden. She cooked and baked everything I taught. She did talk a lot in the cooking class and sometimes I would lose my patience. I always wanted my students to be successful.

She came to my house and sat by my bed and nursed me with affection and love.

When I had my accident in 2016 due to vertigo and fell down 10 steps to the cement basement floor, I was badly hurt. The first one to show up beside my daughter and grandchildren was nurse Kathy Guzzo. She came to my house and sat by my bed and nursed me with affection and love. I was deeply moved by what she did.

Two weeks after my fall the phone rang. Someone was crying on the other end of the phone. I could not believe what they were saying: Kathy had died! They found her on the floor in her living room. Terri and I were heartbroken. When we went to the wake she still looked alive—as if she was sleeping. She looked beautiful.

I think about Kathy all the time and miss her with all my heart.

Dr. Meryl Efron

I FIRST MET MERYL EFRON and her partner at the time, Maureen Skelton, at Carol's Cuisine Cooking School. She was in love with cooking and baking. I knew it meant a lot to her and so I gave her all the attention she needed to thrive. Meryl signed up for many cooking classes and became a serious student. She attended my Techniques & Theory I and II, and Advanced Techniques & Theory of Cooking classes. She also took all my baking workshops.

Meryl was a well-known dentist on Staten Island who became a celebrity when she won the *Staten Island Advance's* Cookbook contest. She became very involved and later became a judge for the annual contest. All the photographs and articles from the newspaper of her cooking wins were framed on the wall of her waiting room. She loved to cook for Historic Richmond Town and often donated her services.

Meryl loved to entertain and hosted fabulous parties at her and Maureen's home; I was often invited. Whenever I needed her, she would invite me to her parties to cheer me up. I particularly remember a party I attended at her mom's house in Todt Hill. Les had moved to Florida and she knew I was feeling down. She told everyone that I would not notice that she bought the shrimp cocktail at the supermarket. It was the first thing I noticed and we had a big laugh about it.

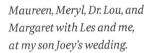

Maureen, Meryl, Dr. Lou, and Margaret with Les and me, at my son Joey's wedding.

PHOTO BY PETER DAMIANI

Dr. Lou Gianvito standing in front of the KitchenAid mixer cake that Meryl commissioned for me for my 40th anniversary party.

Besides being my dentist, she was my dear friend for many years. At the Carol's Cuisine 40th anniversary celebration she sent me a cake made by a famous cake decorator of a KitchenAid® mixer. It was decorated and looked just like a real mixer.

When John Scalia, who was a funeral director, called me late one night to tell me that Meryl had died, I was devastated. She was only 55 years old when she died suddenly in her sleep.

I went to her memorial at the St. George theatre and many people who loved her were there. I still miss my friend every day and wish I could talk to her once again.

Caesar Salad

⅓ cup extra virgin olive oil

2 cloves garlic, coarsely chopped

1 tablespoon fresh lemon juice

1 tablespoon Worcestershire sauce

½ teaspoon salt

¼ teaspoon freshly ground black pepper

1 head romaine lettuce

1 whole egg, lightly beaten

½ cup grated imported Parmesan cheese

¼ cup crumbled blue cheese

4 flat anchovy fillets

Croutons *(see recipe below)*

Place the olive oil and garlic into a small bowl and allow to stand for 30 minutes. Then add the lemon juice, Worcestershire sauce, salt, and pepper, and beat with a fork to mix well.

Wash and dry the lettuce. Tear the leaves into bite-sized pieces and place them in a large salad bowl. Pour on the dressing and toss quickly. Add the egg, Parmesan cheese, and blue cheese, then toss again. Lastly, sprinkle the croutons over the salad and arrange anchovies decoratively across the top.

Croutons

4 slices firm-textured white bread   Vegetable oil for frying

Trim the crusts from the bread and cut the slices into ½-inch cubes. Pour oil into a large skillet for a depth of ½ inch. Heat the oil to 350 degrees (measured with a deep-frying thermometer). Add the bread cubes and fry over medium heat until crisp and golden. Remove the croutons from the skillet with a slotted spoon and drain well on paper towels before serving.

Raised Doughnuts

3½ cups, sifted all purpose unbleached flour (Hecker's Flour is recommended.) *Note: The amount of flour varies with the brand of flour that you use. Start with 3 cups of sifted flour, mix in your sugar and salt, then sift again. You may need to use the additional half cup of sifted flour. Use whatever is needed for a soft, sticky dough.*

3 heaping tablespoons granulated sugar (a heaping ¼ cup)

1 teaspoon salt

¾ cup warm milk (105–115 degrees)

2 large eggs, slightly beaten, room temperature

⅓ cup, melted unsalted butter, cooled to 85–95 degrees

3 tablespoons warm water (105–115 degrees)

1 package of active dry yeast (2¼ teaspoons)

½ teaspoon of sugar

Flour for rolling out dough

Vegetable oil for deep frying

Measure warm water into small bowl, add ½ teaspoon of sugar, and sprinkle yeast over water, allowing yeast to dissolve. Set aside for five minutes.

Sift flour, and lightly spoon into measuring cup, and measure 3½ cups into sifter. Remove a ½ cup and reserve. Use only if needed. Add sugar, salt, and sift into mixing bowl.

Make a well, and add the warm milk, two eggs slightly beaten, melted butter and dissolved yeast

With a flat beater or large spoon, mix the liquids into the flour.

Knead the dough with a dough hook, until the dough wraps around the dough hook, or by slapping dough with your hands. The dough will be sticky. That is the way it should be.

Take the soft dough out of the bowl and put it into a lightly buttered bowl, turning to coat top.

Cover with plastic wrap.

Let dough rise until double or more in volume, about 1–2 hours.

Test by poking two fingers, into dough; if the holes stay, it's double.

Punch dough down. Roll it out on a lightly floured board into a rectangle shape, about ¾ of an inch thick.

With a floured doughnut cutter, cut as many doughnuts as you can. As you cut them, set the doughnuts and holes on a lightly floured board.

Leave enough space between them to rise again. About two inches apart.

Lightly flour a dish towel, and cover the doughnuts and holes to rise again. They should double in size.

Can take about 30 minutes to an hour, depending on what type of yeast you use. Do not let them rise to more than double.

Heat vegetable oil in a large frying pan, or wok, to 375 degrees. About 2–3 inches of oil.

Add one doughnut at a time. When the first one sizzles, add the next one, and repeat.

Do not fry more than three doughnuts at a time or the oil will cool down and the doughnuts will be greasy.

If your oil is too hot the doughnuts will be brown on the outside and raw on the inside.

Turn doughnuts when they are light brown on one side, and brown the other side. Turn doughnuts only once. The holes are difficult to turn, so when they rise to the top, kind of hold them into the oil.

They do not have to be brown all over. Drain on paper towels. Use lots of paper towels. Let them cool until warm.

Dip lightly in granulated sugar on both sides. Shake off excess. Or use a combination of sugar and cinnamon to taste.

Carol's Cafe

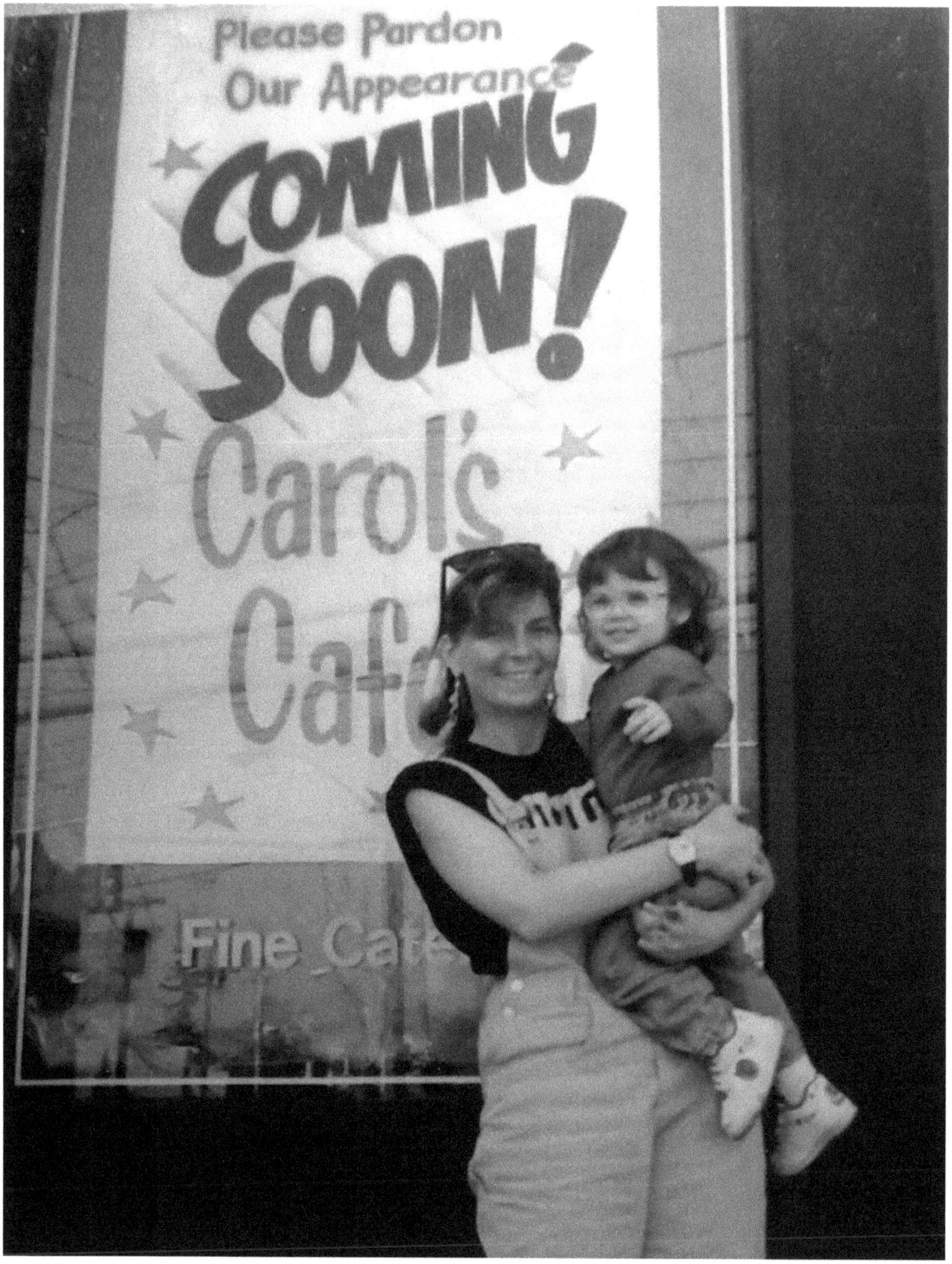
Please Pardon
Our Appearance
COMING
SOON!
Carol's

Why Open a Cafe?

AFTER MY GOURMET FOOD and housewares store closed, I looked at that large empty room for two years. My heart was broken when I looked at that vacant space. I wanted to fill it with something new and exciting. It was a beautiful room with 20-feet-high tin ceilings, interior brick walls, and oak floors from the late 1800s.

Maria and my grand-daughter Amanda in 1993.

I picked out old historic photographs of Staten Island at Richmond Town, had them reprinted, matted, and framed at Mauro Graphics where my daughter Terri had worked. I kept the refrigerated showcase, where I sold prepared food and desserts to customers when I had my store. Now it would hold our wines and beers as well as display my homemade cakes, pies, and other desserts.

When I first bought the building in 1983, we received many types of plants from friends and students, wishing us luck for the grand opening of the new location for Carol's Cuisine Cooking School. These beautiful green plants had grown to a great height against the front windows so they practically blocked the windows completely. We had had those plants for more than 30 years when we closed. When we left the premises, we donated all of our plants and cacti to a senior citizens' home.

When I decided to open the cafe, the city started a sewer replacement project directly in front of my building, effectively shutting down traffic for nearly two years. Fortunately, this project allowed me time to renovate my former housewares store into a beautiful cafe.

The city started a sewer replacement project directly in front of my building, shutting down traffic for nearly two years. Fortunately, this allowed me time to renovate my former housewares store into a beautiful cafe.

I had no idea how much it would cost to open Carol's Cafe. What would I need? I had very little parking. I would need a bar, tables, chairs, refrigeration, and a freezer. I already had a walk-in freezer for my cooking school and catering business and a walk-in refrigerator in the kitchen. Of course the kitchen was for a cooking school, and not for a professional restaurant. I would have to rent tablecloths, linens, napkins, and have fresh flowers delivered each week. I believe I took a $75,000 loan on the mortgage originally to renovate the building. I needed the money to open my restaurant.

The pub would become the smoking section about five years after the restaurant opened. The money I needed for the pub was borrowed from my mother-in-law Dorothy Weinstein. I loved her and she loved me. I ran out of money to finish the pub and she gave me a check for $25,000 dollars. I paid her back, sending her a check every month. My former husband Les

This antique stove was a gift from Dr. Vitolo, a well-known plastic surgeon on Staten Island. It was an important part of my restaurant for many years.

Prigerson, her son, tried to get interest on the money I owed when he moved to Florida to be with his daughters. Before she died, Dorothy had signed a paper saying I did not have to pay her interest.

The restaurant opened in 1993 and some of my customers stayed with me until the very end. I remember that one of my customers, a woman who was a judge on Staten Island, helped me get my liquor license. I was having problems with the application, and kept getting denied. When I told her about the problems I was having, she told me to re-submit the application, and within two weeks, I had my liquor license in hand. She never told me how ill she was, and the day before she died, she came for dinner in my cafe.

I focused on what I needed to do to get the restaurant going. Did I think about the obstacles? I was too busy teaching classes, catering, making appearances, and doing television shows. It was exhausting. I knew I wanted an eclectic restaurant. I bought mahogany-colored tables and chairs, white dishes, and silverware. I had an antique stove that a plastic surgeon, Dr. Robert Vitolo, had given to me, placed in the main dining room. Dr. Vitolo found this antique stove in the basement of a beautiful old white house with a large porch that he purchased for his office. His daughter Noreen was my student for a number of years and is still a good friend.

The stove was a focal point in the main room of the cafe. On it, I placed freshly cut flowers, antique brass candlesticks, and cooking class information. People had to walk up the handicap ramp to come into the restaurant and it was the first thing they would see.

Staff

SOME OF THE EARLY lessons that I learned: we needed to advertise; have a menu that worked; and customers should not have to wait for their food to be served. We needed to get reviewed, have delicious food and desserts, and be different from your typical Staten Island Italian restaurant. I was a female executive chef, and that was unusual. I wanted to be respected for my talent, and I needed a talented sous chef and kitchen staff alongside of me.

The original waitstaff consisted of John and Liz serving, plus a variety of waiters that I had to let go as I learned what service was about. I wanted people to be in a better mood after they left my restaurant. I had a flaky bartender who was fun, but only did bartending on the side. A bartender had to be creative, really know how to make delicious drinks, and understand wine and beer. The waitstaff had to know how to take care of the customers and understand my food. The best waiter I had was Rob, and his friend Rudy was my busboy. Carol Ann came in after a few years, and was an incredible waitress and bartender. She did Cocktail Party classes with me, teaching the students how to make cocktails. Carol Ann taught Terri how to bartend, and she also became a great waitress and party planner.

The kitchen staff was another story. I watched the rivalry and disrespect they had for each other. One group of my staff (who were brothers) resented the rest of my staff, and there were constant battles for dominance in the kitchen. I had an array of sous chefs, and my son Joe was my first sous chef. He worked for me about five years. To be a great chef you need to have patience and talent, and not let the tension and exhaustion get to you.

James Ryan was with me for five years, and left when he had an argument with one of the brothers. He is still my dear friend. My mistake was hiring one brother after the other because they became a sort of mafia at Carol's Cafe. We began to see things that were very upsetting. They drank excessively, did drugs, and fought with each other constantly. Chef Sal rose from dishwasher to sous chef but he was fired along with all of his brothers after an incident with a crazy prep person who tried to attack Carol Ann in the kitchen. I hired Sal back and he was with us until we closed.

I worked many, many, hours to make the restaurant a success. I devoted myself to the quality of the food and desserts. Every season I changed the menu. I learned about wild game like venison, buffalo, wild boar, and about foie gras. I featured it on the menu and developed original recipes that became classics. Carol's Cafe received four stars from the *Staten Island Advance*. It was the highest number review you could receive at the time. We maintained that number for the entire time we were open. The first Zagat review was 27 out of 30 for food. We were listed in the Michelin Guide and were the first restaurant on Staten Island to receive a lovely review. In fact, our final review in 2016 in Zagat was 46 out of 50 for food.

I cooked in the kitchen every night, and developed a reputation for cooking to order. I would come out of the kitchen to ask customers how they wanted their food prepared. I think when they saw this middle-aged female chef, always with makeup and hair done, they were surprised. Instead of a chef's coat I wore embroidered aprons. My aprons that said things like Kitchen Bitch, Don't Make Me Poison Your Dinner, Carol's Bigger and Better Breasts, and Never Trust a Skinny Cook. It shocked them.

I had a spice rating from one to ten and would cook my customers' food the way they wanted it. Of course there were people who thought they should have a level eight or ten spice and did not realize how hot their food would be. The foods I created for my cooking classes was featured on our menus. Our holiday dinners were the best. For example, our Thanksgiving dinner was exactly what I made for my family. The fresh turkeys were reserved in advance from D'Artagnan, where I bought all my wild game for the restaurant. Of course, it was more expensive but it was delicious. My cakes, pies, soufflés, breads, and desserts each developed a great reputation.

We had all kinds of characters and celebrities come into the cafe. As a perfectionist, I just wanted to please them, but other cooks were also preparing dishes for service.

I learned that customers complained the most about waiting too long for their food or food not cooked to their liking. We cooked our food to order so it did take longer for it to reach the table. Some customers complained about bad service if we were very busy or that they wanted to meet me and I was too busy to come out.

We had all kinds of characters and celebrities come into the cafe. As a perfectionist, I just wanted to please them, but other cooks were also preparing dishes for service. One of my other cooks manned the salad and pasta station. I would teach them how to prepare the appetizers and how to plate them. Soups and braised dishes such as my meatballs and lamb shanks were made in advance because they took hours to cook. Once I trained the cook at this station, it was up to them to execute my dishes. It was not easy to see how sometimes shortcuts were taken by them because they thought they knew better. They did not understand my vision and it was very frustrating.

NEVER TRUST
A SKINNY COOK

Don't Make
Me Poison
Your Dinner

FOOD AND SEX:
THE GREATEST
PLEASURES IN LIFE

I CAN GO FROM
ZERO TO BITCH
IN 4.3 SECONDS

Masturbaking
with Carol

A small sampling of my embroidered aprons.

When other chefs were cooking on the line with me, there were times that I wanted to cry when I saw the mistakes they were making. I remember when a large table all ordered Vienna Schnitzel, and I was so busy that my line cook had to make it for me. These customers were my regulars, and I knew that I might lose them because of the crap my cook had sent out. They complained to the waitress and were upset. I am sure they recommended that entrée to their friends and it wasn't delicious. They knew that it was not prepared by me.

Cooking is instinctive to me and I just know how meats should feel. Of course, roasts such as beef, top round of veal, leg of lamb, loin of pork, and wellington are done with a thermometer. Beef Wellington is the toughest, because the beef is seared first and quickly cooled in the freezer and that has to be done properly. Instant-read thermometers were a revelation, but we went through them quickly because often they were mishandled. I began selling them in my cooking school when I was still in my house, and have used them ever since. We would use the instant-read thermometers to test the temperature of the Wellington, to determine if it was rare, medium-rare, medium, or God forbid, medium-well. When the Beef Wellington was over-cooked or undercooked, it was a real problem. It took 30 minutes to make a new one if the customer sent it back.

At the cafe, we made individual Beef Wellingtons. After I seared the meat I made a sauce with the fond. Using a Homemade Brown Beef Stock, I deglazed the pan picking up the fond. We made that ahead and froze it in portions. The beef was cooled and then the individual portions were put together to order. The phyllo sheets were layered and brushed with melted butter. The seared, cooled fillet of beef was put on top, and then the mush-room duxelles and foie gras (if used) was placed on top of the beef. The phyllo was gathered around the meat, and tied with a blanched leek ribbon.

"Well-done" people do not want to see pink or "blood," as they like to say. I always wonder how they became well-done people. My mother cooked all her meat well but that did not make me a well-done person. I love food too much to want to eat it that way. I had a customer, a woman, who had me cook her well-done beef three times. First I seared it on in my cast-iron skillet, and then roasted it in the oven and finally finished it on the grill. She was so happy that I prepared it the way she wanted.

The Beef Wellington became a sensation at Carol's Cafe but customers complained that it took too long to serve. We were never a restaurant that made food ahead of time and that was not for everyone. We were a fine din-ing restaurant, and served eclectic food.

Beef Wellington (Individual)

The most elegant, very popular, entrée served at Carol's Cafe was Individual Beef Wellington. I developed a variation of this recipe with a slice of seared grade A foie gras (when it was affordable), veins removed, cut a ¼-inch thick, and seared very quickly in duck fat, drained on paper towels, placed on the cooked beef, and enclosed in the pastry.

For rare: 120–125 degrees, medium rare 125–128, medium 130–135, medium well, "God forbid" 140 degrees. Do not even go there for well done, have a meatball. Remember the meat must rest for eight minutes after you take it out of the oven. The juices must go back into the meat. If you serve it right away, you will lose the juices.

Place filet mignon in preheated 375–400-degree oven to roast to desired temperature, after searing. There is no thing as a perfect oven, so giving you a time would be silly. Check with an instant-read thermometer after 8–10 minutes for rare, 10–12 minutes for medium rare, 12–14 minutes for medium well. Good luck!

Individual Filet Mignons

6 servings

6 filet mignons, each approximately 8 ounces and cut about 1½-inch thick

Unsalted butter as needed (*I like Land O'Lakes unsalted butter.*) *When it is on sale buy a few extra pounds and freeze it, well wrapped. Unsalted butter freezes for three months. Salted butter freezes for one year.*

Extra virgin olive oil as needed

1½–2 pounds of assorted mushrooms (a mix of wild and domestic) chopped coarsely

½ cup dried porcini mushrooms, soaked in very hot water for at least 20 minutes (optional)

½ cup minced shallots

2 teaspoons minced garlic

Fresh herbs: sage, thyme, fresh oregano, tarragon, Italian parsley, use what you like. *Sage and tarragon are strong flavored, so use just a little.*

½ cup or so of dry Madeira to flame the mushrooms

3 tablespoons fresh chopped chives

2 packages of fresh phyllo dough, left out at room temperature for two hours, before using. (*Note: If using frozen, defrost overnight in the refrigerator and then bring to room temperature, takes about two hours.*)

4 leeks, green parts only, blanched and cut lengthwise into six ½ inch ribbons. (*Note: Blanching is a cooking process, where you place the food substance, usually a vegetable or fruit, to be scalded in boiling water, removed after a brief, timed interval, and plunged into ice water to halt the cooking process.*)

Preheat the oven to 400 degrees.

Season the filet mignons with lots of olive oil, salt, and pepper on both sides. Combine the butter and oil in a large sauté pan over high heat. If your sauté pan is 12 inches, do no more than three pieces at a time. Wait for each one to sizzle well. When the pan is hot and foam has subsided, add the beef, one at a time. Sear until well browned on each side. Reserve pan, do not wash it, to make your sauce. Transfer to a cooling rack on a platter. Cool completely, in the refrigerator, before wrapping in phyllo.

Prepare the Sauce

In the skillet you seared your beef filets make the sauce for Wellington:

Unsalted butter and extra virgin olive oil as needed	Madeira or fine brandy
½ cup or to taste, minced shallots	2 cups or so beef stock
1 teaspoon of minced garlic	2 teaspoons Dijon mustard, only
½ cup shitake mushrooms, sliced or use the mushroom of your choice	½ cup heavy cream
1 tablespoon chopped soaked porcini mushrooms	Fresh chives and Italian parsley, chopped to taste

In the skillet, add two tablespoons unsalted butter and one tablespoon olive oil. Add the shallots and garlic, cook for five minutes, add the shitake mushrooms and cook, slowly, until just colored. Flame with dry Madeira or cook until completely reduced. Add the beef stock and bring to a full simmer. Add the cream and mustard. Reduce until thickened. Taste for seasoning, add the herbs, salt and pepper, and correct. If needed, add a pinch of sugar. Set aside. Cool completely. This sauce freezes very well.

Make the Beef Wellingtons

Melt two sticks of unsalted butter and keep over hot water. Use a double boiler. It must stay warm or it will congeal.

Blanch leek, green part only, in boiling water for a few seconds, until wilted. Drain on paper towels. Now you are ready to proceed.

continued

Beef Wellington (Individual), *continued*

Each Beef Wellington will need five sheets of phyllo. Keep phyllo covered with a slightly damp towel while working with it. On a clean board, place your first sheet of phyllo. Butter it lightly with melted butter, repeat until you have five sheets. Place a couple of tablespoons of cooled Mushroom Mixture in center of sheets. Place tenderloins on top of mushrooms. Top tenderloin with another couple of tablespoons of mushrooms. Gather edges of phyllo together and gently twist. Tie with leek ribbons. Gently brush with warm melted butter.

Roast in preheated oven at 400 degrees, until you reach the desired temperature. Place on a warm plate. Drizzle hot sauce around the Beef Wellingtons. (The word drizzle is to be taken seriously. If you are heavy-handed, your phyllo will become too wet.)

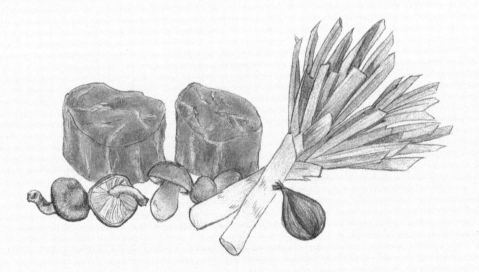

Favorite Recipes

EVERYONE HAD THEIR FAVORITES but I was a seasonal chef so if someone wanted a blueberry pie in January, they had to wait until July. Of course, now everything is available all year long, but I would not change my ways.

My Mussels in White Wine became my most ordered dish. I made them in White Wine Sauce with a touch of concasse (fresh tomatoes) or in a Red Sauce with a mixture of fresh tomato and Italian canned tomatoes. The ingredients included extra virgin olive oil, onion, lots of garlic, shallots, lemon wedges, and fresh chiles, if they wanted spice. Then simmered slowly, until sweet and golden. It took about 20 minutes. I added white wine and reduced the sauce until the wine was gone. I added fresh tomatoes for color or I used canned tomatoes for red mussels. We made our fish stock fresh and that was added to the mixture. I used kosher salt, freshly ground black pepper, a touch of sugar, Italian parsley, basil, fresh oregano, and dry oregano. The mussels were spiced to order according to the customer's liking.

A few people loved the sauce over just-cooked linguine. I offered half portions or full portions which we served in a large bowl, family style. It was shocking that I had never had mussels in my life when I was growing up. When I first prepared the mussels, they had to be cleaned and the beards had to be removed. We had to make sure they were still alive. We had to scrub them under cold running water and make sure all the sand was removed. Later, we purchased cultivated mussels called P.E.I. (for Prince Edward Island) and they only had to be rinsed in cold water. Then we threw out the open ones, because they were dead.

We developed a reputation for being expensive, because we had ingredients on the menu that were expensive, like foie gras and wild game, but we also had affordable dishes, like our mussels. I think being an eclectic restaurant was hurtful in the sense that people were confused and didn't know how to categorize us.

It would upset me when customers in the restaurant would ask me, "Where is the foie gras? Why don't you have it on your menu anymore?" What they didn't understand is that foie gras, grade A, is $114 a pound. It is very difficult to have a fine dining restaurant, and not be able to buy these ingredients anymore because you cannot pass that expense on to the customer.

I loved to make food from all over the world, just like the way I taught my classes. It made me happy. I know financially my business would have made more money if I focused on one subject, like Sicilian or Northern Italian cooking but that bored me, and I loved to create new dishes or desserts. I made Apple Pie in a Paper Bag. I made New Orleans Bread Pudding into a soufflé for a special customer, Maureen, for her birthday. Recently when she heard I was retiring, she wrote me a letter about her birthday soufflé and recalled that I wrote the recipe out for her that night and how she treasured it.

Our homemade potato gnocchi with brown butter sauce and fresh sage.

One of my most famous dishes was Penne with Shrimp, Broccoli Rabe, and Fresh Tomatoes, that I created for a customer named Camille. One day she said, "Can you make me something with shrimp, broccoli rabe, and tomatoes?" She came every Sunday and would ask for a dish that wasn't on the menu. This dish became a classic, and was never taken off the menu. I made it for Bobby Flay, *Neighborhood Eats* (Channel 7), on my show *The Happy Cooker,* and on many other television shows. Reporters loved how dramatic it was when I flambéed the shrimp with brandy.

Now I'm going to talk about calf's liver. My mother made calf's liver just for me. It was sautéed in a frying pan. I think she floured the liver, and then fried the onions in the same pan. When I went on a diet, she placed the liver under the broiler and cooked it to death. It was terrible but I did lose weight.

I am the only one in my family who loves liver. I was determined to put liver on the menu at Carol's Cafe. Johnny Carson used to joke that he doesn't care what you do to liver, it is still liver! I wanted to prove him wrong, and I developed a recipe for the restaurant.

When customers in the Cafe ordered my liver entrée, I gave them a diploma saying that they were a "Member of Carol's Liver Club" which I would autograph for them. It was done with a sense of humor, and the customers loved it. We used calf's liver. We would buy the whole piece of liver, clean it by removing the cellophane skin, and then portion it by cutting it into half-inch-thick steak slices.

To prepare the dish, the liver was soaked in milk to remove some of the bitterness. In a 10-inch cast-iron frying pan, I slowly cooked three slices of bacon. The bacon was drained on paper towels and set aside under a heat lamp. Lots of sliced onions were cooked in the bacon fat until they were caramelized, sweet, and golden brown. The onions were set aside and put under the heat lamp. The soaked liver was dried on paper towels, then coated in seasoned flour. A tablespoon of butter was added to the pan and when it was hot, I put the liver in. It was cooked to order. The customer would tell me if they wanted it rare, medium rare, or well done. Usually people who order the liver well done do so because their mother made it that way. I would try to talk them out of it, and say, "Let me make it for you medium." Sometimes they would try it that way and then tell me how much more delicious it was.

The liver was flambéed with port wine and then set aside. To make the sauce, rich beef stock was added to the pan, a little fresh tarragon and chives, a teaspoon of glacé, Dijon mustard, and heavy cream. The liver was presented on a large white plate with the caramelized onions and cooked bacon placed on top.

> **When customers in the Cafe ordered my liver entrée, I gave them a diploma saying that they were a "Member of Carol's Liver Club" which I would autograph for them.**

Sweet Pastry

3 cups all-purpose flour, sifted

1 teaspoon salt

12 tablespoons unsalted butter, cut up into small chunks and chilled

6 tablespoons Crisco shortening, chilled

6 to 8 tablespoons ice water

4 tablespoons granulated sugar

In a large bowl, combine the dry ingredients (flour, salt, sugar) with the cut-up, chilled butter and Crisco. Working quickly and lightly, pinch and slide the lumps of dough between your fingertips until the mixture resembles dry rice. This process layers the shortening and flour together, creating "leaves" that will form flakes when baked. Fingertips are used instead of the warmer palm of your hand because warmth melts shortening, which can then be absorbed by the flour, causing the dough to toughen. The rule: keep everything as cold as possible. Instead of using your fingertips to blend the dough, you can also use a pastry blender.

At this point, add the ice water. Take care not to overwork the dough. Lightly combine the dough until it just begins to cling together in clumps, but before it forms a ball. Sprinkle on a tiny bit more water if the dough looks too dry. Dough should feel pliable like clay, but not sticky. If you catch the dough at this point, even if you are using a machine, you will not overwork the pastry.

Divide the dough into equal pieces and press into two disk shapes. Lightly flour two pieces of plastic wrap and wrap the two disks. Chill in the refrigerator at least 30 minutes. The dough may be refrigerated for three to four days, or may be frozen for up to six months. **Note:** Allow chilled dough to sit out at room temperature for a few minutes to loosen its extreme hardness before rolling out.

Preparation:

After the dough is made and chilled, it is ready to be rolled out. Set the dough in the center of a lightly floured work surface. Sprinkle the top of the dough with a little flour, and rub some flour onto your rolling pin. Remember that too much flour toughens dough, so use only enough to prevent sticking.

continued

Sweet Pastry, *continued*

Rolling out Dough:

Roll out dough with short, even strokes, from the center of the dough disk to the edges. Lift rolling pin as you approach the dough edge; rolling over the edges will cause them to be too thin. To keep dough from sticking and to make an even circle, lift and turn the dough after every few strokes. At this time, toss a fine dusting of flour beneath the dough if it is needed. If dough sticks to the work surface, use a spatula to gently ease it up. Roll dough to ⅛-inch thickness and two to three inches larger than the pie or baking pan. You can set your baking pan upside down over the dough in order to better measure your dough.

Fitting the Dough:

Loosen rolled dough from surface and fold dough in half onto itself, then fold in quarters. Pick up this folded dough triangle and position it over the baking pan so the center point of the folded dough triangle is in the center of the pan. Unfold the dough, allowing it to drape evenly across the pan. Alternatively, you can roll dough up onto the rolling pin, lift it into place, and unroll it over the pan.

Apple Pie in a Paper Bag

**One unbaked nine-inch fluted
pie shell**

Prepare Sweet Pastry (page 207) and chill for at least 30 minutes.

Roll pastry out and place in a nine-inch aluminum pie pan. Flute the edges. Cover lightly and place in the refrigerator while preparing filling and topping.

You will need about a ½ cup of apricot preserves to paint on pie shell.

Apple Pie Filling

About 6–8 large apples. *Choose the apples carefully. Granny Smith, Jonathan, Cortland are some of the best.*

¾–1 cup sugar or to taste, depending on the apple of your choice

3 tablespoons all-purpose flour

1 teaspoon cinnamon or to taste

¼ teaspoon, freshly grated nutmeg

¼ teaspoon salt

2 teaspoons fresh lemon juice

2 tablespoons apple brandy (optional)

Peel the apples and cut them into quarters. Remove the cores, then cut each quarter into four or five lengthwise slices, each about ½-inch thick and then cut again into ¼-inch slices.

Place in a large bowl and drizzle with lemon juice. Toss well and cover with plastic wrap pressed into apples, and refrigerate if not using immediately. This will help the apples retain their color and not turn brown.

Combine sugar, flour, cinnamon, and nutmeg with a whisk. Sprinkle over apple slices and toss gently. Add apple brandy if using. Set aside.

Have ready a large heavy, brown supermarket paper bag. Do not double the bags.

LEAVE ONLY ONE RACK IN THE CENTER OF THE OVEN.
DO NOT LINE THE RACK WITH TIN FOIL, OR YOU CAN CAUSE A FIRE.

Preheat the oven to 425–450 degrees. Only you know your oven. If it is a fast, hot oven, leave at 425 degrees. If it is a slow oven, then go to 450 degrees. Use an oven thermometer to check.

continued

Apple Pie in a Paper Bag, *continued*

Topping for Pie

Scant ¾ cup sugar

¼ cup light brown sugar

¾ cup flour, plus ⅛ of a cup

1 teaspoon cinnamon or to taste

¾ cup cold unsalted butter

Combine sugars, flour, cinnamon, and salt. Cut cold butter into small pieces and blend into dry ingredients with your fingertips, or a pastry blender. Do not over blend, there should still be small pieces of cold butter in mixture. Taste for seasoning and add whatever is needed. Set aside in the refrigerator.

Now you are ready to put the pie together. Taste the apples for seasoning and add whatever is needed, sugar, cinnamon, or nutmeg. Paint the pie shell with the apricot preserves. You may need to warm the preserves to thin them out. Put the apples in the cold pie shell, do not pile too high. Use only what is needed. Sprinkle on the topping carefully.

Carefully slip pie into heavy brown paper bag. Fold top of bag under.

Bake in preheated oven for 50 minutes to one hour.

DO NOT OPEN OVEN UNTIL THE 50 MINUTES ARE UP.

Carefully peek in bag and see if pie is done. It should be a deep, golden brown with juices flowing. If not, leave another five to ten minutes.

Note: You will smell the bag the first 10 minutes; do not open the oven or you can cause a fire.

Remove pie in the bag, and place carefully onto cooling rack. Remove pie from bag immediately and leave to cool on cooling rack. Serve warm.

Calf's Liver Flambéed in Port Wine

When I decided to put calf's liver on the menu at Carol's Cafe, my cooks thought I was crazy, but I love liver—so I decided to have a "Liver Club." My menu stated: "Become a member of Carol's Liver Club." After a diner ate my liver dish, I would come out of the kitchen, and shake their hand. Then I would welcome them as a member, and present them with a signed certificate. I had so many members that I lost count! This recipe was a favorite of Rosalind Atkinson.

This recipe serves 4

8 slices calf's liver, cleaned of any membranes, sliced ½ inch thick

2 cups milk

12 slices bacon

5 large yellow onions, sliced thin

5 tablespoons unsalted butter

5 tablespoons extra virgin oil

1 teaspoon sugar

½ teaspoon kosher salt

2 cups all-purpose flour

1 cup port wine

1 cup beef or veal stock

1 cup heavy cream

¼ cup chopped flat-leaf parsley

¼ cup chopped fresh chives, plus 8 long chives for garnish

5 leaves of fresh sage

1 sprig fresh tarragon

2 tablespoons Dijon mustard

Kosher salt and freshly ground black pepper

1 tablespoon reduced balsamic vinegar

Place the calf's liver slices in a shallow bowl with the milk and set aside. Allow the liver to soak while you cook the bacon. This technique will help to remove the bitterness from the liver.

In one large, or two medium, sauté or cast-iron pans, place the bacon in a single layer. The pan should be cold. Prick the bacon with a fork to prevent curling. Cook over low heat, turning occasionally, until crispy. Drain bacon on paper towel and set aside in a warm place.

In the same pan(s) as the bacon fat, add two or three tablespoons of the butter and olive oil along with the sliced onions, sugar, and ½ teaspoon salt. Cook slowly over medium-low heat, stirring occasionally with tongs. The onions should be golden brown and caramelized. This process may take as long as 20 minutes. Set aside in a warm place.

Remove the soaked livers from the milk and dry on paper towels. Season the flour with salt and pepper and place in a flat dish. Dredge the liver in the flour and place on a rack to dry.

continued

Calf's Liver Flambéed in Port Wine, *continued*

Using the same pan(s) as the onions were cooked in, heat the remaining butter and olive oil over medium heat. Add the liver slices one at a time making sure not to crowd the pan. Cook until golden brown, turning as needed until the livers are medium rare (see note). Drizzle with reduced balsamic vinegar and turn to coat. Quickly flambé with port wine. Remove the liver from the pan and set aside.

Add beef or veal stock to the pan(s) and reduce over high heat. Add fresh herbs, mustard, and salt and pepper to taste. Finish the sauce with the heavy cream and reduce until thickened. Taste for seasoning, adding additional salt and a pinch of sugar if sauce is a little bitter.

To serve, place livers on four individual dinner plates. Divide sauce evenly over each portion. Pile on warmed caramelized onions and warmed bacon. Garnish with fresh parsley or two long chives on top.

NOTE:

- To test the "doneness" of the cooked liver, use this technique: Tense your hand, spread it out like a fan and touch the part between your thumb and pointer finger— that is well-done. Relax your hand just a little for medium-well, a little more for medium, and so on.

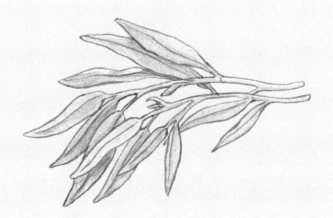

Favorite Classes

I DID BIRTHDAY PARTY cooking classes for children for many years. It started when I did Maria's birthday party at P.S. 48. That is how I began to teach cooking classes for kids. I taught them how to make Crepes and Butterfly Vanilla Cupcakes filled with Chocolate Buttercream. It was a hands-on class so the kids actually prepared their own food. The children really enjoyed that.

The other party options were French Bread Pizza and Tacos. For many years we did these cooking parties, mostly on Fridays. Once we opened the restaurant, it was difficult to do both things so we stopped doing them. People continued to request the children's parties until we closed.

In one of the rooms at the cafe hung a photo of a girl wearing big glasses that was taken during one of these private birthday parties. That "girl" grew up to be a food critic later on in her life. She wrote a lovely review about Carol's Cafe, mentioning how she felt that the best day in her life was her cooking class birthday party. She went on to say how much that party influenced her life, and how she loved that a picture from her birthday party hung in the cafe, for so many years.

Many of my customer's came to the cafe with their children, and I watched them grow up. They became attached to me, and would run into the kitchen to bring me cards and flowers. In my classes, I had mentally challenged kids and adults who were allotted money to take my classes once a month. They knew how much I cared about them, and now that I'm retired I worry that I'm not there for them.

*Coconut Custard Pie
in the cafe.*

Butterfly Cupcakes

This recipe yields 18–24 cupcakes depending on how much you fill your cupcake tins.

2 cups of sifted Presto Self-Rising Cake Flour

1 cup sugar

½ cup unsalted butter (room temperature)

1 cup minus 2 tablespoons milk

3 egg yolks (room temperature)

1 full teaspoon pure vanilla extract

Sift flour and measure two cups into a strainer. Add one cup sugar into the strainer and set aside. Place ½ cup butter into a mixing bowl and beat for about one minute. Sift in flour and sugar, add milk, yolks, and vanilla. Beat for three minutes. Scrape down the sides of the mixing bowl with a rubber spatula twice while beating.

Line cupcake tins with paper liners. Fill the cups ⅔ full with batter. Preheat your oven to 375 degrees for at least 10 minutes. Bake for about 20 minutes or until a toothpick inserted in each cupcake comes out clean. Remove cupcakes from tins and place on cooling racks.

Chocolate Filling

½ cup unsalted butter (room temperature)

½ cup sugar

2 ounces unsweetened chocolate, melted and cooled

1 teaspoon vanilla

3 large eggs

Cream butter and sugar until light and fluffy, about 10–15 minutes. Beat in melted chocolate and vanilla, then add eggs one at a time, beating two minutes after each addition. Continue to beat until sugar is thoroughly dissolved. Chill until firm enough to use.

Making the Butterflies

With a paring knife, holding it at a 45 degree angle, cut a cone-shaped piece from the top of each cupcake. Placing the top part of cone down, cut each piece in half. Fill the hollow with the prepared chocolate filling. Place the cut pieces of cupcake on top of the filling to resemble butterfly wings. Sprinkle with confectioners' sugar and serve. If not serving immediately, refrigerate.

Note: Any unused chocolate filling may be frozen for later use.

Interesting Classes

WITH MY LIFE IN CHAOS, I concentrated on my cooking school. It was my job to write two brochures a year and along with the classic classes that we did every year, to come up with new classes so the students would come back. Having single-session classes made it very difficult to come up with new ideas. Unlike schools in Manhattan that had a turnover of students, we had repeat students that took many different classes.

My Blueberry Crumb Pies.

Writing the brochure took at least three weeks of working through the night, after I came home from work. In my opinion, some of the most interesting classes did not book. Things changed when I no longer answered the phone and had someone who did not have the passion or knowledge to discuss the classes with the potential student. This started in my home when my assistant at that time would register students over the phone. I know because I received complaints about the tone of her voice, even though in person she was a very nice woman. I had no choice, I could not do everything.

Beer Today, Gone Tomorrow

I tried to create interesting classes that reflected my lifestyle and all that I was learning from others. One was about beer for anyone who was serious about beer. The class was called "Beer Appreciation with Sal Pennachio." Sal was the owner and brew master of New York Harbor Ale, and a friend and business partner of my son-in-law, Jeff.

Sal led the class on a trip through the world of beer, with tastings of eight classic beer styles and eight microbrewery beers, including all the classic beer styles. Sal also brought a sampling of his own beers, New York Harbor Ale and New York Harbor Porter.

On a quiet Sunday, when the restaurant was closed, my son-in-law Jeff, a home brewer himself (who is also a Recognized Beer Judge by the A.H.A., and President of the local Homebrewers Club, "The Outlaws of Homebrew") hosted an American Homebrewers Association Sanctioned Beer Judging Competition, that had homebrewers come from all over the United States to compete. We set up tables all around the room and people went from table to table to taste the beer. Jeff and a panel of judges picked the Best in Show, and many other awards were handed out that day. The room smelled of beer for a long time and it made me smile. I tried to have another beer class and of course there was no interest. Mostly women took my cooking classes, and they just didn't like beer.

Teenage Survival

I thought it would be interesting to have a class for teenagers. In many households both parents wanted or needed to work. Life was so hectic that many meals consisted of prepared and/or take-out food, which is neither nutritious or delicious. I thought, wouldn't it be terrific if teenagers felt enough confidence in the kitchen that they could not only help the family, but learn how to help themselves? I called the class "Teenage Survival Cooking." I picked dishes I thought they would like such as Chicken Parmesan; Crispy Shrimp with Homemade Tartar Sauce; Homemade French Fries; Nachos with Refried Beans, Cheddar Cheese, and Green Chiles; Garlic Toast; Penne with Marinara Sauce; Make your own Pizza, anyway you like it; Carol's Chocolate Chip Cookies; and Confetti Rice Krispy Treats. I always began the class with how to behave in the kitchen and gave them safety tips.

A highlight from the class was catching a 13-year-old girl, and a 14-year-old young man making out in my walk-in refrigerator.

A highlight from the class was catching a 13-year-old girl and a 14-year-old young man making out in my walk-in refrigerator. Her mother told me she had an eating disorder and hoped that her taking cooking classes would help her. She was a very slim, pretty girl with braces. The young man also had braces. When I walked in their braces had locked and she was embarrassed. I think the surprise of me walking in jerked them apart. During the class, she moved her food around on the plate and did not eat anything. I said, "Try something that you might like" so she did. She was surprised that the Penne with Marinara Sauce tasted delicious. Perhaps she had never tasted tomato sauce made from scratch before and was used to store-bought sauce in a jar. I was only with her for two lessons and I wonder if I helped her.

I remember once twin boys in foster care from the city attended a class but could not sit still. I was frying french fries in a wok when one of the boys walked by and stuck his hand in the hot oil to get a french fry. I screamed at him quickly and he removed his hand. I said the kitchen is a dangerous place, and you must be careful.

I am so proud of the young people who studied seriously with me and became chefs, food critics, and had careers in the food industry. I told them how I first knew that I wanted to be a chef and when I met my first cooking teacher in public school. I explained that my parents did not encourage me, and they were very fortunate that their parents took them to my cooking school at such a young age. I explained that even if they didn't become a chef, they would know what a joy a well-cooked meal is.

Korean

I offered another class called "Korean Food with a Twist with Dinah Surh," but it was a difficult class to book. Martha Stewart had called Dinah the "Korean Martha Stewart." We only registered a handful of students for her class but she was so sweet that I proceeded with the class anyway. She made BBQ Beef using simple techniques, a Korean Lettuce Taco, and a sumptuous Korean Philly Cheese Steak Sandwich packed with beef, lettuce, American cheese, zucchini "coins," pan-fried fish fillets with a special dipping sauce, and a refreshing cucumber salad. Her dessert was Naked Cupcakes with crystallized ginger, pine nuts, and red dates. She currently lives on Staten Island and is very involved in the food scene. She has also appeared on the *Food Network*.

I am so proud of the young people who studied seriously with me and became chefs, food critics, and had careers in the food industry.

Others

Not all of the guest teachers were accepted by my students. I tried to offer courses like "Professional Bread Techniques with Holiday Breads, with Chef Carmen Jones and Dee Gelles." Another class, "Strawberry Jam with Nancy Slowik," was about the fundamentals of safe canning. Not even Norman Weinstein's spectacular "Peking Duck" class attracted enough students. What did book were our own classes so soon guest teachers were no longer invited.

*Advanced Techniques &
Theory of Cooking Class,
"Finale."*

I loved American cooking (as did James Beard) so I put a class together called "Real American Food." I made Quick 'N Easy Chili, Carol's Corn Chowder, Southern Fried Chicken, Carol's Delicious Meatloaf, Crispy Soft Shell Crabs with Cajun Wine Sauce, Clam Box Fried Clams with Homemade Tartar Sauce, Carol's Potato Salad and Coleslaw, All-in-the Family Corn Fritters, and Carol's Delicious Crab Cakes. For dessert I included Rich Strawberry Shortcake with Chantilly Whipped Cream and our Homemade Vanilla Bean Ice Cream.

"Dining On Lobster" was a class that became so popular that it was televised for Time Warner Cable. The class began with live and kicking lobsters. In this full participation class, each student prepared their own lobster. We began with our superb Lobster Bisque and proceeded to Grilled Lobster with Pesto Sauce Stuffing, Poached Lobster, and Steamed Lobster served with drawn butter. For a grand finale, I prepared a scrumptious Blueberry Crumb Pie.

Trip to Sicily

Teaching a class at the Italian Culinary Institute in Manhattan.

I had always wanted to go to Sicily because that was where my father was born. While I was teaching a class at the Italian Culinary Institute in Manhattan, I met an Italian woman who was a travel agent. She heard about my interest in Sicily and offered to arrange a trip for myself and a group of my students to go there.

She set up a ten-day tour for seven of us. Upon our arrival in Sicily, she had promised that a tour guide would meet us at the airport but that didn't happen. We were not off to a good start. Eventually a new guide was sent to replace him but we were on our own for a while.

We went to a Sicilian family restaurant that was like a large wedding hall. We arrived early and were told that they did not start serving until 7:00 PM. At 7:00 PM exactly, the doors swung open and everyone came in at once. I saw a sea of women in black dresses with pearls around their necks. The chefs had to cook everything all at the same time. I felt like I was back home in Brooklyn with the black dresses, and all my aunts and relatives were walking in.

I called the handsome young waiter (who did not speak English) over to our table, and said that my grilled octopus is not cooked. He brought it back to the kitchen and was back in a minute or two with the exact same hard

Carol Ann and me teaching a class at a firehouse in Staten Island after 9/11.

piece of octopus. All they did was make grill marks on it. My knife bent as I tried cutting into it. We all laughed! It was funny and disappointing. Not what I expected in this Sicilian family restaurant. The octopus needed to be boiled until it was tender, and then grilled. At Carol's Cafe, I developed a delicious grilled octopus dish with poached pears or figs that stayed on the menu for years.

One of my favorite days was spent at the salt mines in Sicily. You cannot imagine how beautiful the scenery was. I bought my little salt pig cardholder from an old Sicilian man who had a cart. Everything on the cart was made out of salt. He was taken with me and showed me a old, yellow, wrinkled newspaper article about his work. I wanted to shop and buy more things, but his body odor was intolerable. I treasure that little salt pig and wish now I had purchased more of his creations.

I was happy when we left the villa where we were staying and went to Palermo. We then stayed in a modern hotel and beautiful beach was not far away. Finally, one of our group who was driving me crazy about going to the beach could do that. I got my camera ready, and thought she was going to dive into the ocean like Esther Williams. There she was in her pale blue bikini, and she only tiptoed into the water and ran out. I asked, "Is that it?"

We did go to Taormina, and climbed the steps where at every step, we found little shops where they made the most beautiful pottery. I loved shopping and chatting with the local storekeepers. I wanted to buy everything, but remembered my experience shopping in London when I had to buy more luggage to accommodate my purchases. So I controlled myself and now the beautiful pottery I bought has a home in my china closet where I can admire it everyday.

I wish I could remember the names of the places that we visited. I do recall going to the post office and having to leave because of the horrible body odor. Deodorant is not used in Sicily. I can honestly say that I will never forget my time in Sicily, but as far as the cooking was concerned, it was not a learning experience. It was beautiful but it is not easy traveling with a group of people who didn't necessarily get along with each other. It is not the same as vacationing with family or being by yourself. I was happy to be home.

Chocolate Angel Food Cake with Espresso Buttercream.

Crab Cakes

*Yield: approximately
9 appetizer-sized cakes.*

1 pound fresh lump crabmeat, picked over for cartilage

1 egg

5 tablespoons mayonnaise

4 slices soft textured white bread (such as Wonder bread), crusts removed and cut into 1-inch squares

1½ teaspoons Worcestershire sauce or to taste

4 heaping teaspoons honey mustard

1 teaspoon Old Bay Seasoning

1 scallion, chopped fine

1 celery stalk, peeled and finely diced

Tabasco sauce to taste, about ½ teaspoon

½ lemon, juiced

¼ cup minced chives

½ cup chopped flat-leaf parsley

Salt and pepper to taste

⅛ teaspoon ancho chile powder

Optional: ⅛ teaspoon jalapeño powder or minced serrano chile

Peanut or corn oil for frying

Place crabmeat in a large bowl. In a smaller bowl whisk together egg, mayonnaise, bread cubes, Worcestershire sauce, mustard, and seasonings. Pour contents of smaller bowl over crabmeat and mix well. Add remaining ingredients and stir to combine.

In a small skillet, heat some of the cooking oil. When the pan is hot, add a small amount of the crab mixture, sautéing on both sides until golden. Taste your patty for seasoning, adding salt, pepper, lemon, or chiles as needed.

Line a cookie sheet with parchment paper or foil. Spoon heaping tablespoons of the crab mixture onto the cookie sheet, forming chubby cakes. Cover with plastic wrap and chill until ready to cook. In a large cast-iron skillet, heat about one inch of oil over medium high heat. Carefully add crab cakes and fry three to four minutes per side or until browned. Remove cooked crab cakes and place on paper towels or on a cooling rack.

Optional: Dip chilled crab cakes into panko breadcrumbs for added texture before frying.

Serve with sherry wine sauce (on next page).

continued

Crab Cakes, *continued*

Sherry Wine Sauce

Yield: about 1 cup

1 egg yolk

¼ cup ketchup

3 tablespoons finely chopped scallions

2 tablespoons dry sherry

1 teaspoon creole or brown mustard

¼ teaspoon salt

¼ teaspoon pepper

¼ teaspoon Tabasco sauce or to taste

½ cup vegetable oil

Place all the ingredients except the oil in a blender or food processor and process about 30 seconds. With the machine still running, add the oil in a thin steady stream and continue processing until the mixture is smooth and slightly thickened, about one minute. Make sure to scrape down the sides of the bowl with a rubber spatula at least once while blending. Taste for seasoning. Chill before serving.

Vanilla Ice Cream

7 large egg yolks	1 vanilla bean, split in half
1 cup sugar	1 cup heavy cream
2 cups whole milk	Pinch of salt

In a stand mixer, beat the yolks and sugar together until thick and pale yellow, about 10 minutes.

After splitting the vanilla bean pod, use a small spoon to scrape the inside, reserving the seeds. Add the seeds and the pod into the milk.

In a four-quart heavyweight saucepan, bring the milk and vanilla bean to a simmer. Remove from the heat.

While the mixer is on low, slowly add about one cup of the hot milk into the egg yolk mixture to temper the custard. Beat for a few minutes to combine, scraping once with a rubber spatula.

Pour the tempered mixture back into the hot milk while whisking to prevent curdling. Cook over medium heat, stirring continuously with a heat-proof rubber spatula until the custard has thickened. You can test this by running a spoon along the side of the spatula to see if it leaves a distinct trail.

Whisk in the heavy cream and salt. Taste for seasoning, adding pure vanilla extract if needed.

Pour the mixture into a bowl and refrigerate overnight, chilling completely.

Remove the vanilla bean pods and freeze the custard in an ice cream machine, according to the manufacturer's instructions.

NOTE:

· This custard curdles easily. This usually occurs while you are cooking the mixture. If this happens you can save it by quickly transferring the hot custard into the bowl of a stand mixer with a whisk attachment. Beat the mixture to cool it down. Alternatively, you can do this in a food processor. In most cases, unless you have made "scrambled eggs," your mixture will recombine, and you can proceed with the recipe.

Blueberry Double Crust Pie

For two 9-inch pies

Sweet Pastry *(page 207)*

½ cup raspberry preserves (warm and strain if there are seeds, cool) to coat bottom of pie crust

4 cups fresh, picked-over berries, rinsed and destemmed and dried with paper towels

1 cup granulated sugar

A pinch of salt

3 tablespoons quick cooking tapioca or 3 tablespoons cornstarch, *measured very carefully, by pressing hard on the cornstarch in the measuring spoon and leveling off*

2 tablespoons fresh lemon juice, strained

Zest of a small orange or zest of a lemon

Freshly ground nutmeg to taste

1–2 tablespoons Chambord liqueur (optional)

2 tablespoons unsalted butter, cut into small pieces, for top of blueberries

Prepare the pastry for double crust pie and divide into two portions, equally. Chill for at least an hour or overnight.

Make filling for pie while dough chills. Dress blueberries without the tapioca and taste for seasoning. Correct seasoning, it may need more sugar or trust your palate. Do not dump, always season with caution. Add tapioca carefully, only after you have fully seasoned the mixture.

Roll bottom pastry out and line the pie plate with the dough, trim and leave an inch of pastry around the rim.

Put raspberry preserves evenly on the pastry with a pastry brush or the back of a spoon. Chill while rolling out top crust. Put blueberry mixture into bottom crust and top with two tablespoons unsalted butter cut into ½-inch pieces.

DON'T FORGET THE BUTTER! I did quite a few times and had to somehow get it under the top crust! You know when it's 4:00 AM and you're tired, you make mistakes.

Put top crust on and trim evenly with bottom crust.

Fold the edge under the bottom crust overhang and pinch together to seal, making a raised rim all around. If too much pastry dough, trim again. If the flute is too thick, it will fall off.

Flute pastry and cut a center vent hole. Cut slits with scissors or knife around the middle of the crust or as an option, cut rolled pastry into ½-inch strips and arrange in a lattice topping. Flute edges as desired.

Preheat oven to 400 degrees. Chill for a ½ hour or place in freezer for a ½ hour for a more defined flute.

Sprinkle lightly with granulated sugar and set pie in the lower third of the pre-heated oven and bake for 10 minutes. Reduce heat to 350 degrees and raise the pie to center of the oven rack and bake an additional 40 to 45 minutes or until the juices that run from the pie begin to caramelize and pastry is golden brown.

Check the pie every 12 minutes and turn carefully for even baking. If the pastry gets too dark, cover loosely with a sheet of aluminum foil. Cool on a wire rack.

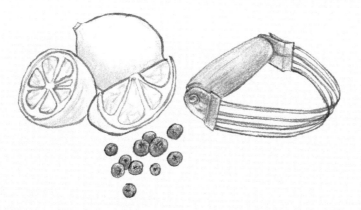

Blueberry Crumb Pie

Make recipe for Double Crust Blueberry Pie (page 228). You will need one pastry round. Freeze the other or make two Blueberry Crumb Pies. Roll out one pastry and place in pie plate. Chill for 30 minutes in refrigerator.

Crumb Topping for Fruit Pies

For two 9-inch pies

3 cups sifted all-purpose flour

Freshly grated nutmeg to taste

3–4 teaspoons cinnamon or to taste

1⅓ cups packed light brown sugar or more if you like it sweeter

1 cup + 4 tablespoons unsalted butter, cold from the refrigerator

Combine flour, nutmeg, cinnamon, and packed brown sugar.

Place in food processor. With steel blade, cut in cold butter with pulse button until crumbs form.

If you do not have a food processor, cut butter in with pastry blender by hand. Do not overwork! Taste for seasoning and correct if necessary.

Do not over mix. Place in bowl, and with fingers form large crumbs. Do not overwork!

Can be made ahead and refrigerated or frozen.

When making a fruit crumb pie, do not put butter on top of the fruit like the Double Crust Blueberry Pie. Just carefully place the crumbs on top and place on a cookie sheet to catch the drippings. Bake until juices flow and caramelize and crumbs and crust are golden brown.

Place in a preheated 400-degree oven for 10 minutes and then reduce the temperature to 350 degrees for 35–45 minutes.

If the crumbs are getting too dark, tent with tin foil until juices flow and caramelize.

NOTE:

- These crumbs can be used for any fruit pie using fruit that is in season.

Guest Teachers

Most Favorite

NORMAN WEINSTEIN IS A native New Yorker, former musician, and a wonderful cooking teacher. He was the founder of Hot Wok, a cooking school and catering business, and the author of *Chinese Cooking* and Barron's *32 Wok Dishes*. I was a guest in his home and he was a guest in my home.

He taught Chinese cooking and knife skills classes at my cooking school. His knife skills class taught you how to choose the right knife for the right job, and the simple secrets of keeping your knife sharp. He guaranteed that you'd learn to slice, shred, and dice your way to great meals. I studied Chinese cooking, and made Peking duck with him in Manhattan.

Norman's duck class was my favorite class that I ever took in Manhattan. Of course it is a very complicated procedure, but Norman made it fun, interesting, and delicious. He made the whole class laugh. Peking duck takes about five days to make! I may not remember every step but I do remember him pumping air into the duck to separate the skin from the meat, and hanging the duck so the skin would be dry and crisp. He had prepared the duck ahead that we were going to eat. I had never tasted Peking duck before and it was delicious. Crisp skin served separate from the meat, scallion flowers, the sauces and Norman—what could be better! He gave me some Peking duck to take home in a brown bag. I got on the bus to go back to Staten Island. The bag started to leak duck fat and the perfume of the duck started a conversation with the people on the bus. What a glorious day!

I made Peking duck in our house on Scranton Street. The first time I hung it in my garage on a hook to dry, my husband came home and opened the garage door and was fit to be tied. After he complained, the next time I hung the duck in the shower. He got up to take a shower and when he opened the shower door he screamed and woke up the whole house. He just didn't understand. My children love when I tell them this story!

Least Favorite

THE WORST, MOST HUMILIATING class ever taught at my cooking school was a Japanese cooking class taught by a teacher from the New School in Manhattan.

I watched her class in disbelief. She was so unprepared. She did not bring in the right ingredients and was not very knowledgeable about the subject she was supposed to teach. It was a farce! She might have fooled people in Manhattan, but not my students. Her sushi rolls were missing ingredients and tasted ordinary. I wanted to stop her in the middle of the class. I was embarrassed that I had hired her. I decided to teach my students a Charlotte Russe Cake to make up for this horror. I did that in the back of the room while she was teaching. I showed them how to use a pastry bag to decorate the cake with Chantilly Whipped Cream, Strawberries, and Blueberries. I did not know if that made up for this mess, but they loved the cake. I was beginning to get discouraged with guest teachers because many of them were not qualified to teach.

My Favorite Cooking Teachers

Jack Lirio

MANY COOKING TEACHERS AND personalities taught at Carol's Cuisine Cooking School. Jack Lirio taught at my school on April 29, 1982. He was charming, experienced, and talented. He had his own cooking school based in San Francisco and he specialized in French Cuisine and European Baking.

We loved his finale: Chocolate Covered Strawberries and a favorite recipe from his book, *Cooking with Jack Lirio*: Chocolate Squares with Chocolate Cream. They were really elegant brownies that were spread with smooth chocolate whipped cream and finished with a white whipped cream rosette. They were delicious and made in a food processor. A traditionalist when it came to baking, Jack was happy to use a food processor when-ever possible. His Crème Caramel, Viennese Tortes, and Fruit Tarts were famous. "If you don't have a food processor," he told the class of cooking students, "buy one."

After his class, Jack asked me if he could spend the night at the cooking school before he flew back to San Francisco. I had a sofa bed in my office, but there wasn't a window and he felt claustrophobic, He carried the mattress out to the kitchen, and placed it

A traditionalist when it came to baking, Jack was happy to use a food processor whenever possible. His Crème Caramel, Viennese Tortes, and Fruit Tarts were famous.

on the floor where there was a very large mirror overhead. He laid down on the mattress and saw his reflection and began to giggle. We both laughed uncontrollably.

I never saw him again. He autographed his cookbook for me and wrote, "Carol, it is a pleasure to know you and Joe. I love your school and I love you both, too. Thanks for inviting me in to do the classes. Your students are great. I'd love to see you teach someday. You must be good or you wouldn't have such a wonderful following. Best regards and love, Jack Lirio." Of course, I wanted him to come back and teach another class, but he disappeared from the teaching scene. I wondered about him to this day. I googled him recently, and to my surprise he is 88 years old now, and lives in Honolulu.

Jack Ubaldi

JACK UBALDI WAS THE FOUNDER of the Florence Prime Meat Mar-ket in New York City's Greenwich Village and operated it for over 40 years. In 1974, he sold that business and became an instructor in cooking and butch-ering at the New School's New York Restaurant School. He was a butcher's butcher. He also reminded me of my father. He was from Northern Italy and my father was Sicilian. He was petite like my father and quite handsome. He was the kindest person I met and you just wanted to hug him.

In his first class, he made a Boned Leg of Lamb with Kidney Beans. This dish was like a cassoulet with lamb and beans flavored with salt pork and pork skins. At his second class, he made a variety of homemade sausages. I can still see him standing patiently by the grinder filling the casings with the seasoned sausage meat.

Jack's next class was called "A Meat Encounter" and it was demonstration and participation. Each student brought in two chickens, one for boning and the other to be glove-boned. Basically, this means to crack the chicken open like a book, remove the spine and rib cage and whittle down the leg quarters from the inside. This is a great technique for serving a stuffed bird. My students loved him and wanted him to come back. He lived in Queens and drove himself to Staten Island. The next time I called him he said he had a problem with his eyes and was no longer driving or teaching at night. I was so sad that we would no longer experience this loving man.

Richard Sax

RICHARD SAX WAS AN ESTEEMED culinary writer long before the days of food blogs. He founded *Food and Wine*'s test kitchen, as well as being the author of numerous cookbooks including the acclaimed *Classic Home Desserts*. Sax served as IACP's ethics chairman and was well known for his enthusiasm for straightforward, healthy cooking. He passed away at the age of 46 from lung cancer. A quote from the *New York Times* obituary said, "As a cooking teacher he was down-to-earth, generous and willing to share his skills and knowledge." I know how much my cooking students and I enjoyed every moment we shared with him when he taught at my school.

Thelma Pressman

I MET THELMA PRESSMAN in San Francisco at a meeting for the International Association of Cooking Schools. We had a lot in common and I asked her if she would like to do a class for me in Staten Island. She was the president of the Microwave Cooking Center in Encino, California. She was recognized as the authority on the subject. Her *Microwave Cooking—Meals in Minutes* was a must. Her class for me was called "The Art of Microwave

Cooking." She was informative, smart, and fun. I wished we did not live so far apart. I would have loved to be her friend. She was often called "the Julia Child of microwave cooking."

Rose Levy Beranbaum

ROSE LEVY BERANBAUM HAS BEEN writing about breads, cakes, and pies for many years and taught baking for more than a decade as director of the Cordon Rose Cooking School. Her book *The Cake Bible* won the Book of the Year award from the International Association of Culinary Professionals.

I asked her to teach a baking class at my cooking school. I charged the students $30 for the class. It was 1984! Her fee was $650 and it was the most expensive class ever at Carol's Cuisine Cooking School. We had to rearrange the kitchen. She wanted all the students in chairs in rows. We had to move the two tables against the back wall. There was no coffee break allowed. During my classes, my students were able to get up and have coffee any time or have a bathroom break.

Rose demonstrated two of her favorites: The Chocolate Oblivion Truffle Torte with Raspberry Sauce and a Golden Layer Cake

> **I told her how happy I was for her success and she said, "I would rather look like you."**

with Praline Buttercream and Hazelnuts. Her books and her recipes are very long and scientifically explained. She was brilliant and nice, but people who are not professional just want to read a working recipe and bake a delicious cake. The class went on too long and ended at 12:30 AM. Rose was selling her expensive thermometer, which was made out of glass and very fragile. It was about two feet long, and she charged $25 or more, which was expensive in those days. I felt uncomfortable when none of my students bought it so I bought one. It broke in a million pieces the next day. At the end of the evening, I told her how happy I was for her success and she said, "I would rather look like you."

Peter Kump called me to discuss the high fees that guest teachers were charging. In Manhattan they charged more for classes than I did in Staten Island. The owners of all the cooking schools made an agreement that it was getting out of hand and we needed to regulate the prices or we wouldn't be able to afford guest teachers. I agreed but also began to hire local people and my family to teach classes instead.

Mrs. Terri Lewis

MY DAUGHTER TERRI GIUDICE-LEWIS is the wife of Jeff Lewis (her best friend from high school, and the love of her life!), mother of Amanda and Keith, artist, waitress, bartender, sous chef, party planner, and pastry chef. Terri has been baking since she was four years old. She prepped my classes and was my teaching assistant. After I bought the building, she did her own cooking classes. We were a team, even though our personalities were the opposite of each other. What we had in common was our love for food and our love for each other.

Terri teaching the students how to decorate gingerbread cookies.

I liked to tell stories about my experiences or my Italian family in Brooklyn and she wanted to get on with it. If I went on too long, she would tell people to just ignore me. We were quite funny! There was a lot of laughter in the classes. We gave them knowledge, experience, and delicious food. Some of the students came for years.

Terri's traditional class was "The Christmas Cookie Jar (for Parent and Child)." We taught it every year. It was described as "Great fun, great cookies, and memories that last long after the Christmas cookies are gone. Christmas Butter Cutout Cookies decorated with Royal Icing, Gingerbread Angels, and Delicious Giant Chocolate Spice Cookies." We charged $65 for both parent and child. I wanted it to be affordable because I knew what these classes meant to the kids and their parents. Many of those kids grew up to be adult customers at Carol's Cafe. They told me it was one of their happiest days in their lives baking cookies with their parents.

Joseph Giudice

MY SON JOSEPH GIUDICE was a chef at Carol's Cafe for several years. He taught a class called "How to Cook Fish." Two of his dishes were Red Snapper Marechiara (seared red snapper, clams, mussels in a light plum tomato sauce) served with pasta and Soft Shell Crabs Francese.

His most popular class, we taught together. I introduced him and chatted about the dishes he would do. He did everything else himself. It was called "Make Your Own Mozzarella." I wrote "Come and learn how to make

Joe behind the line at the cafe.

Joe and his wife Theresa.

Joe's creamy, delectable homemade mozzarella. It included Mozzarella Balls, Stuffed Mozzarella with Broccoli Rabe in Garlic and Oil, Mozzarella and Roasted Red Pepper Salad, and Mozzarella en Carozza."

The first thing he did was put three very large pots of water on the stove and bring the water to a boil. He bought his cheese curd at Pastosa, a local Italian grocery store that had everything Italian you ever dreamed of. His 18–20 students would all make their own mozzarella ball to take home at the end of each class. First they would eat the delicious dishes that he made. My son never held back and was very personable. He told them

My son never held back and was very personable. He told stories about being an Italian chef in Staten Island, with some embellishments.

stories about being an Italian chef in Staten Island, with some embellishments. He gave people a good time and really taught them how to make delicious fresh mozzarella. I remember one woman student in particular, while stretching her mozzarella, laughed uncontrollably. Her black mascara ran down her face and she wet her pants. It didn't faze Joe at all. He just helped her make her own ball of mozzarella. No one went home empty-handed. His classes always booked, unlike some of the guest teachers who sometimes didn't understand what middle-class Staten Islanders wanted.

Chocolate Spice Cookies

2 cups sifted all-purpose flour

1 ½ teaspoons baking powder

½ teaspoon baking soda

¼ teaspoon salt

¾ teaspoon cinnamon

½ cup unsalted butter, room temperature

1 cup granulated sugar

2 eggs, well beaten

3 squares unsweetened chocolate, melted

Preheat oven to 350 degrees.

In a bowl, combine flour, baking powder, baking soda, salt, and cinnamon and sift well. With a mixer, cream butter and granulated sugar together for 15 minutes, scraping down the sides of the bowl every five minutes. Creamed butter mixture should be light and fluffy. Add beaten eggs and melted chocolate and mix well. Begin to add the flour a small amount at a time, mixing well after each addition.

Divide dough into two disks. Roll each disk between two sheets of parchment paper until ¼-inch thick, then chill thoroughly. Once chilled, dough may be cut with a floured cookie cutter in the shape of your choosing.

Bake on an ungreased cookie sheet for about 10 minutes. Do not place cookies too close to each other on baking sheet. Cool the cookies for five minutes on the baking sheet, then remove to a wire cooling rack to finish cooling.

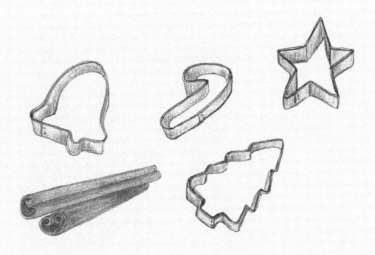

Sauté of Soft Shell Crabs with Plum Tomatoes and Lemons

Serves 2

2 soft shell crabs, cleaned and dredged in a seasoned flour

2 plum tomatoes, cut into 8 wedges, seeds removed, seasoned with sugar and salt. *(Note: if the tomatoes are large, you might want to use 1 tomato, quartered)*

1 lemon wedge, cut into 3 crosswise, seasoned with sugar and salt

2 garlic cloves, thinly sliced

1 or 2 shallots, thinly sliced

Brandy to flame (optional)

1 teaspoon serrano chiles, chopped fine (optional) or to taste

½ cup white wine

1 cup fish stock, or whatever is needed

½ cup water, if sauce is too fishy

Kosher salt and freshly ground black pepper and sugar to taste

Herbs: fresh basil, Italian parsley, 1 sprig of thyme (just the leaves), fresh oregano

1 tablespoon butter

In a heavy skillet (about 10 inches), add olive oil and butter, add tomatoes and lemons.

Sear the tomatoes until caramelized, remove to a platter.

Add butter and olive oil to the pan, and heat till hot; add crabs, shell side down.

Brown on both sides. Flame with brandy, if desired.

Set crabs aside.

In the same skillet, add shallots and garlic and cook for a couple of minutes until golden.

Return tomatoes and lemons to pan. Add chiles if desired. Add white wine and reduce until gone.

Add fish stock, water, and herbs. Reduce and season. Add fresh herbs of your choice.

Put crabs back into pan and turn to coat with sauce.

Finish with cold butter and taste again.

Mike Azzara
First Review

ALTHOUGH WE OPENED THE cafe in 1993, after three years in business we still had not been reviewed by our local newspaper, the *Staten Island Advance*. I couldn't understand it. Was it because we were both a part-time restaurant and also a cooking school? I called the paper to request a review and a critic who called himself "Gordon Hall" showed up at the restaurant on Halloween night. He came with his wife. I explained to him that we closed early and I had sent my staff home to have fun on Halloween. He was annoyed but his wife, who was very nice, said, "You heard her. It's Halloween."

Braised Lamb Shank with Orzo Risotto and Roasted Tomatoes.

He came back a week or so later, and our first review appeared on Friday, November 22, 1996. I opened up the newspaper and this is what I read:

"How does one define the thrill of the art connoisseur who comes upon a masterpiece or the satisfaction of a scientist who makes an important discovery? Such emotions may not be terribly different from the ecstasy of the lover of food who encounters the cuisine at Carol's Cafe/Pub (the pub is a smoking section), the cozy little restaurant that started out as a cooking school.

Manhattanites and Staten Islanders who cling to the notion that the best of everything starts at the Battery may scoff, but we would argue that some of the best restaurant food in the city can be sampled on Staten Island at Carol's. The just-published 1997 Zagat survey, which this year includes a record 14 Island restaurants says, "It's the best Staten Island has to offer." For innovative, imaginative and uniquely delicious fare, all cooked to order, it is in a class by itself.

For owner-chef Carol Frazzetta, who has been operating a cooking school for 25 years, the onsite kitchen is her art studio or laboratory. Give her some leeway and a meal becomes an adventure. Unlike the stereotypical temperamental chef who brooks no tampering with his sacred recipes, Ms. Frazzetta is willing to vary dishes to accommodate individual likes and dislikes.

More often than not, however, we have found it wise to stick to her versions. Even the lowly sausage, the stuff of hero sandwiches and pizza, is transformed into haute cuisine in her hands. For example, the D'Artagnan wild game sausage ($9.50) offers the diner the chef's choice of three among five meats. On our most recent visit, the choices were Wild Boar, Rabbit and duck Foie Gras. The three links wonderfully spiced, were presented

"We would argue that some of the best restaurant food in the city can be sampled on Staten Island at Carol's."

in a rich brown gravy. After a good deal of vacillation we settled on the duck as our favorite.

Sweet potato and butternut squash soup ($6.95) is another taste sensation. A rich ochre color, the velvety concoction drizzled with cream blends the flavors of the potato and squash in a way that pleases the palate and comforts the palate and comforts the soul on a crisp autumn evening. There was something crunchy in the soup, which, we were told, was a French pancetta, a new product from D'Artagnan.

Layers of thinly sliced potatoes cooked just enough to bring out the flavor are combined with fresh tomatoes, Gruyère cheese, fresh spinach and ham to create the

"The lamb shank was not just grilled but braised and seared first. The flavors hinted at a little bit of India, a touch of Italy and a pinch of China."

potato torte ($6.95). It is then baked to a golden brown and crusted with what seemed to be Parmesan cheese.

The unique touch lies in the mysterious blend of spices in an entrée of penne with shrimp, broccoli rabe and fresh tomato ($16.95). The sauce was thin, almost soupy, but flavorful as were the shrimp.

From the evening's specials list, grilled lamb shank with lemon preserves and arugula ($21.95) came with either a side of couscous or vegetables. Talk about different. It becomes an instant favorite. The lamb shank was not just grilled but braised and seared first.

The flavors hinted at a little bit of India, a touch of Italy and a pinch of China. The meat was served on a bed of arugula. Choosing the vegetables, we were presented with mashed potatoes topped with haystack fried onions, Sicilian string beans cooked in a slightly spicy tomato sauce and rum glazed carrots.

Although we didn't have room, we had to sample a dessert, all of which are made by Carol. Our server mentioned that Lemon Meringue Pie ($5.00) is a big favorite. A thin, flaky crust with a fresh lemon pudding that imparted just the right degree of tartness.

Carol's Cafe/Pub is one of an all-too-small handful of Island restaurants that cater to the beer drinker. There are now 18 superior brews available in bottles and another four on tap.

Unfortunately, the restaurant is not open to the public Sunday through Tuesday, but Sunday is a big day for private parties. Ms. Frazzetta is as hands-on an owner as you'll find, from the decorating to the music. During our last visit, the CD player shuffled among Billie Holiday, Billy Eckstine, Sarah Vaughan and—get this—Leon Redbone. Dinner for two, including cocktails and beer, amounted to $103 plus tip."

We received 4 stars, and I cried with joy and relief.

Oven Roasted Lamb Shanks with Roasted Tomatoes and Toasted Orzo

Lamb Shanks

Serves 4

3 tablespoons extra virgin olive oil

Kosher salt and freshly ground pepper

4 lamb shanks

2 carrots, peeled, and coarsely chopped

2 stalks celery, coarsely chopped

1 large onion, coarsely chopped

24 cloves garlic, smashed

2 cups port wine

1 cup red wine

4 cups beef stock or chicken stock

Preheat oven to 350 degrees.

Heat oil in a medium Dutch oven until smoking.

Season the shanks on both sides with salt and pepper and sear until golden brown on both sides, remove to a platter. Add the celery, carrots, onions, and garlic and cook until caramelized, about 20 minutes or so.

Add the port and red wine and reduce by half. Add the beef or chicken stock and shanks and bring to a boil.

Cover and bake in oven for two hours or until tender. Remove shanks, strain, and reduce by half.

Orzo Pasta

1 stick of unsalted butter (4 ounces)

2 tablespoons extra virgin olive oil

1 pound orzo

1 cup onion, finely chopped

2 tablespoons shallots

2 teaspoons garlic

½ cup white wine

4 to 6 cups beef or chicken stock

¼ cup finely chopped parsley and fresh herbs of your choice

Heavy cream to taste, optional

Heat oil and butter in a pan. Add half of the orzo, and toast until golden brown. Add onions and cook until golden.

Add shallots and garlic and cook for another eight minutes or so. Add remaining orzo and sauté for two minutes.

Add white wine and reduce until gone.

Add beef or chicken stock, a half a cup at a time, as if you were making risotto, until the pasta is al dente.

Finish with additional butter, fresh herbs, and a small amount of the braising liquid.

Add chopped parsley and salt and pepper to taste. Add heavy cream to taste.

Slow Roasted Tomatoes

4 plum tomatoes, core removed

1 tablespoon extra virgin olive oil

Salt, pepper and a big pinch of sugar

Toss the tomatoes in the olive oil and season.

On a parchment-paper-lined cookie sheet, place seasoned tomatoes.

Roast in a 200-degree oven for one hour or longer, turning every 15 minutes until caramelized.

Roasted Garlic Bulbs

4 heads garlic, tops removed

1 cup water

2 tablespoons unsalted butter

Preheat oven to 350 degrees.

Place water and butter in a roasting pan, add garlic heads, cut side down, cover, and roast for 1½ hours .

Or

Wrap bulbs of garlic in foil with herbs and oil, and season with salt and pepper.

Roast in 350-degree oven for at least an hour, or until tender.

Glazed Carrots

5 pounds carrots cut on an angle,
Asian style (about ¼ inch thick)

2 sticks unsalted butter

3 cinnamon sticks

½ cup sugar

½ cup dark rum

½ cup chicken stock

Herbs to taste: parsley, dried oregano,
fresh oregano, fresh thyme, fresh
rosemary, or whatever you like

Put everything in a large saucepan or deep frying pan. Cook over moderate heat
until carrots are just tender. Do not overcook.

Taste them for seasoning and for doneness. When done, remove carrots with a
slotted spoon. Cook remaining liquid to a glaze. Toss carrots with a rubber spatula
into glaze.

Coat well. Taste for seasoning again. Garnish with chopped parsley.

Cafe and Pub Take Off

AFTER THAT REVIEW APPEARED in the *Advance*, the restaurant became very busy, and the weekends were jam-packed. We served the same food in the pub as we did in the main dining room. Our bar was in the pub, and the smokers loved that they had their own private room. People who were having affairs liked that room a lot. Luckily our bartender and waitress were also smokers. We even had special cigar nights, where an expert would come in and talk about cigars and give out samples. I could not stand the smell, as I had given up smoking in my 30s. The room seated 20 comfortably. On the walls were antiques and historical pictures of Staten Island. They had their own restroom and felt this was their private place. It was very difficult to get a reservation on Friday and Saturday nights.

Chocolate Orgasm Cake was a cafe favorite.

In the kitchen, at that time, we had two line cooks (including me), two people working on the appetizer-salad station, and a dishwasher. We had someone plating desserts on the other side of the kitchen and one of my baking students came in on Friday and Saturday to make soufflés. We also had an expediter who told us when to fire our dishes.

The refrigerated showcase in the main dining room had on display all the desserts, which were seasonal. I made fresh fruit pies, apple crisps, a variety of different cakes, like the cafe favorites, Chocolate Orgasm Cake and New Orleans Bread Pudding. Often I would prepare delicious Tiramisu, Chocolate or Butterscotch Pudding or panna cotta. My customers would check the showcase when they walked in, to see what new desserts I had made. We also had available different homemade ice creams like French Vanilla, Chocolate Fudge, Maple Butter Pecan, and Banana Oreo. We made the most decadent chocolate sorbet that our regular customers ordered every time they came in for dinner. Each night we offered a soufflé of the day. The soufflé choices could be peanut butter, vanilla bean, Grand Marnier, or fresh fruit soufflé, such as raspberry, strawberry, or peach, which were made without yolks (so they had no fat). The most popular soufflé was the chocolate soufflé. We had to make double orders of the chocolate soufflé many times for large tables. We served them in individual porcelain ramekins, with Chantilly whipped cream on the side.

Chocolate Orgasm Cake

Serves 12

3½ ounces unsweetened chocolate, chopped

1 can of beets (8¼ ounces)

4 ounces unsalted butter, at room temperature

2½ cups firmly packed light brown sugar

Three large eggs, at room temperature

2 full teaspoons pure vanilla extract

2 cups all-purpose flour, lightly spoon into a cup, level off

2 teaspoons baking soda

½ teaspoon salt

½ cup buttermilk, room temperature

Baking pans needed: two 9×2 inch round cake pans

Preheat oven to 350 degrees.

Grease bottom and sides of pans. Dust with flour and shake out excess. Line with parchment paper and grease and flour again. Shake out excess flour.

Melt chocolate over double boiler or in microwave. Cool slightly.

Drain beet juice in a strainer. Set aside. Chop beets in a food processor or by hand into very small pieces. Add to beet juices and set aside.

Cream butter, sugar, eggs, and vanilla in a large bowl with an electric mixer on high speed until very fluffy, about 10 minutes, occasionally scraping down with a rubber spatula. Reduce speed to low and beat in melted chocolate.

Sift together flour, baking soda, and salt on wax paper or bowl. With mixer on low speed, alternately beat flour in fourths, and buttermilk in thirds, into chocolate mixture, beginning and ending with flour. Mix until incorporated, about one minute.

Add beets and juice and beat on medium speed until blended, about one minute. The batter will be thin and you will see pieces of beets.

Divide the batter equally between the two prepared pans. Bake in the 350-degree oven for 25–35 minutes or until toothpick inserted in center comes out clean with a little smear of chocolate clinging to toothpick. Do not over bake or cake will be dry.

Cool cakes on rack for 10 minutes and then invert onto a cooling rack.

I like to make a double recipe, cool cakes completely, and wrap in plastic wrap and tin foil, label, date, and freeze. Defrost wrapped cake at room temperature before frosting.

continued

Chocolate Orgasm Cake, *continued*

Chocolate Ganache

2 cups heavy cream

2 teaspoons pure vanilla extract

1 pound semisweet chocolate, chopped fine or use chips

Heat cream in a medium saucepan just until it comes to a boil.

Remove from heat and add chocolate and vanilla, stirring until mixture is smooth and chocolate is melted.

Transfer mixture to a stainless steel or glass bowl. Taste for seasoning and place in freezer for four minutes, then remove and stir with a whisk. Place back in freezer for four more minutes.

Whisk again, and decorate the Orgasm Cake.

Alternately, the frosting may be placed over ice water and stirred constantly until spreading consistency. If it starts to set too thick, immediately remove from water.

Assembling the cake

To assemble the cake, place one cake layer topside down on serving platter. Spread with a third of the frosting and top with second layer, bottom-side up. Spread remaining frosting over top and sides. Let stand at room temperature for frosting to set.

The frosted cake may be kept at room temperature to allow frosting to set.

I like to refrigerate overnight uncovered until set, then dome it with a cake server.

Ganache keeps well for a week. Bring it back to room temperature to serve.

Cafe Entertainment

WE HAD MUSICIANS ON Saturday nights, some holidays, and for special dinners that we did during the week. I especially liked Vinnie Ruggieri, who played jazz piano, and Betty Miller, a vocalist who sang a lot like Billie Holiday. The musicians we had during the week included a doo wop group that all wore the same outfits, a jazz quintet (featuring Nino Morreale, Vinny Dee, and Lou Siani for our New Orleans dinner), and a classical guitarist for our French dinner.

Michelin Review

I WAS VERY HAPPY to read this review in the *Michelin Guide*:

"This is the kind of place that you'd only find in New York and, in particular, Staten Island. Carol's Cafe is a local institution, and there is a Carol here. She warmly entreats you to try her Neapolitan-style fried ravioli appetizer filled with ricotta, Parmesan, mozzarella, and Soppressata, before moving onto a hearty plate of rigatoni tossed with Wild Mushrooms and Spinach in a creamy Gorgonzola sauce. While these are great choices, and ideal for sharing, Carol's spin on a sautéed broccoli rabe (with the addition of pan-roasted garlic and candied lemon wedges) makes eating your greens a delightful proposition. Quirky selections like Dr. Lou Gianvito's Fish (Who is he? Who cares … the dish is great!) add to the charm of this unique mainstay."

Neopolitan Fried Ravioli with Salsa Rosa

Pasta Dough

Make the pasta dough first; it needs to rest at least an hour at room temperature.

2 cups "00" flour. Use Napole brand, available at fine Italian grocery stores.

3 large eggs at room temperature

½ teaspoon kosher salt

2 teaspoons extra virgin olive oil

One lemon at room temperature, zested

The strained juice of one lemon

Freshly ground black pepper to taste

Ancho chile powder for color, about ½ teaspoon (optional)

One tablespoon chopped fresh chives (optional)

Place eggs, black pepper, salt, olive oil, lemon juice and zest, in food processor with steel blade. Mix for two minutes. Add the flour and ancho chile if using. Pulse on and off, until flour forms a ball.

Touch, it should be soft and moist. If you like, pulsate a tablespoon of chopped chives, carefully, just till scattered through the dough. Taste the dough for seasoning.

Be careful with the flour, measure by spooning into a measuring cup and level off. Wrap in plastic wrap and let sit at room temperature for at least an hour. Only if you must, refrigerate the dough. You must bring it to room temperature again, at least an hour.

Oh My God if you still do not own a food processor!

Pour the flour on the work surface, shape into a mound, and make a well in the center. Lightly beat the eggs with the rest of the ingredients.

Add flour gradually to the egg, drawing it in from the inside wall of the well.

When the mass is ready for kneading, knead until it reaches the right consistency.

continued

Neopolitan Fried Ravioli with Salsa Rosa, *continued*

Filling for Fried Ravioli or Manicotti

This filling is for two times the recipe for pasta dough. Do not put a double recipe into the food processor.

Do one recipe of the pasta dough at a time.

Yield: approximately 120 ravioli

2 pounds impastata, a thick ricotta available at Pastosa *(I find whole milk ricotta, wrapped in cheese cloth and strained overnight, very risky.)*

¾ pound fresh or homemade mozzarella chopped in small cubes

½ cup grated Parmesan cheese

¼ cup grated Romano cheese

2 large eggs, whole

2 egg yolks

2 tablespoons freshly chopped parsley

¼ pound chunk Genoa salami or soppressata preferred, diced into very small cubes

Freshly ground black pepper; if salt is needed, be very cautious

Freshly ground nutmeg to taste (very careful, do not overdo)

Combine all ingredients. Taste and adjust the seasoning.

Preparing the Ravioli

After your pasta dough has rested for at least 30 minutes, divide it into four pieces. Work with one piece of dough at a time and keep the other pieces wrapped in plastic. Use a pasta machine to roll out the dough in sheets, starting with the widest setting, flouring as needed; gradually decrease the thickness. Stop rolling when you can see the outline of your hand through the dough.

Use a ravioli press to form 12 small ravioli at a time. Continue this process until all the dough is used up, placing the formed ravioli, in a single layer on lightly floured, parchment-lined, cookie sheets.

You can freeze the ravioli at this point on the cookie sheets. Once frozen, dip each ravioli in buttermilk and then dredge in panko breadcrumbs which have been seasoned with salt, pepper, and a little Parmesan cheese.

Return the breaded ravioli to the freezer. Once they have frozen completely, you can portion them into Ziploc® bags for later use.

Frying Your Ravioli

You can deep fry your ravioli in corn oil but this usually requires that you finish them in a 400 degree oven, in order to make sure that the cheese has melted and they are hot inside. Alternatively you can shallow fry them in olive oil until they are golden brown.

Remove the fried ravioli to a paper-towel-lined cooling rack or cookie sheet. Serve them hot with Salsa Rosa. In the cafe, we put some sauce on the serving dish first, then placed the ravioli on top and garnished with fresh basil leaves.

Salsa Rosa

Yield: about 4 cups

4–7 small-medium red bell peppers. You need 2 cups puree.

Extra virgin olive oil, for coating, plus 1 tablespoon, plus ¼ cup

Kosher salt as needed

Sugar to taste

2 whole serrano chiles, remove seeds

3–4 cloves garlic

¼ cup tomato puree

1 sprig of fresh oregano

About ¼ cup white balsamic vinegar, or to taste

Preheat oven to 450 degrees.

Coat peppers with olive oil and place on a foil-lined baking sheet. Salt liberally. Bake in the oven, turning every 10 minutes until peppers are blistered and black, about 20 to 30 minutes total.

Meanwhile, add 2 tablespoons of olive oil to a sauté pan. Add the serrano chiles and the garlic. Cook over moderate heat, turning occasionally, until the chiles are softened, lightly browned, and blistered on all sides. Remove the pan from the heat and let the chiles cool in the oil for several minutes. Reserve oil !

When the roasted bell peppers are blistered and blackened, remove them from the oven, place in a glass bowl, and cover with plastic wrap. This will steam the skins off and make them easier to remove.

After 20 minutes, remove the peppers and peel. Remove the seeds, stem, and ribs. Do not run under water ! This will just wash the flavor off.

NOTE:

- You can roast the peppers under the broiler or over a gas flame, if you prefer, but I like to do them in a hot oven. It takes a little longer, but you don't have to watch them as closely.

Dr. Lou Gianvito's Fish of the Day in a Light Tomato Sauce with Sweet or Hot Cherry Peppers

Serves 2

2 filets of mahi mahi, skin removed, the meat should be firm and pink
Season fish with salt and pepper on both sides and a squeeze of lemon.

Salt and pepper and sugar to taste

½ teaspoon dry oregano

Lemon cut into wedges

Extra virgin olive oil as needed

Red pepper flakes to taste

½ cup of chopped onion or more to taste

2 shallots, minced

2 teaspoons of garlic, minced

Serrano chile chopped fine to taste (optional)

½ cup white wine

1 ½ cups diced canned tomatoes or fresh ripe tomatoes, blanched, peeled, seeds removed and cut into ½-inch dice

Fresh basil, oregano and Italian parsley

Fish stock or water or pasta water as needed to thin out the sauce

Sweet cherry or hot peppers in vinegar (about a half a cup or to taste)

In a 10-inch heavy frying pan, add a couple of tablespoons olive oil, onions, two wedges of lemon, red pepper flakes, oregano, pinch of sugar, pinch of salt and cook slowly until onions are sweet and golden. Add shallots and garlic, cook about five minutes.

Add the white wine and reduce till gone. Add the diced tomatoes, basil leaves, ripped, oregano leaves, pinch of salt, black pepper, and sugar if needed.

Cook slowly for 10 minutes. Add some fish stock or water to thin out the mixture.

Taste for seasoning and adjust.

If you like it spicy, add some chopped serrano chiles to taste.

Lower it to a simmer and place seasoned fish in pan, spoon some sauce on top. Cover and poach about 10 minutes. It depends on the thickness of the fish.

Check for doneness by carefully making a slit in the thickest part of the fish and see if it is cooked through. Add the sweet or hot cherry peppers with a little of the vinegar and sprinkle with fresh parsley, basil, and oregano. Taste and adjust seasoning. Add a pinch of sugar if needed.

On the Isle

IN MIKE AZZARA'S FOOD column called, "On the Isle," in the *Staten Island Advance* on June 15, 2000, Mike wrote:

"You've heard that Carol's Cafe and Pub serves the most delicious food in the tri-state area, or maybe even the Western Hemisphere, and you've been dying to try it, but for one reason or another, you haven't gotten around to it.

Here's a golden opportunity to send your palate to Paradise, and do good at the same time. Tomorrow is Restaurant Day 2000 and participating restaurants will offer special sidewalk tastings of their signature dishes for $3, $4 or $5, with $1 from each sale donated to one of two hunger-fighting organizations: Citymeals on Wheels and Share Our Strength. Stroll by tomorrow between 6pm and 9pm and taste some goodies. The restaurant is on Richmond Road at the intersection of Four Corners Road."

Consulting: John Scalia

IN 2001, I MET John Vincent Scalia, a very successful funeral director, and owner of the Old Bermuda Inn. He came to my restaurant for dinner with his wife, and my student and friend-to-be, Doctor Lou Gianvito. I had no idea what he was there for, and the way he looked at me made me nervous. If only I understood what I was getting into.

He asked me to come down to the Bermuda Inn to talk to him and see his facilities. In his kitchen, which was in the basement, I noticed the windows were boarded up. It was August and the air conditioning was not on. All the chefs were Mexican and some did not speak English. He wanted me to give them cooking lessons. He didn't hesitate when I told him what my fee would be. He also asked me to be a partner in his restaurant and pub. I would not get paid or invest any money until we made a profit. I had my accountant come for the signing of the contract and he agreed with John. He had no idea how hard I would work for the next year.

The announcement went out in the *Staten Island Advance* about our partnership. John and I had our picture taken professionally for the ad. The nightmare began with the cooking lessons that I gave to the staff. The cooks had no interest in what I had to say. They only came because John told them they had to be there. To my horror, I watched them deep-fry Chicken Francese. Their chicken stock was loaded with yellow fat from the chicken, and they did not degrease it. John wanted to hire a Mexican chef who spoke English, to be in charge of the kitchen. I met with the chef prospect at Carol's Cafe and asked him to make me a sauté dish, but he had no idea of the technique. I patiently tried to explain to him what he was doing wrong, and hoped that I was helping him. He was a very nice, patient man, and I thought he would be a good influence in that kitchen. I made the right decision and John Scalia was pleased. The chef that I recommended was also named John and I believe he is still working at the Old Bermuda Inn.

At Christmas, one of John's cooks gave me a Christmas present, which I did not open until I got home. It was a large shoebox, wrapped nicely with a red bow. I opened the box and he had sculpted a very large penis with testicles out of flour and butter, and kneaded it into a dough (called a beurre manié). He probably used Crisco and lots of flour to make it so hard. I rewrapped his "gift" in the same box, with the same the red bow, and walked up to this chef in the kitchen and said, "Merry Christmas!" He was so surprised that I gave him a present, that he opened it in front of the kitchen staff. Little did this terrible cook know that I had placed a hand-written note inside the box that said, "A Dick, for a Dick!" I had to tell him what it said because he couldn't read. The whole kitchen laughed!

What I was not prepared for was the sabotage that would be deliberately done to get rid of me. I will start with the brunch. I baked my cakes and breads for my first Sunday brunch. I made Apple Cranberry Pecan Crisps, Chocolate Syrup Cakes, Ode to Ebinger's Crumb Cakes, Honey Whole Wheat Braids, and Perfect White Breads in Miniature Shapes. I made my

New Orleans Bread Pudding. I baked at Carol's Cafe with my assistant, Theresa, every night after my restaurant closed. It was a tremendous amount of work. We had changed the desserts from store-bought to homemade. At the very first brunch this woman walked in with a large group of people, yelling, "I hate this brunch!" She wanted the old brunch with the store-bought cakes and breads. Of course, it was planned by the people who did not want me there. I remember, I actually went over to the woman and said, "I baked all those cakes." She looked at me with disgust and said, "I like the store-bought better."

I hired Terri's best friend Vanessa, who was very close to me and my family. She and Terri were little girls at P.S. 48 and are friends to this day. Her job was to help me and I made her the manager of catering, the staff, and the restaurant. She had a lot of experience working as a manager and waitress. I asked John to have a meeting with the staff and Vanessa and me. At the meeting was John's daughter and she verbally attacked me in front of everyone. I said I would be happy to leave. John jumped up and in her face, told her off. That was the moment I should have left, but John's protecting me made me reconsider. With all my heart, I wanted to convert the restaurant to fine dining, but I was up against his family and the kitchen staff. I designed a new menu, and tried to teach them how to make my dishes. John's son-in-law would come into the kitchen where I was cooking and would disrespect me by basically ignoring me and calling all the cooks "chef" but me. He was married to the daughter who yelled at me.

With all my heart, I wanted to convert the restaurant to fine dining, but I was up against his family and the kitchen staff.

For the first Thanksgiving, I had to cook for both Carol's Cafe and the Bermuda Inn. I had made a big pot of Harvest Soup and put it in the walk-in refrigerator at the Bermuda Inn and left for the night. The next day when I came back, someone had emptied the stock pot and left only a couple of inches of the soup in the pot. I knew I could not take this much longer. The icing on the cake was when they put heavy objects on top of my cakes that I had baked for the restaurant to squash them. On Thanksgiving Day, the service people didn't show up, and Vanessa and I served the meal, having grave-diggers from John's funeral home who didn't speak English, as the busboys.

While I was working at Carol's Cafe, I learned that at the staff Christmas party, one of the only people that I trusted who worked there, ends up in the parking lot in the backseat of a car, hooking up with one of the maintenance men who worked for John. That did me in! Carol's Cafe needed to be my priority, and I was driving myself into the ground. For what? Other than the time I spent teaching his cooks some basic cooking techniques, I was never paid. I decided to tell John I didn't want to do this anymore. I sat with him in a Chinese restaurant and with tears in my eyes, I told him that I was done. I said I would help him find a new executive chef who I would help train.

For two weeks, I interviewed chefs in my apartment. The chef that I respected, and wanted to hire, was told by John that he didn't want to pay the salary he asked for. Notice, I said he. Women chefs weren't even considered. The chef I did pick was African American, highly intelligent, and experienced. He met John and was hired with the salary they agreed on. He also wanted a fine-dining restaurant; I warned him about the difficulties I had, and how the staff would try to sabotage him. He said, "Not me. I could handle this." His menu was lovely. I enjoyed his food and stayed with him for a couple of weeks. I tried my best to help him. He worked for John for about six months and without warning, John fired him on Christmas Eve.

John's family members and the cooks who hated me got what they wanted, which was me out of the picture.

John's family members and the cooks who hated me got what they wanted, which was me out of the picture. I was so relieved to be out of there.

I was so relieved to be out of there. It was an experience that I will never forget! I truly believed this man when he told me that I would be rich and successful like him. I learned I was not like him and I never could be.

The next time I was a consultant, this customer came to me with an idea he had about having a gourmet hot dog truck. He asked me to put a menu together, and we sat for over two hours and discussed it. My fee for consulting was $250 an hour, and when he left he gave me $600. I told him that it was difficult to get a license for a food truck in New York City, and to be successful he needed a chef that could cook what I was going to create.

What I learned is that he had dreams, but had no idea how difficult it was to be in the New York food industry. I always told people the truth, though sometimes they did not want to hear it. I worked many hours after work creating original hot dogs, like The Elvis Dog, (stuffed with peanut butter and banana, and wrapped in crispy bacon and fried in butter), Let's Be Frank Dog–Invent Your Own (plain grilled or add some toppings), Deep Fried Hot Dog (with New York style onions and creamy coleslaw), South Of The Border Dog (with roasted poblano chile peppers and topped with crushed potato chips), Staten Island Italian Stallion Dog (with broccoli rabe with garlic and olive oil, fresh tomato, and Parmesan cheese sauce).

When I tried to reach him to give him my ideas for his menu, and get paid for all the hours I put into creating his menu so he could follow his dream, he was nowhere to be found. It was like he was a Mafia wiseguy who just disappeared. I decided to take this new menu I created and put it to good use. I opened "Pub Grub" in the pub section of my restaurant.

> **What I learned is that he had dreams, but had no idea how difficult it was to be in the New York food industry. I always told people the truth, though sometimes they did not want to hear it.**

I announced, "Now available in Carol's Pub: we offer fun, affordable, family-friendly Gourmet Hot Dogs, Burgers, and Sandwiches. Stop by. . . and give it a try!"

We had a grand opening and it was a big hit. What went wrong was my service people did not want to work on Sunday. My young busboys were given an opportunity to be waiters but were doing drugs, and when I wanted to take off on Sunday to catch up on my work, they took advantage and had their friends eat for free.

Sadly, a handsome, intelligent waiter named Steven died of alcoholism at 37 years old. When I went to his wake, I could not believe that this young man who had everything to live for was dead in that coffin. He had had his party in the restaurant the day he graduated college and he and his family were so proud. He was 15 years old when he first worked for me as a busboy. Kevin was his friend, who also worked for me, but was fired when I found out he sold drugs in my restaurant to the nephew of one of my best customers. My customer never knew! I recently wrote to Kevin and he went into rehab and is doing fine. He said I am a beautiful person and he learned a lot about life from me.

This group of young people were working in the pub and I trusted them. I taught my cooks the menu but once I wasn't there to cook, the quality of the food suffered. If I had the money, I would have hired a professional sous chef that I could trust who was able to execute my menu. That has always been the main problem, not enough money! I knew I could operate a cheaper restaurant but I was creative and that would not challenge me.

That is why restaurant owners have partners. According to a frequently cited study by Ohio State University on failed restaurants, 60% do not make it past the first year, and 80% go under in five years. It's not from lack of personal taste or quality. More often it's because of a breakdown in the chain of command and quality control. Or as chef Robert Irvine once said, "Very slowly your most popular dish can start to veer off its intended flavor profile and your cherished execution can stray from what is best for the end product."

A Christmas dinner with some of my staff and students. The two young men on the left who started as my busboys, Woody and Steven, each passed away at a young age.

Big Hungry Shelby

BIG HUNGRY SHELBY IS a blogger and food critic who wrote this about us:

PHOTO BY SHELBY COHEN (BIG HUNGRY SHELBY)

BBQ Duck with Peanut Sauce and Napa Cabbage Slaw.

"Back in 2012, we visited Carol's Cafe, in the Dongan Hills neighborhood of Staten Island, after a really long day of Miss New York prep. Dining at this elegant yet comfortable bistro was a treat, and we've been meaning to return ever since.

This year, we brought a whole gang with us, and once again felt enveloped by the hospitality and fine fare owner Carol Frazzetta dishes up.

We started with two appetizers. First off, Carol's caramel shrimp. The shrimp are brined, then go for a swim in a complex, sweet and sharp brown sauce with fiery ginger and garlic, plus bright scallions in the mix. There's a lot of sugar in this dish, but it never becomes cloying—the sign of a chef who understands how to balance flavors like a master. Slices of crusty bread dragged through that glorious elixir were like turning the flavor dial up to 20 and ripping it off. But the plump, sweet, salty shrimp were no slouch, either. The fresh torn basil up on top made the dish, balancing the sweet, rich garlic with bright notes.

Our next starter was the BBQ duck with ginger and satay sauce; but folks, I've had satay at a million weddings and even in Amsterdam, where Indonesian food is a big deal, and I've never had satay this refined. It was light, slightly sweet and sharp from the ginger, earthy from the peanuts, and just a little spicy. Once again, the sauce was delectable, and it was impossible for us to leave any on the plate. It begged to be licked (which we did not do, but it was tempting).

The last time we ate at Carol's, I somehow missed the chocolate soufflé. I am a soufflé junky. You just can't beat a dessert that captures such intense chocolate flavor in such an ethereal texture. Man oh man, eggs are miracles. This soufflé was light as a feather, and just ever so slightly undercooked in the middle, to add creaminess to the fluffy, cocoa rich, sweet confection. This dessert has to be ordered when you select your entrées because it must be prepped in real time, and it's totally worth it. It was the best thing I ate all weekend in Staten Island this time around."

—Shelby Cohen
Big Hungry Shelby

Media

CAROL'S CAFE, OUR LITTLE four-star restaurant on Richmond Road in Dongan Hills received a call from the TV Food Network! On a Wednesday night a camera crew from the TV Food Network had cameras go behind the scenes in the kitchen, from 5:00 until 6:30 PM, and also pan across the dining room, which I hoped would be filled with diners. I was a wreck prior to their visit. As far as I knew, it was the first time the network focused on a Staten Island restaurant.

The show was called "Dining Around," and was hosted by Nina Griscom and Alan Richman. I believe Len Pickell, founder and president of the James Beard Foundation, recommended our cafe to Nina Griscom, who was his friend from The James Beard House. Of course, the very positive comments in the 1997 Zagat Restaurant Guide could not have hurt our chances of being picked for the show. Our food rating was 27. Food, Décor and Service were rated on a 30-point scale so we were very proud that we received such a high rating.

In addition to having them film in the restaurant, I prepared some dishes for the hosts to sample and comment on, while they were on the air. My son-in-law Jeff drove into Manhattan at 6:00 in the morning on the day of the show to hand deliver my Wild Game Sausage Sampler and my Vienna Schnitzel with Homemade Spaetzle. We also provided micro-brewed beers to pair with the food. The segment started off with them showing the film they shot of the cafe, and me cooking in the kitchen. When they tasted my food, and tried the sausages we bought from D'Artagnan, Nina put her hand to her mouth, pulled something out of it, and said, "Bone." I had no control over the ingredients D'Artagnan put in the sausages that I chose for my Wild Game Sausage Sampler plate. I sent arugula along as a garnish for the Vienna Schnitzel but one of their assistants put iceberg lettuce on the side instead, which basically ruined the whole presentation.

I was proud to be part of the International Who's Who of Chefs *book.*

Vienna Schnitzel with Lemon Sauce and Arugula

1½ pounds boneless top round of veal, trimmed and cleaned

2 large eggs

½ cup flour

2 cups fresh bread crumbs

2 tablespoons unsalted butter

2 tablespoons extra virgin olive oil

Kosher salt and freshly ground black pepper to taste

To prepare the veal, slice the veal across the grain into four equal pieces. Then butterfly each piece by cutting horizontally through the middle of each without cutting all the way through.

Open each piece up (it will resemble the shape of a butterfly) and place it between two sheets of plastic wrap on a flat surface. Using a meat pounder, or the flat side of the cleaver, pound the meat until it is uniformly about ¼" thick. After the meat has been pounded, sprinkle even amounts of salt and pepper over both sides of each piece of meat.

To bread the veal, you will need three separate, wide, shallow containers such as plates. Crack the eggs into one of the containers, add one teaspoon olive oil and one teaspoon water to loosen the eggs, and beat well. Place the flour into one container, and the bread crumbs in the other.

Season the flour with salt and pepper. Have ready a cooling rack to place the veal on. Dredge each piece of veal in the flour, then dip the floured meat into the egg, turning to coat both sides.

Lift the meat out of the pan, allowing the excess to drip back into the pan. Lay the veal in the bread crumbs, pressing gently to coat the meat. Turn each piece over and repeat, making sure they are evenly coated with the crumbs.

Transfer the breaded cutlets to the cooling rack. Rack should have a cookie sheet underneath so crumbs to not fall on the floor. Do not cover.

Preheat the oven to 250 degrees. Heat the olive oil and butter in a large skillet over medium heat until a basil or parsley sprig sizzles in the oil.

Place one piece of veal at a time in the pan, waiting for each piece to sizzle, before putting the other one in. Cook until golden brown on the bottom. Flip the veal over and cook until golden brown on the other side. Do not crowd pan.

Remove from the pan, and place on cooling rack over a baking sheet and place in the oven while making the sauce.

Lemon Sauce

2 tablespoons unsalted butter

2 tablespoons extra virgin olive oil

1 onion, finely chopped

1 cup shallots, chopped fine

¼ cup garlic, minced

1 cup sliced mushrooms, white or shitake

¼ cup dried porcini mushrooms, soaked in very hot water for 20 minutes and then chopped

1 cup fresh tomatoes, peeled, seeded and cut into ½-inch cubes (concasse)

½ cup dry Marsala wine

About 2 cups beef stock

2 lemon wedges

Fresh herbs: basil, parsley, oregano, a sprig of tarragon, just the leaves

Unsalted butter to finish, about 2 tablespoons

2 tablespoons beef glaze

Salt and freshly ground black pepper to taste

Pinch of sugar

In the same skillet, add olive oil and butter. Add the onions and cook until golden. Add the shallots and garlic and cook for about five minutes more. Add the tomatoes and cook for five minutes more.

Add the mushrooms and cook until well colored. Flame with the Marsala or add Marsala and reduce until gone. Add enough stock to make a sauce. Squeeze the lemon wedges into the sauce and add them to the sauce. Add the herbs and concentrated beef stock if you have it. Reduce until the right consistency and season with salt and pepper. Add the butter just before serving.

Arugula

If using arugula, leave the small leaves whole and rip the larger ones. Season with salt and pepper, and dress with vinegar and extra virgin olive oil. Place the reserved veal onto your serving dishes and divide the lemon sauce evenly on top. Place the dressed arugula alongside the veal.

Spaetzle

3 eggs, beaten till frothy

3 cups sifted flour

Freshly grated nutmeg to taste
(*I prefer just a touch*) (optional)

½ teaspoon salt or to taste

Freshly ground black pepper to taste

½ tablespoon baking powder

1 cup milk, use only what is needed to make a thick cake batter

Fresh chopped herbs, like chives, basil, parsley, oregano or whatever you like

Place eggs in a bowl and gradually add flour (sifted with the salt), until the mixture is well blended. Add only enough milk to make a thick cake batter. Add herbs to taste and taste for seasoning. Add salt if needed. The dough tastes better if you let it rest in the refrigerator overnight or at least an hour. I taste the spaetzle batter before I do the full batch. Just drop a few in the boiling water to taste and adjust the seasoning. Do not put too much batter in at a time. Do it in batches.

Make spaetzle

Bring a large pot of water to a boil. Press spaetzle through a spaetzle maker (spaetzle maker is $5.00 on Amazon) or through a sieve with large holes, into boiling water and when they rise to the top, take them out with a Chinese strainer. Make a brown butter sauce and sauté till golden brown. Serve as a side dish with the Vienna Schnitzel.

Brown Butter Sauce

½ stick unsalted butter

1 or 2 fresh sage leaves

Salt and pepper

Slowly simmer butter mixture in a frying pan, stirring frequently, until it turns a nutty, golden brown. Taste for seasoning! You may like a teaspoon of minced garlic or minced shallots, added with the butter. You do not want the garlic or shallots to burn.

Wild Game Sausage Sampler

Serves 2–3

6 wild game sausages of your choice
(Available at D'Artagnan. I like duck, lamb, rabbit, venison, or wild boar.)

1 tablespoon duck fat, or extra virgin olive oil or more if needed

1 cup sliced onions

½ cup thinly sliced red bell pepper

1 teaspoon chopped fresh chile of your choice, depending on how much spice you like (optional)

½ cup finely chopped shallots

1 tablespoon minced garlic

1 cup sliced shitake mushrooms, or mushrooms of your choice

½ cup fine port

1 cup veal, beef, or chicken stock

1 teaspoon of glaze (reduced beef stock)

Fresh herbs: You can use rosemary, sage, thyme, tarragon, or Italian parsley to taste

Kosher salt and freshly ground black pepper to taste and a pinch of sugar

Prick sausages and set aside.

In a heavy 10-inch skillet add duck fat or olive oil, gently heat with sprigs of herbs of your choice.

Add sausages and cook slowly until browned on all sides. Set aside.

If needed, add more duck fat or olive oil to the pan, add onions, sprinkle with a pinch of sugar, salt, pepper. Cook over low-medium heat until sweet and golden. Add peppers, cook until tender. Add chile (if using). Add mushrooms and cook until well colored, add shallots, garlic and cook about five minutes more. Put sausages back in pan and pour port over top and flame.

Reduce port to a glaze. Add stock and reduce to about half. Season with salt, pepper, a pinch of sugar, and serve.

We garnish this dish with toasted pignoli nuts, or toasted walnuts, if you like. Garnish with one of the herbs you used in the sauce. Flamed rosemary is dramatic.

WOR Radio

I THINK I SHOULD talk about the first time the media noticed me. On WOR radio there is a show called the Joan Hamburg show. In the '70s, I received a phone call and was asked to bake something for her show. I believe I made her a Christmas stollen. My whole family gathered around the radio to listen to her talk about how delicious it was and that I was a talented baker. It was so exciting and meant so much to me. The next time she called the topic was low-fat baking. I made brownies with a delicious dark cocoa. It was something new at the time to try to make flavorful desserts that were lower in calories and fat. She had a variety of bakers make different products.

_____

Carol's Cafe Vanilla Soufflé.

Another radio personality walked in while she was tasting the different desserts, and commented on how disgusting they were. I knew my brownies were delicious because I had been teaching them in my low-fat class and the students loved them. I called the radio station and complained that he had grouped all the desserts into one category. He never forgot and became my bitter enemy.

Years later he came to my restaurant with a writer from the *Advance* and a friend. I was at the Old Bermuda Inn working as a consultant the night they arrived. If I had known he was coming I would have been there to cook their entrées. My son Joe, who was a chef at the restaurant, did not know who he was.

I came back in time to make their vanilla soufflés for dessert. He asked me for the recipe. I took it directly out of my file and gave it to him. I went to the table to say hello and he asked, "Did you give me the correct recipe?" On his Saturday radio show, he talked about food and had guest chefs. He devoted a half hour to ripping me apart as a person and a chef. I had no idea how much he hated me. I laid on my bed listening to this early morning show and cried my eyes out. He said I walked over to their table with a glass of whiskey in my hand and interrupted his conversation with his friends at the table and implied that I was drunk.

He had an agenda and wanted to punish me for calling WOR radio so many years before that. He was a nasty son of a bitch.

I am not a drinker because I do not tolerate alcohol well. I do enjoy fine wine and brandy on appropriate occasions. He said I wasn't invited to sit down and the flank steak that my son prepared was over marinated. He suggested that I prepared the steak when I wasn't even there. He never mentioned that I gave him three free Vanilla Soufflés with Chantilly Cream and the recipe. He had an agenda and wanted to punish me for calling WOR radio so many years before that. He was a nasty son of a bitch.

My friend Len Pickell called me and tried to console me. It was terrible and I will never forget it. The good news is that eventually he was fired from that radio show after putting me down on the radio. Len Pickell called to tell me that wonderful news. He was fired because of something he said about another person, and his hatred for the James Beard House. He was mad that he was never invited to cook there, so he would disrespect the Foundation on the air. Good riddance!

Vanilla Soufflé

3 tablespoons butter	5 egg yolks
3 tablespoons flour	6 eggs whites
1 cup milk, hot	1 teaspoon cream of tartar
½ cup sugar	1–2 inch section fresh vanilla bean, or
	1 teaspoon pure vanilla extract

Melt the butter in the top part of a double boiler (over boiling water). Mix in the flour. Cook a minute. Add the hot milk, the sugar and, if you have it, a piece of vanilla bean. If you do not have a vanilla bean, use vanilla extract, but after the mixture is cooked.

Stir this constantly until it is thick and smooth. Remove from the fire and discard the vanilla bean. (Now add the vanilla extract, if that's what you're doing.) Beat the egg yolks and add to the sauce. Allow the mixture to cool at least 15 minutes. Beat the egg whites until they are stiff and creamy. Sprinkle the cream of tartar over them as you beat.

When the egg whites are stiff, add a large spoonful of them to the vanilla mixture and beat it in thoroughly until the mixture has a slightly foamy texture. Now, dribble all over the remaining egg whites, and fold carefully, until it is mixed thoroughly.

Slide this into a buttered and sugared two-quart soufflé dish, and place in a pre-heated 350-degree oven.

This should be done in about 25 minutes, but test it.

Crushed raspberries, or strawberries sugared with a little kirsch makes a good sauce for this.

You may also serve sprinkled with confectioners' sugar and a dollop of whipped cream.

Bobby Flay

MY EXPERIENCE WITH BOBBY FLAY was delightful. I appeared on his show, *Boy Meets Grill*. I decided that I would cook one of my signature dishes at Carol's Cafe. I made Broccoli Rabe with 40 cloves of garlic. It had fresh lemon wedges sprinkled with sugar, and ancho chile powder, extra virgin olive oil, concasse (fresh tomatoes, blanched, peeled and cut into a half-inch dice), homemade chicken stock, fresh basil, and lots of freshly grated Parmesan cheese. The other dish I chose was my most famous dish to this day: Mussels in White Wine served with lots of crusty warm bread.

_____

Bobby Flay and me filming his show at the cafe.

My hair and makeup were done by a lovely hairdresser from A.F. Bennett, a local salon. The owner, Frank Bennett, was one of my customers and he sent the stylist to take care of me at no charge. Of course I gave her a big tip. I wore a white chef's jacket. I was at the stove when Bobby Flay arrived. In my large cast-iron frying pan was extra virgin olive oil, 40 cloves of smashed garlic, lemon wedges that were caramelizing from the sugar, with the flame very low. He looked in the frying pan and began to giggle. I knew he was amazed at the 40 cloves of garlic. I explained to him that I was pan-roasting the garlic for about 40 minutes until they were sweet like candy. I told him that most of the customers at Carol's Cafe ate the garlic because it was healthy and delicious cooked that way. The other thing I did differently was that I did not blanch my broccoli rabe. I trimmed it, cut off the stems and then cooked it in chicken stock until it was barely tender. In the restaurant, I would use vegetable stock for vegetarians. Doing it this way, all the flavor and nutrients stayed in the dish.

I made arrangements with my fishmonger, Tommy, to bring fresh sardines for Bobby Flay to cook. He was supposed to be there at nine in the morning, and he was very late. He walks in up the ramp and says to Bobby Flay, "I did not get the sardines but I will get them the next time you come." I said, "There will not be a next time." He said, "I have swordfish!" Bobby Flay was gracious enough to change his plans, and make the swordfish on the grill with a Sicilian caponata dressing.

Bobby Flay said I was one of the best Italian chefs he worked with in New York City.

Bobby did all of the things his entourage said he would not do. They said he would only be there for an hour, and he was there three hours. He signed autographs; he spoke to the whole staff and kissed me many times. He allowed us to take many photographs of him and the show while it was going on. Many things have changed for Bobby Flay since I met him. He is a major chef on the Food Network now with many shows.

The story with photographs of Bobby Flay made headlines in the *Advance*. The show was repeated many times on the Food Network and it really made everyone so happy in Staten Island. I was very proud, and my experience with him was unforgettable. He is a fabulous chef.

Years later I discovered a review on the Food Network website where Bobby Flay said I was one of the best Italian chefs he worked with in New York City.

Mussels in White Wine

Serves 3–4

3 pounds mussels *(I prefer cultivated mussels. P.E.I. Prince Edward Island are best. They are tiny, sweet, and clean.)*

½ cup extra virgin olive oil

1 large yellow onion, finely chopped

Pinch of salt and sugar, added to the onions while cooking

1 teaspoon kosher salt

8 large shallots, finely minced

14 cloves of garlic, finely minced *(You can use more or less garlic, if you prefer.)*

1 cup fresh tomatoes, peeled, seeded, and cut into ½-inch pieces *(In a pinch, you can use a couple of plum tomatoes from a can, seeded and chopped.)*

1 fresh serrano pepper, seeds removed, and finely chopped (optional)

½ teaspoon red pepper flakes, or to taste (optional)

1 cup dry white vermouth or dry white wine

3 cups of fish stock, or 1½ cups clam juice and 1½ cups water, or vegetable stock if you prefer

½ to 1 cup fresh italian parsley, chopped

½ cup fresh basil (Tear the leaves, do not chop, or the leaves will turn black.)

A sprig of fresh oregano, or 1 teaspoon dry oregano

Salt and freshly ground pepper to taste

NOTES:

- Uncooked shellfish should always be closed. They should be clean smelling, like the ocean. Rinse mussels under cold water, removing any "beards" and discarding any open (dead) mussels.

- Tap the mussels to see if they close; if they do, they are alive and good to use; if they do not close, they are dead, and must be discarded.

- The shells will open during cooking. If they do not open, you haven't cooked it long enough, or they are dead.

- Shellfish should always be eaten fresh. If you cannot be sure of their freshness, don't eat them.

Preparation

In a large saucepan, add the extra virgin olive oil, red pepper flakes, and onion. Slowly sauté until they are soft, and golden, stirring occasionally. This can take about 10–15 minutes.

continued

Mussels in White Wine, *continued*

Add the shallots, chopped garlic, and fresh serrano pepper and red pepper flakes. Sauté just until the shallots and garlic are a pale golden color. Do not brown.

Add the tomatoes, and cook for five minutes.

Add the white wine, and reduce until it is almost all gone.

Add one teaspoon kosher salt and the fish stock, and bring to a boil for about five minutes, reducing the liquid.

Add the salt, pepper, parsley, basil, and oregano.

Over a high flame, add the mussels. Stir, and cover tightly. Cook quickly on a high temperature, stirring several times, just until the mussels open their shells.

Do not overcook the mussels, or they will become very tough.

Serve over fresh-cooked linguine, or in soup bowls, with crusty italian bread.

Garnish with fresh parsley and serve.

Mussels in White Wine

Sautéed Broccoli Rabe with Garlic and Oil

Serves 4

2 pounds broccoli rabe

½ cup extra virgin olive oil

20 garlic cloves or more, lightly smashed

1 cup chicken stock, or more

¾ of a cup fresh tomatoes, peeled, seeded and cut into ½-inch dice

2 teaspoons lemon juice, or to taste

Freshly grated nutmeg, salt, and pepper, to taste

½ teaspoon red pepper flakes (optional)

½ cup freshly grated Parmesan cheese, or more to taste

¼ cup fresh basil or Italian parsley, chopped

Wash broccoli rabe and dry on paper towels. Remove the large tough leaves, leaving just tender leaves and flower buds. Cut off and discard lower part of the stems, leaving the broccoli rabe about six inches long.

Add olive oil and garlic cloves to a large heavy frying pan.

Over low heat, slowly sauté garlic until golden on all sides. This can take about 20 minutes.

Roughly line up broccoli rabe, and slice into three-inch lengths.

Raise the heat to medium, and add the broccoli rabe to the pan, tossing to coat with garlic and oil.

Add tomatoes and toss for a minute or so to remove excess water from the tomatoes.

Add chicken stock; cook for about five minutes, or until the broccoli rabe is "al dente."

Add lemon juice, nutmeg, red pepper flakes, fresh herbs, salt and pepper.

Taste for seasoning; adjust if necessary.

Add Parmesan cheese just before serving or the cheese will become stringy.

NOTE:

- Broccoli rabe is an unusual medium-sharp flavored green widely grown in Italy. It has edible stems and small bud clusters. Peel the stems before using if desired.

The Happy Cooker

THE HAPPY COOKER WAS the name of a television show that was on Staten Island, for the Time Warner Network, *NY 1*. Every week, I would shoot a cooking or baking segment with the anchor woman, Alicia Vitarelli, a reporter who did the news at that time. The name of the show came about because I told them that when I attended the College of Staten Island, I wrote a column about cooking and baking, with a recipe for the college newspaper. The name of that column was "The Happy Cooker."

Because I am so short, when we were standing behind the kitchen table Alicia would take her shoes off because of the difference in our height. She said it did not photograph well when she was looking down at me and she wanted to be able to look at my face. On one of the shows, I made a beautiful blueberry crumb pie. I wore a black lace long-sleeved blouse. The cuffs and collar were solid black. When they took the show back to the studio to look at it, they discovered that the lace part of the blouse disappeared and all that they saw was the collar and cuffs. It looked like I was standing there in my black bra rolling out a pie crust. I still have a copy of that show, and I still hear them laughing. I did that show for a year. Alicia Vitarelli is now an anchorwoman in Philadelphia for ABC.

It looked like I was standing there in my black bra rolling out a pie crust.

Then, Time Warner Cable asked me to do a half-hour cooking show, with 13 segments. I worked on all the shows, planned them and brought them to the studio for approval. It was going to happen and I was so happy. Then the news came, which was that this young, handsome producer, a health fanatic who went to the gym every day, had leukemia. He said when he recovered, we would do the show. Sadly, he died in less than a year.

In January 2000, AOL announced plans to acquire Time Warner. Shortly after that I learned that there would be no show. Here I was, devastated about losing the show, but I was still alive. I wanted the people of Staten Island to have the opportunity to have a free cooking lesson. I knew how important it was for me to be able to watch the Julia Child television show on Channel 13 when I was learning to cook. I kind of thought that this was the last opportunity at my age to have a television show.

I needed a publicist to get the word out. I knew that, but I could not afford one. Publicists started to come to my house in the '70s, pursuing me. I remember this particular female publicist, who came down my basement stairs when I still taught in my home. She wore a hat with a feather and smoked cigars.

She concluded that I needed to divorce my husband because he was holding me back and that I should lose 20 pounds. I was a size 10 and quite attractive. An Italian girl from Brooklyn, who worked so hard, seven days a week, and I needed to divorce my husband Joe. I always felt that I had the talent, but not the confidence, and these publicists who did not have talent made a lot of money on people like me.

Through the years, whenever these publicists came to me, I did not have the money to hire them. One of the publicists who came to me spent a lot of time in my restaurant talking to me. She gave me a tape recorder and having limited experience with tape recorders, it never worked properly. I get so frustrated with mechanical things and remembering people's names. She finally got to the point, that her fee was $3500 a month and that did not include stamps, envelopes, and paper. I told her I could afford the stamps but not her fee. There goes my temper again.

The last publicist I met took a private cooking lesson with her husband. My private lessons are $100 an hour. This publicist was very impressed and wanted me to work with her. She said she knew someone at NBC and that there was an afternoon show called *New York Live* that she wanted me to be on. Unfortunately, she wasn't able to get me on the show because she said I wasn't known to the hostesses.

When my timer went off for the pie, I instinctively jumped off the box, and took the pie out of the oven. For a brief moment I was tall, and then I was short. We all had a good laugh.

I was approached to do two shows for NBC without the help of a publicist.

One was a documentary about Staten Island; Ralph Penza, the anchorman, was the moderator. When they called about the show, I was thrilled. It was a 15 minute to 30 minute segment. I knew we would be closed for vacation, and we were having the floors sanded and polished. I told them that I wanted to do the show, but we would have to film in the kitchen.

They said they really just wanted to do a show with me cooking. When NBC arrived, I was in the kitchen by myself. I had no help, but NBC and the staff were wonderful people, and so I calmed down and got to work. I made Sizzling Shrimp Scampi with couscous while Ralph Penza interviewed me. I remember I had an apple pie in the oven. Ralph Penza was 6 foot 4, and I am under 5 feet tall, so behind my counter that had an overhead mirror, they made me stand on a box to talk to Ralph Penza. When my timer went off for the pie, I instinctively jumped off the box and took the pie out of the oven. For a brief moment I was tall, and then I was short. We all had a good laugh. I was so proud of that program, but I'm sorry I don't have a copy of it.

Wednesday's Child

THE OTHER SHOW I DID for NBC was a local spotlight segment on the news called *Wednesday's Child*, hosted by Janice Huff. She had been doing the segment for at least 15 years. *Wednesday's Child* highlights local children who are up for adoption. Janice was very lovely and kind, but when she tried to speak to a young man during the segment, he didn't respond to her. So I left the kitchen and joined in the conversation, and then the young man relaxed.

When they asked me to do *Wednesday's Child,* they said that they wanted to highlight a child who was up for adoption, who wanted to learn how to cook. So they wanted me to give him a cooking lesson. I had no idea that the child they wanted me to teach would be a young man 16 years old who was handsome and shy. I thought hard about it, and decided to do a stuffed burger. But it wasn't going to be an ordinary stuffed burger. The meat was freshly ground chuck stuffed with a combination of blue cheese, mayonnaise, and butter, kneaded together. The burger was topped with caramelized onions that I slowly sautéed in butter and extra virgin olive oil. The bun was a brioche roll. The "special sauce" was my homemade fresh orange mayonnaise. It is so complicated that I was the only one in the restaurant who could make it. I never made it the same way twice and never measured any of the ingredients except with my hands, grabbing this and that.

The young man and I made the burger together for the first time. He stuffed and shaped the meat patty, and placed it in the hot pan. His face lit up, and he smiled for the first time. He was a quiet and shy young person, but cooking food changed his whole demeanor. On his plate were homemade potato chips, a dill pickle, and this masterpiece of a hamburger. He brought it out to Janice Huff and was proud of his accomplishment.

This burger became a mainstay on my menu. The ultimate compliment was when a customer would tell me that the burger was so delicious that they weren't even going to put ketchup on it. I didn't comment, except that I wanted to say, God forbid! This hamburger became so famous that chefs came to the restaurant and tried to duplicate it. All they had to do was take my grilling class. The hamburger is seared in a hot cast-iron pan to order. I recommended that customers order the burger medium rare. I would reserve the drippings in the pan, so I could toast the bun in all those delicious juices.

> **The "special sauce" was my homemade fresh orange mayonnaise. It is so complicated that I was the only one that could make it in the restaurant.**

Carol's Most Delicious Blue Cheese Hamburger with Caramelized Onions

2 pounds of ground chuck only. Do not buy lean meat.

Kosher salt and freshly ground black pepper

Olive oil for hamburgers

Caramelized Onions

About 5 large onions, sliced thinly

2 tablespoons unsalted butter

2 tablespoons olive oil

1 teaspoon sugar

1 teaspoon of kosher salt

Fresh herbs (optional)

Place all the ingredients in a heavy frying pan and slowly simmer for at least an hour or until sweet and golden.

Add more butter and oil to the pan, if needed.

If you like, put a couple of sprigs of fresh herbs in the pan for extra flavor.

Stir about every five minutes.

Stuffing for Burgers

5 tablespoons unsalted butter, at room temperature

1 cup crumbled blue cheese, more if you like

3 tablespoons mayonnaise

For the Hamburger Rolls

Hamburgers rolls of good quality

Ancho chile (optional)

Herbal Mayonnaise: *Use a commercial mayonnaise and doctor it up. You may add Dijon mustard, lemon juice, chile peppers (chopped fine), horseradish, ketchup, and fresh herbs to taste.*

continued

Carol's Most Delicious Blue Cheese Hamburger, *continued*

Divide the meat into four patties.

With a spoon, take out the center of the patty, not going through the bottom. Reserve the centers.

Mix the butter, blue cheese, and the mayonnaise with your clean fingers. Place a heaping tablespoon of this mixture into the center of the hamburgers. Cover with the reserved centers.

Season the hamburgers with salt and pepper, and the ancho chile powder, if you like.

Lubricate the hamburgers well with olive oil.

Cooking the Burgers

When you are ready, heat the grill until it is very hot, about 30 minutes.

Your hand should be carefully held above the grill. If you have to remove your hand after 20 seconds, the grill is hot enough. If you are using a grill pan, spray with no-stick cooking spray. If you are using a gas grill, lubricate it very well with oil.

Place the burgers on the grill and cook until you reach the temperature of your choice. Be sure to give your burgers a quarter turn, to make beautiful marks.

When the burgers are done, place the rolls on the grill to toast them on both sides. Be careful not to burn them.

Now you are ready to fill the rolls.

On both sides of the rolls, spread some of the prepared herbal mayonnaise. Place the hamburger on top of the roll, and pile caramelized onions on top of the burger.

Serve immediately.

Neighborhood Eats

ABC CALLED ME AND wanted to do a television show about my cooking school and the restaurant. The show was called *Neighborhood Eats* and the moderator was Lauren Glassman. They needed to shoot the show in the afternoon and they asked me to put a cooking class together. I did not teach in the afternoon anymore, so I called some of my students to put together a special class. They were so happy that I thought of them. I was very nervous, and the room was filled with 18 students, the camera crew, the moderator, my daughter Terri, and me.

PHOTO BY SHELBY COHEN (BIG HUNGRY SHELBY)

I wore a red chef's jacket for the show. I say that because I only wear a chef's jacket for television shows and for appearances like cooking for Mayor Bloomberg. It's always been difficult for me to find jackets that fit me properly because they are designed for people of average height or taller. Also they make me feel over-heated so I preferred wearing my embroidered black aprons that my customers enjoyed reading.

That afternoon I taught Penne with Shrimp and Broccoli Rabe and Vienna Schnitzel with homemade Spaetzle. The pro-ducer for the show told me that I was one of the only chefs to give them an accurate recipe of what was demonstrated at the taping.

Host Lauren Glassman walked around the kitchen and interviewed my students. One of the students she interviewed was Dr. Louis Gianvito. He became my student a year after his wife died. He was 75 years old at that time. He continued to be my student until I closed, 10 years later. The moderator asked him, "What have you learned from Carol?" Dr. Lou (as I call him) put his finger on his chin, thought a moment, and said, "Carol taught me how to turn the stove on." At the time, NYC cabs had just begun installing video displays in the back of taxis that ran human interest stories, and Dr. Lou's segment was shown inside the cabs in Manhattan. My Staten Island customers could not wait to tell me about seeing him in the taxis. It was so funny because Dr. Lou became my biggest fan, my doctor, and one of my dearest friends.

Penne with Shrimp, Broccoli Rabe, and Fresh Tomatoes

Breaking Bread

I APPEARED ON A show that aired on Wednesday nights at 8:00 PM on NYC TV called *Breaking Bread*. Monsignor Jamie Gigantiello graduated from culinary school before becoming a priest, and he hosted the show with Tati Amare who grew up in her mother's restaurant. They shared "a passion for food and faith" and would visit a different parish on each episode and discover various restaurants in the vicinity of each church. On the day the show was filmed, two of my chefs were there cooking on the back stove. Chefs Sal and Rami could not believe their eyes when Tati showed up wearing a tight red dress. She is a stunning woman with long black hair. I prepared Filet of Beef Stroganoff with Pan Seared Noodles in Brown Butter Sauce. When I flambéed the beef, she got so excited. Needless to say, my chefs did as well!

Beef Stroganoff with Pan Seared Noodles in a Brown Butter Sage Sauce

Serves 4

1½ pounds, fillet of beef, cut into strips, 2" × ⅜" × ⅜"

Kosher salt and freshly ground black pepper to taste

Unsalted butter (whatever is needed)

Extra virgin olive oil (whatever is needed)

2 large onions, sliced thin (3–4 cups of onions or more to taste)

½ pound of thinly sliced mushrooms, any kind will do

½ cup brandy

About 1 cup beef stock, or more if needed

1 cup sour cream

Fresh herbs

In a heavy cast-iron frying pan, heat one tablespoon olive oil and one tablespoon butter. Add onions, a pinch of salt and sugar, some herbs.

Cook slowly until caramelized and sweet, about 20 minutes. Set aside. In the same pan add one tablespoon olive oil and one tablespoon butter.

When very hot, add mushrooms, sage, tarragon, and parsley. Cook over high heat until colored and liquid has evaporated. Season with salt and pepper. Set aside.

Do not wash pan.

NOTES:

· If the meat is partially frozen, it is easier to slice. The slices will be irregular, that is to be expected. Just before cooking, season on both sides with salt and pepper.

· Watch point: The beef must be seared quickly, not fully cooked.

Heat same pan until very hot; melt olive oil and butter, whatever is needed and sear a few pieces of beef at a time, turning it quickly, until just brown on all sides. Set aside, do not pile. Continue until all the meat is seared.

Put all the meat back into the pan, pour over the brandy, and flame. Add the onions and mushrooms, and a little beef stock, about a cup.

It is a good idea to heat the stock first, so meat does not overcook.

Stir in the sour cream and quickly bring to a boil. Add fresh herbs, salt, and pepper to taste and serve with Pan Seared Noodles.

Pan Seared Noodles

1 pound of egg noodles (like fettucine)

1 stick (4 ounces) unsalted butter

Fresh sage

Chives

Parsley

Kosher salt and freshly ground pepper, to taste

Cook noodles in salted boiling water until al dente. Drain, set aside in a bowl and toss with some additional butter to prevent the noodles from sticking.

In one large or two medium sauté pans, preferably cast iron, melt butter with a sage leaf. When butter begins to brown, add noodles and toss in butter until they begin to crisp and become lightly browned.

Season with fresh herbs, salt, and pepper. Serve alongside Beef Stroganoff.

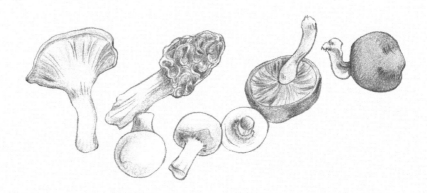

Good Day New York

ONE OF MY LAST television appearances was on Fox Channel 5's *Good Day New York*. The hosts were Rosanna Scotto and Greg Kelly, and they interviewed me while I made my famous Mussels in White Wine. It was a very hectic day, as I had to be at the Fox TV Studio on 42nd Street by 7:00 AM. Jeff was worried that we would get stuck in traffic, so we decided to leave at 5:30 AM. Of course, we made it to the studio in under 45 minutes, and had to wait out front until they called me in. It was a blessing in disguise, as the extra 45 minutes we sat in front of the studio gave me a chance to relax. I decided not to sleep the night before the appearance, saving myself the time of having to get up, and get ready to travel to Manhattan so early in the morning.

Once the producer came down to the street to get Terri and me, they loaded up all the ingredients and prepared mussels that I had brought with me. They asked that I bring a completed dish of mussels, along with all the raw ingredients so that I could demonstrate to Rosanna and Greg how to prepare and cook the mussels, and have a completed dish for the hosts to taste while I was demonstrating it.

Terri and I sat in the green room for an hour and a half, until they finally came and brought us into the studio. We watched the televangelist Joel Osteen and his wife being interviewed before I was introduced. I was expecting some kind of decent cooktop, but was instead greeted by a propane hot plate. In these situations, you just have to make the best of things, and just forge ahead.

Greg was fascinated by the fact that I was using Prince Edward Island Cultured Mussels and he kept asking, "What does cultured mussels mean?"

The segment started off with me explaining how to prep the mussels, and Greg was fascinated by the fact that I was using Prince Edward Island cultured mussels and he kept asking, "What does cultured mussels mean?" The funniest part of the segment was how Greg was raving over how delicious the mussels were, dunking pieces of Italian bread into the broth, moaning in ecstasy every time he took a bite, and saying, "I'm definitely coming to your restaurant, these are delicious!"

Of course, he never came to the cafe!

So Long, Farewell

Chefs and Students Who Worked for Me

Michael Howell, Chef

MICHAEL HOWELL, A NOVA SCOTIA native, was an interesting and talented chef, who worked for me for about a year and a half. I was 20 years his senior and he liked to tell people that I was on the line, and he was expediting, which means he was telling the chefs when to fire their dishes.

Greg Roach and James Ryan.

His wife, Mary Harwell, worked on Broadway in a production capacity. Michael was a talented chef and my favorite dish that he made at Carol's Cafe was Lazy Man Lobster with Two Sauces. He was meticulous and took his time, and the dish was intricate and beautiful. I do remember a staff meal that was his very brave attempt to make eggplant parmesan. The eggplant was cut into slices about one-inch thick and placed raw in a roasting pan. I believe he put tomato slices or tomato sauce on top and layered it with mozzarella. He placed it in the oven until the cheese melted. His effort was not appreciated by the staff.

Michael left Carol's Cafe for a position as head chef in the Bahamas. My heart was broken because he is a fine man and chef. We did keep in touch and we saw each other again, years later, when he was asked to do a dinner at the James Beard House. He asked me if he could use my kitchen to prep. We also maintain a friendship to this day through Facebook. He told Anthony Bourdain that I was the finest Italian chef he worked for in New York City. I am so appreciative of that since I was always one of Anthony Bourdain's biggest admirers.

George Willis, Line Cook

THE BEST CHEFS who worked for me were my students. They understood what I expected because I taught them in my classes and those that took the classes seriously went way beyond recreational cooking. George Willis was one of those students.

George Willis is a big guy who is intelligent, sweet, and honest. He sold pharmaceuticals. He took classes for several years before he started working with me on the weekends as a line cook. In the Technique and Theory classes, he showed me his talent when he brought in his homework. In the Baking Workshop, he always brought in his baked goods that had to be finished at home. He made no excuses. He just did what he was supposed to do to become a fine cook.

A line cook is what makes the executive chef succeed. Knowing he was there plating my dishes, I never feared that he would not enhance my cooking. It was so hectic on the weekend that when you had someone like George on the line, it was so reassuring. He had to stop working at the cafe because of his job. He became very successful in his career for the pharmaceutical company, did a lot of traveling, and he is a wonderful husband and father. We are still dear friends, and keep in touch on Facebook.

James Ryan, Sous Chef

JAMES RYAN WAS MY SOUS CHEF, working for me for five years. He was like a son to me. His mother died when he was 12 years old. My son Joe was friends with him, and they went to school together. As a young man, James spent time in my house, and would eat dinner with us. Perhaps I influenced him! He graduated from culinary school and did an internship in Europe. He was very honest, efficient, and responsible, and his knowledge of the food industry is vast.

In those days, we were very busy. James was expediting when one of my line cooks, Benny, treated James brutally and so James gave notice. He is now a teacher at Port Richmond High School where he's the head of the culinary program, and is loved by his students. I have volunteered my services and mentored the students whenever he has asked me. I made his wedding cake. He has two sons and is a very involved father. He coaches a wrestling team and acts as a baseball umpire as well. He is very involved in the Careers through Culinary Arts Program (CCAP), a national nonprofit that works with public high schools to prepare underserved students for the workforce.

Over the years James would help us with catering whenever we needed a chef to go on off-premises catering jobs, or to work in the restaurant when we were short-handed. I always appreciated that he was willing to help, no questions asked.

Rick, Sous Chef

RICK WAS A VERY TALENTED, experienced chef who had owned his own restaurant before he came to Carol's Cafe. I was thrilled to have him and gave him two weeks' paid vacation after just a short time he was with us. His prepping, stocks, and sauces were impeccable. He had many years of experience. I felt relief that finally I had someone who could alleviate all my responsibilities. One night he asked if Les and I would like to go to his friend's restaurant on Bay Street in Staten Island. It was called Aesop's Tables, and was run by a woman named Wendy who allowed her big dog to walk around the dining room while you ate. She had a backyard garden where guests were allowed to sit and eat in the nice weather.

Les, Rick, and I were sitting in the backyard having a drink. It was a lovely evening, and boom, Rick looked into my eyes and told me that Wendy needed him to be a chef at this restaurant. Les pushed his chair back in shock and almost fell to the floor. I just looked at this piece of crap and realized what a con man he was. He had just received two weeks' vacation and we were so nice to him. Of course it was too good to be true. At this point in my life, nothing in this business shocked me. Eventually, he opened his own restaurant again, and it only lasted a year or less.

Then I heard he was the head chef of a French restaurant opened by the girl who stole hundreds of dollars from my store many years ago. They invested a fortune in renovations, equipment, and food stuffs and yet they failed in a year. It amazes me that there are so many bullshit artists in the restaurant business who think that it's so easy.

When I look back on all our reviews and accolades and how we were loved by the people who counted, I am very proud.

So many investors have been taken in by this dream. I did not want investors, even though they came in and out of my life over the years. I would listen to their proposals but I wanted to be my own boss and I did not want to alter my dreams of delicious food and comfort. I am proud to say that Carol's Cafe maintained that for 25 years. When I look back on all our reviews and accolades and how we were loved by the people who counted, I am very proud.

David Feis, Sous Chef

WE HAD MANY COOKS and chefs coming in and out of my restaurant because I couldn't afford to pay the salary of a qualified chef de cuisine. The way I would hire a chef was to interview them and have them prepare a dish that they considered to be their best. There were talented, sweet chefs like David Feis, who was my sous chef. He worked very hard in the busiest times of Carol's Cafe and wanted to advance, but I was the executive chef and customers wanted to see me in the kitchen, cooking for them. He left to become an executive chef of the Staten Island Hotel Restaurant. The next time I saw him, he became a regular customer at Carol's Cafe. He came with his wife and two children for their special occasions. He told me he was no longer a chef and worked as a longshoremen. He came to the restaurant one night for his daughter's birthday. His son and daughter always made me cards to show their love. Before he left he spoke to me privately and said he stopped cooking because his wife wanted him to. He still loved to cook and wanted to try again. I told him I know how difficult it is for a chef to have a normal life. I did tell him if that's what makes him happy, he needed to make a decision.

I know the sacrifices people make who are in this profession. A happy marriage is a difficult thing to accomplish. A true chef who loves to cook and has an understanding partner is a rare thing. There are no holidays with your family. You work long hours and you have to deal with tremendous stress. When you do come home and crawl into bed, wiped out, you have to listen to your husband telling you, "You smell like garlic," which mine did. When I announced my retirement, David wrote to tell me how fond he was of me.

Joseph Giudice, Sous Chef

MY RELATIONSHIP WITH MY SON JOE is best described as a roller-coaster ride. Despite his talent and professional training, his A.D.D. and substance and alcohol addictions caused many problems in our family and the cafe.

He was my sous chef when the cafe opened, but it became impossible for him to maintain that position given his personal issues. Over the years he continued to teach his "How to make Mozzarella" class, and work in the restaurant on occasion until we closed.

In 2011, after his father died, Joe and his wife Theresa moved to Missouri for a fresh start at the urging of their close friend, Matt. Tragically Matt, who was a veteran, took his own life in 2016. Joe credits his friend with saving his life by helping him to get clean.

Joe currently works as a cook in the kitchen of a hospital and donates his time to the veterans in his community in honor of Matt.

Nick, Sous Chef

NICK WAS MY FORMER STUDENT who took many classes as a boy and young man, and then went on to study at the Culinary Institute. I was very fond of him and so wanted him to succeed. It was just a matter of timing, and when he was available to become a sous chef at Carol's Cafe, he accepted the position. He did a good job, managing the orders and prepping what was needed. Everything was fine until he began to cook on the line.

He wanted a bigger role, and felt I was not giving him the chance to cook for the customers.

My original recipes were not learned in school and so the intricacies are not classic French techniques. I never kept my recipes to myself and all he had to do was ask or ask me to teach him. I think that because he had graduated from the Culinary Institute, he felt that he could prepare my dishes without my input. The success of Carol's Cafe was my creations. My customers wanted and eagerly anticipated my dishes and did not want them changed, especially dishes like the Stuffed Calamari in Tomato Sauce. It was not handed down to me by my mother or grandmother. It took me a long time to perfect the recipe.

My customers wanted and eagerly anticipated my dishes and did not want them changed.

The way I cook is with a feeling and I had to create dishes without ever seeing them before. I would make my stuffing and do test patties until it was divine. He went ahead and made this dish from a recipe that was typed for my classes. He then froze it in portions for the cafe. He should have asked my advice and asked me to taste the stuffing before he went ahead. When a regular customer who had the dish before complained, and said that Carol did not make this, I had a problem. I could not use it and it was discarded after he left.

Once we were cooking on the line together, and I watched him making one of my classic dishes. I knew it was not going well. I took the pan out of his hands to finish the dish and of course he was insulted. When you are busy on the line, you have to make quick decisions.

The customer comes first and your goal is to always please the customer. He gave notice and I believe it was two weeks. That was not enough time to find someone and I knew he did not have another position waiting for him. I asked him to give me more time after all we meant to each other. I taught him many things and always went out of my way to look at his work when he studied with me. I also was his friend, like a grandmother, and believe he went on to culinary school because of my influences. I wanted him to be a better chef but that didn't matter.

That was also the end of our friendship. He was with us only six months. Some of the best chefs in the world have never gone to culinary school and learned by working in restaurants. You must have the passion, natural talent, creativity, and love of food. I devoted myself to making people happy and it made me so fulfilled when my customers swooned.

Stuffed Calamari in Tomato Sauce

12 large squid *(The sac should measure about 5 inches long.)*

Sauce Ingredients

4 cans (28 ounces each) plum tomatoes in juice, chopped fine in a food processor

½ cup extra virgin olive oil

2 large pinches of kosher salt

2 large pinches of sugar

2 large onions, chopped fine

2 large shallots, minced

12 cloves garlic, minced, or more to taste

½ teaspoon red pepper flakes (optional)

1 cup white wine

Fresh basil to taste

½ cup fresh Italian parsley, chopped

2 sprigs fresh oregano, leaves only

1 teaspoon dry oregano

Kosher salt, freshly ground pepper, and a large pinch of sugar

Stuffing

1 loaf Italian bread

Water to soak the bread

¼ cup extra virgin olive oil

1 cup finely chopped onions

¾ cup finely chopped shallots

¼ cup minced garlic or to taste

4 ounces mozzarella, chopped coarsely

¾ cup Parmesan cheese

6 large eggs, lightly beaten

2 tablespoons extra virgin olive oil

½ pound shrimp

Tentacles, from squid

¼ cup brandy

½ cup fresh flat-leaf parsley

¼ cup fresh chives

½ cup fresh basil, cut into chiffonade

2 teaspoons fresh oregano leaves, chopped

½ teaspoon fresh thyme leaves

2 teaspoons lemon juice or to taste

1 teaspoon minced fresh chile pepper (optional)

2 ounces prosciutto, chopped fine, (optional)

Wash the squid sacs thoroughly inside and out and reserve tentacles. Dry very well with cloth towels and set aside in refrigerator.

continued

Stuffed Calamari in Tomato Sauce, *continued*

Make Stuffing: In a heavy frying pan, cook onions, adding pinches of sugar and salt, slowly in olive oil, until golden. Do not brown, takes about 20 minutes. Add shallots and garlic and cook for another 5 to 10 minutes. Set aside. Soak bread while onions are cooking. When bread is soft, squeeze out the water very well. Break or chop bread up into small pieces. Set aside.

Season cleaned shrimp with kosher salt and freshly ground black pepper. Heat a skillet until very hot, add olive oil and sear shrimp quickly on both sides; add brandy and flame, or reduce for two to four minutes. Set aside. When cool, chop coarsely. Season tentacles with kosher salt and freshly ground black pepper.

Heat a skillet until very hot, add olive oil and sear tentacles until nicely colored. Flame with brandy and set aside until cool. Chop coarsely and set aside.

In a very large bowl, add all stuffing ingredients, mix well with hands. Take a small piece of stuffing and place on a small dish and warm for a few seconds in the microwave, taste for seasoning and correct. Can be done ahead and set aside in refrigerator.

You can stuff squid sacks with a pastry bag or with a small spatula or spoon. Do not fill completely, allow for expansion. About ⅔ full. Set aside.

Heat a very large heavy frying pan until hot, add olive oil and sauté filled squid sacs, without crowding pan, until golden brown on all sides. Set aside when all sacs are done.

In same pan add olive oil and onions for sauce, and sauté until golden; add shallots and garlic and sauté for another 5 to 10 minutes. Add white wine and reduce until gone. Add tomatoes and bring to a boil, lower to a simmer, add stuffed sacs and cook uncovered for about two to three hours or until sacs are very tender. Add fresh herbs, season with salt, pepper, red pepper flakes, a large pinch of sugar, or to taste. If frying pan is not large enough, transfer all ingredients to a large saucepan.

NOTES:

- Can be served as an appetizer or an entrée with spaghetti on the side, using the delicious squid sauce.
- This dish keeps very well in the refrigerator and can be made a week ahead.
- The sauce freezes very well.

Fried calamari with spicy
tomato sauce.

Margaret, Terri, me, Sal, and
Carol Ann at the Italian
Culinary Institute.

Assistants

Jeff Frank

JEFF FRANK, WHO STUDIED with me in my house, became my assistant accidently. He helped me after I was in an automobile accident on my way to the gym. The way to get rid of my stress was to be physically fit. I started doing yoga first, and studied with a 70-year-old teacher who was amazing, and was the best teacher I ever had. She knew I ate too much beef after she studied me standing on my head. She said she knew that because my face turned red.

I was so frightened that I would gain weight that I would grill a plain burger for lunch every day with a salad. If I gained weight, my husband Joe, who never had a weight problem, would touch my stomach and ask, "What is this?"

After my yoga teacher left Staten Island, I joined Gold's Gym, and would have to travel on the expressway to get there. One day I became stuck in traffic just before the exit on the expressway, and was at a complete stop. My foot was on the brake and the car behind me had been struck so hard by another car that it slammed into mine, causing serious damage. I was so physically fit that I did not realize how badly hurt I was. My husband arrived and did not take me to the hospital, even though the police officer told him I was hit very hard. My injuries affected me for the rest of my life. I began to have hip, back, and right-leg problems.

> **I made an arrangement with Jeff that if my head went down, he would get up and start talking to the students until I recovered.**

Jeff, who was my cooking student, became involved because after my accident I became dizzy and had fainting spells. I made an arrangement with him that if my head went down, he would get up and start talking to the students until I recovered. I would go upstairs to my kitchen, and sit for a little while until it passed.

When I moved to the new building on Richmond Road, Jeff Frank came with me. He became one of my employees, helped me cater the big parties, and assisted me in the classes. Late at night while we were working, we would listen to Pavarotti and Tchaikovsky; Terri lived in one of the apartments upstairs with her husband Jeff (no, not Jeff Frank, Jeff Lewis), and would call down to shut that damn music off! We would work through the night to complete the overwhelming amount of work we had to do.

He wanted to further his education so he went to Paris to study baking. When he came back, he studied at Peter Kump's Cooking School in Manhattan. He also went to work as an unpaid assistant for Sara Moulton for many months. She was a cooking teacher who was Julia Child's assistant and a contributor to *Gourmet* magazine.

When he was not offered a paid position, Jeff became a chef at a restaurant in Staten Island where he did all the baking himself. When the review for the restaurant came out, the critic was cruel and he got negative feedback about his pastry which he had always taken great pride in. It upset him so much that he left the restaurant business, moved away from Staten Island with his wife, and became a salesman selling law books. His heart was not in it. We remained dear friends and he never forgets Mother's Day or my birthday. He came to visit me in Staten Island a couple of times over the years with his son.

About two years ago, we had a conversation on the phone about how unhappy he was selling law books. I encouraged him to go out and look for a job in the restaurant business. He said they were offering him very little money and I told him to do it anyway. He had been out of the business for awhile and he needed to get his foot in the door. He now sends me pictures of his beautiful pastries and he himself looks great. You have to have a passion in your work and he lost that for a while. Now he is back and doing was he loves to do. I love him and I am very proud of him.

Carl, Chef and Assistant Caterer

CARL WAS THE FIRST professional assistant/chef that I hired after I bought the building. He was an excellent African-American chef who worked for me for about a year, because travelling from the Bronx to Staten Island every day was just too much for him. He had his own catering business in the Bronx when I hired him.

I had to learn so much about the food business to take my catering business to the next level, so I went to all the food shows at the Javits Convention Center. I wanted to use new foods and products that Staten Islanders never saw before. My catering menu had to reflect what I created for my cooking classes and little did I know that *eclectic* was an unusual word in Staten Island. In the long run, I should have played it safe and opened an Italian restaurant. But that would have been too easy, and I liked to learn and challenge myself to learn new things.

It was at one of the conventions that I met John Profaci from Staten Island, who was owner of Colavita Imports. Colavita was one of the first companies that I ended up having a long relationship with. I bought all of their specialty imports, like their extra virgin olive oil, pastas, Italian cheeses like fresh wheels of Parmesan, and balsamic vinegars.

John Profaci became my biggest fan (when my first book, *Carol's Cafe Pasta Sauces* came out, he bought a case of them!), and now Colavita products are known worldwide. John had asked me to cater Colavita's grand opening party, and one of the menu items he wanted was a large poached salmon. Unfortunately, I didn't have a pan large enough to poach the oversized salmon, and that's when Carl came to the rescue by improvising a pan big enough to poach the salmon, by taping two disposable tin-foil pans together, and it worked!

Carl would try new and different techniques. He loved to dye onions blue, and put them on food trays for a decoration. I was fond of picking them up, taking them off the trays, and putting them in my apron pocket, so as not to insult him. He was very nice and hard-working and helped me do many catering jobs before he moved on.

Janet Gallo

JANET GALLO, A VERY PRETTY girl, became my student, and took Tech and Theory I and II, the Advanced Tech and Theory classes, and all of my baking workshops. I saw how dedicated she was, and I asked her if she would like to work for me in the restaurant. We were together several years and I felt she was like a daughter to me. She was dedicated to our restaurant and cooking school and helped make it a success. After she left Carol's Cafe, she went back to school and began teaching in public schools, first as a culinary instructor and later as a special ed teacher. I missed her terribly when she left, but was very proud that she followed her dream to pursue a career in the culinary field.

Brian

BRIAN WAS A YOUNG CHEF, only eighteen, who cooked with me at the beginning of Carol's Cafe after graduating from culinary school. Brian was talented, handsome, and really would rather have been involved with music instead of cooking. He would put food in the oven and leave without telling anyone. Then I would smell something burning. Brian just refused to use a timer even though I had timers everywhere. I believed in timers because as a mother I would get distracted and they would remind me of what I was cooking.

Brian also made the biggest filet of Chicken Fingers (with Honey Mustard Dip) for a very fancy party we did at an important, ritzy, architect's house. I was so busy preparing for this party, I did not see how large he had cut the chicken. I knew he had seen me make this before but then I saw this giant piece of chicken hanging out of this woman's mouth. It should have been about two inches in size not eight inches long. The host asked me about the appetizer and said it was delicious but asked, "Is it usually this big?" "Yes" I said. Never let a client know something is wrong. It is my job to make them happy, whatever the situation.

Never let a client know something is wrong. It is my job to make them happy, whatever the situation.

This was an appetizer that I catered many times before. The breast of chicken was coated with cornmeal, flour, salt, pepper, and paprika, southern style, then deep fried, and served room temperature with a delicious dip. When Brian saw my face, he knew he made a big mistake.

We still keep in touch through Facebook and he now works for a wine and spirits company, and travels often.

Greg Roach

GREG ROACH IS A FUNNY redhead who I was very fond of. He was another student of mine who loved to cook and bake. His intelligence, sense of humor, and talent, led me to ask him if he wanted to work for me in the restaurant, on a part-time basis. He was concerned about how his wife would feel if he worked at night in the restaurant, but he took the job anyway.

Most nights we worked till 5:00 AM. He worked slowly and meticulously. I did not know how he got up to go work for Brooklyn Union as a manager, or if he just went straight there. He kept my spirits up through the bad and good times. He worked for me about two years. He then told me his wife did not want him to work for me anymore because it was affecting her mentally and physically. We have remained friends, and he and his family used to come to the restaurant for dinner.

Sandra and Mark

SANDRA WAS A STUDENT who rescued me by teaching a soul-food class with me, when Mark, our chef, quit suddenly. Mark started as a dish-washer, and one day I asked him to help me prep a delicious lemon butter cake. I quickly noticed how naturally talented he was. I asked him if he would like to prep and cook with me. What I did not know was that he had problems. I was told he had a son when he was a teenager, and his father was married many times. He did not take care of Mark, and Mark developed a drinking problem. Mark was handsome and talented, but could not take any kind of criticism. He was so talented, and his soul food like Pulled Pork, Southern Fried Chicken and Waffles, Collard Greens, Oxtail Stew, and Banana Pudding were superb. I quickly wrote a class into the cooking class brochure, starring Mark as the cooking teacher. This was months before he left.

He worked for me at least a couple of years. One day he came in at 2:00 PM instead of the morning shift. He arrived with a hangover and was throwing food around. He was making a brown veal stock. The bones and vegetables were put into the oven, he slammed the door, and cooked at such a high temperature

> **I met Sandra, a large woman with a great smile, in my classes. I asked her if she would like to do the class with me, because she was a talented cook.**

that everything burned. I told Mark that he had to be more responsible and come in on time. He quit and walked out of the restaurant. My heart was broken because he had so much potential and could have been a great chef. I was very fond of him and could have taught him so much.

I did not cancel the soul-food class although I had never made any of his dishes. That would not be the first time I challenged myself into cooking or baking something I never did before. I met Sandra, a large woman with a great smile, who was a parole officer and social worker, in my classes. I asked her if she would like to do the class with me because she was a talented cook. I made oxtail stew for the first time and it was so delicious. Of course, the pulled pork was in the oven for many hours and we started a new one in front of them. Sandra helped me with the waffles, using her antique waffle iron, and banana pudding, and told stories about the dishes, and it was wonderful. I was so pleased that I asked her to work for me in the evenings in the restaurant, plating desserts and making soufflés.

Sandra worked for me for about a year, and on New Year's Eve, when she was scheduled to work, she did not show up. The rumors were that she had some personal problems and I never saw her again. Her son did call and ask me for her waffle iron, which Sandra thought I still had. I told him I never saw it again after the night of the class. In the restaurant business, equipment and things are stolen, broken, and disrespected. I thought Sandra was an intelligent, talented woman, and I respected her talent and personality.

The Estudillo Brothers

SAL ESTUDILLO WAS ONE of the chefs that worked for me the longest, for more than 20 years. His brother Bernardo worked for me first. Benny (as we called him) was a talented cook but his drinking and his relationship with a woman named Maria helped end his job at Carol's Cafe. There was a third brother, named Ramiro, who also worked at the cafe.

I met Sal when he was 18 years old, when he worked in a small super-market. He had a smile that lit up the room. He knew nothing about being a chef. I saw something in him that made me want to teach him to cook. He started as a dishwasher and soon began prepping. Then he moved to the

Me and Sal cooking together.

appetizer and salad station. Eventually he worked his way up to line cook and sous chef.

The three Estudillo brothers taught a class on Mexican cuisine. The food they made was wonderful and delicious. Of course what they didn't understand was this was a cooking class and they did too much. My favorite dish was Mexican Shrimp Cocktail, a delicious appetizer we had on the menu on and off many times. The dish varied in flavor and seasoning depending on who made it.

After the class, Sal said to me, "Momma" (that is what he called me), "I am so tired." He never wanted to do another class again. I explained to him that he made it very difficult for himself.

Teaching is not easy, and you need to plan what you can do in three hours, because three hours go by very quickly. You have to be informative, funny, entertaining, and make delicious food to feed the students. I tried to have Sal teach again, but I believe it made him very nervous. I told him that it was his first class and he was charming and informative. The students really enjoyed his food. He just made too much of it!

I had no time to cry. I had to do all the cooking at the cafe that night, virtually by myself, with a room full of customers. Just another day at the office!

You had to be very careful when speaking to the Mexican chefs, or they thought you were being disrespectful. Sal told me he had very little education, and that he was a father at 16 but he was quick to learn my dishes and had an excellent palate.

Sal asked me to help him become a U.S. citizen, because he wanted to start a landscaping business. Today he has several businesses and is quite successful. He became very busy and worked for us when he could, until I retired. He even helped us clean up when we closed the business. I believe he is the hardest working man I know.

During the time the Estudillo Brothers worked for me, the daily drama became a circus, and helped seal their fate. Ramiro (Rami) started as a dishwasher. While he washed dishes, he looked to his left, watching me as I cooked on the line. He never took his eyes off me. He impressed me and so I began teaching him. He was talented, but had a drinking and drug problem just like his older brother Benny.

My cooks in the cafe (left to right: Jose, my student Joe Perlstein, and the Estudillo brothers: Rami, Benny, and Sal).

I remember once when most of my staff were in the city doing a large catering job, for a very important client, a nightmare happened. I came to work, walked into the kitchen, and realized that Rami, and his brother Benny, were falling over drunk. I had no time to cry. I had to do all the cooking at the cafe that night, virtually by myself, with a room full of customers. Just another day at the office!

Another day they called me and told me to come in because Rami had an accident. Rami and this young man, who now was the dishwasher, got into a fight because Rami was teasing him. The fight escalated into the backyard and they ran up the steps onto a retaining wall. They were wrestling and Rami fell 10 feet onto the cement, where he landed on his head. He was bleeding profusely and looked at me with tears in his eyes. We had to call an ambulance. That was the end for Rami and I think he knew it.

After his head injury, he was never the same. He loved me and knew he had disappointed me. He had a drug problem, and was arrested and held at Rikers Island jail, until his trial. Of course Sal ended up being responsible for him, financially and otherwise. Rami was deported to Mexico and now is a chef in a restaurant there. He calls me occasionally and I can tell by his voice that he is doing much better.

One Saturday morning at the restaurant, Benny and Maria, his girl-friend, got into a brawl. He was abusive and she was as strong as any man in the kitchen. They broke wine and cocktail glasses, and whatever else they could throw at each other. The police came and arrested both of them. That night I should have closed. One of my chefs was in jail and I did not have a dishwasher. A cooking student and good friend who is now a superior court judge came to the restaurant with eight of his important friends. He wanted to impress them! But I had dishes piled up in the sink and on all of the work tables. I was missing my line cook and dishwasher. I did the best I could and just kept cooking. It was a Saturday night and we were packed with customers, and his table had to wait. At his table, this doctor couple were very angry and were making a scene. My waitress and bartender told me not to go out. I listened to them and made the decision not to address the problem. It was one of the biggest mistakes of my life. I was not experienced enough to know what to do. I lost a dear friend and the judge never spoke to me again.

Teresa

TERESA CAME IN FOR an interview and I hired her. She had an energy and a great work ethic and came into Carol's Cafe at just the right time. Not only was I cooking at Carol's Cafe, I was also involved with the Bermuda Inn. That was a decision I regretted, working at two restaurants. That restaurant was at least a half hour's drive, without traffic, from my restaurant. I had to double my baking and cooking and deal with the staff who did not want me there. Teresa and I worked into the night and watched the sun come up. To relax at the end of the work day, we would walk from Carol's Cafe to New Dorp Lane. She would always touch a pole when we got there and then we would head back to the restaurant. I am not sure how many miles we walked, if I had to guess, it was at least five miles.

We even became best friends and traveled to San Francisco to visit my daughter Maria and her family.

We even became best friends and traveled to San Francisco to visit my daughter Maria and her family. We walked everywhere and stayed in a fine hotel in separate rooms. Our trip to the wine country in Napa Valley was an adventure I will never forget. We got a little drunk and laughed the entire time we were there. Coming back on the bus, we had this annoying couple in front of us who wanted to argue with us about the shade being up or down, and I said, "I'm from Brooklyn, you better not." That made Teresa laugh even more. That was the best day I ever had in Napa Valley! Maria had a great party at her house, and Teresa and I cooked.

When we got back, everything changed! She got romantically involved with my married chef, Sal. She was 10 years older than Sal and should have known better. They made love in the basement, walk-in refrigerator, or any nook and cranny they could find. They were two of the best and hardest working cooks I had at Carol's Cafe but their relationship hurt the restaurant. One day they came up to my apartment above the restaurant with a list of demands for her and Sal that were totally unreasonable. Sal did not speak or have an opinion. Teresa wanted me to fire two other cooks or she threatened to quit. I was

No matter how much I cared for Teresa as a cook and a person, I was not going to be blackmailed so I fired her on the spot. I think she was shocked.

sponsoring Sal to become a citizen so he did not back her up. No matter how much I cared for Teresa as a cook and a person, I was not going to be blackmailed so I fired her on the spot. I think she was shocked.

She went back to the cafe into the basement where the files were kept, and took piles of my recipes and three loose-leaf books, filled with my recipes that we used in the kitchen. My heart was broken for the loss of our friendship. I was very hurt that she took recipes from me and that she put Sal in that position.

My son-in-law Jeff called her at 6:30 AM, and threatened to bring the police to her doorstep if he did not get all of the recipes back within an hour. By 7:30, Jeff was banging on her door, and got every single recipe back.

She was the best assistant I ever had and was with me for about two years. She got a job with Mario Batali in the city and I still miss her til this day. Her relationship with Sal ended. I wanted to ask him if he ever spoke to her, but I knew this was an uncomfortable question for him, so I never asked again.

And Last, But Not Least ... Margaret Strauss

I FIRST MET MARGARET STRAUSS in the '70s as a student in my cooking school in my home. Her husband John drove her to the classes. She laughed at all my jokes and was the kindest and most unselfish woman I'd ever met. Her husband was 20 years older than she and had a daughter from a previous marriage. John didn't want to have children with Margaret which is a shame because she would have been a good mother. She told me that he liked to show her porn but she was indifferent, and thought it was funny. She did not understand why he was doing that.

A couple of years after I met Margaret, her husband died from breast cancer. Coincidentally, Margaret was also later diagnosed with breast cancer. They removed half of one of her breasts as well as the surrounding tissue. Margaret underwent radiation treatments, and took medication for years. She was a trooper and survived. I called her Margo. Many years later, she had a hysterectomy when cancer was discovered again. I asked her, "Why don't you do some filing for me?" She did have a job working in an office for many years. When she retired, she came to work at the cafe helping me prep my desserts in addition to the filing.

Of all the recipes I taught her, for brownies for her family she preferred to make her recipe. I would say, "Bake them just until a toothpick would come out with streaks of chocolate on it." She did not deviate and continued to overbake them. I soon learned that she was set in her ways. She was a also hoarder, who loved to drive, shop, and work at Carol's Cafe. She loved me very much. Just as I

Margaret holding a small shopping cart that she was given at Christmas.

Teaching my grandchildren, Max and Olivia, how to make truffles. Margaret is prepping in the back.

loved her, for her unselfishness. Margo saw Terri and I through the best and worst of times. She became my official prepper, and prepped all my desserts for the cooking classes and restaurant.

I remember one Saturday night when a customer said his Lemon Meringue Pie was salty, and it was one of his favorite desserts. I said, "That's impossible!" Another customer complained about his dessert and I knew something was wrong. I found out that Margo had accidentally thrown a cup of salt into the sugar bucket, thinking it was sugar and all the desserts were ruined.

She loved me very much. Just as I loved her, for her unselfishness. Margo saw Terri and I through the best and worst of times.

The filing cabinets were in the basement and there were 8000 recipes at the time. Margaret's job was to list the recipes in the index book, and file them. As the years went by, she began to repeat the same recipe in the file and soon did not like going to the basement at all. She stopped filing and began to make mistakes with the prepping. Baking is an exact science and when the flour measurement, salt, and other dry ingredients were wrong, it affected my baking.

Caramel Shrimp with
Ginger and Garlic.

PHOTO BY SHELBY COHEN (BIG HUNGRY SHELBY)

Soon we noticed that shopping for the restaurant and cooking school had became too difficult for her. It was something we just had to just deal with. We knew that at 80-plus years old, this was very important to her, and we could not take that away from her. She would drive all over Staten Island to do the shopping, even though some stores were more than a half hour away.

When Margo became too ill to work, it was the end for her. Over the next few months she deteriorated. Her weight went down from 160 pounds to 106 pounds. Four days before she died, I called her, and she said something was wrong with her blood, and she couldn't stop coughing. She was still optimistic and said, "You know I am going to be 85 years old." That was the last time I spoke to her. She died three weeks before her 85th birthday. At her wake, her family told me she had leukemia and I wondered why no one had told her. She lived at the doctor's and constantly went for tests of all kinds. She had six siblings and one of her brothers had died of leukemia at 50 years old.

I was never invited to Margo's house because she was a hoarder, and so she wanted no visitors. Her family knew that, and nothing was done about it. Her brother asked her to sell the house but she had all her treasures, like her thousands of cookbooks, and her cat. We would get together in my house, or go shopping, or go to the movies. Her family told me that they were going to sell her home to a builder. Most likely he would knock her house down and build two townhouses on her land. I thought, thank God she is not alive to see that. I will miss her! She was a true friend.

Chicken Fingers with Honey Mustard Dip

2 pounds boneless, skinless chicken breasts

Trim fat and remove gristle. Slice the breasts on a diagonal into inch-wide strips. Wash chicken and dry on paper towels.

Ingredients for Coating

½ cup yellow cornmeal

⅓ cup all-purpose flour

½ teaspoon salt

¼ teaspoon paprika

Combine ingredients in a shallow bowl. Working with several pieces of chicken at a time, drop the chicken into the mixture and coat them. Remove the breaded filets to a cooling rack. Let dry in the refrigerator for at least one hour.

Deep fry the chicken in patches in a large frying pan containing about one inch of corn oil. The oil must reach 350 degrees before you start adding the filets or the chicken will be oily. Cook the chicken over medium-high heat until golden brown.

Place the fried chicken onto a clean cooling rack in a single layer, transferring the filets to a serving platter when slightly cooled. The chicken is delicious hot or at room temperature. Serve with honey mustard dip.

Honey Mustard Dip

½ cup good quality Dijon mustard

⅓ cup honey

1 tablespoon balsamic vinegar

Combine ingredients in a small bowl and taste for seasoning, adding more honey if desired. Refrigerate until use.

Terri and Maria in the cafe
in November of 2016.

Terri

HOW WAS IT TO work with my daughter Terri? That is a difficult question to answer. Terri and I are very different, but in many ways, alike.

Terri began working with me at Carol's Cuisine Cooking School from the very beginning, assisting me with the classes in our house. She worked part-time for me through college, and also had a full-time job at Mauro Graphics art gallery, framing artwork.

Terri graduated in 1982 from Parsons School of Design in NYC, with a B.F.A. That summer, Terri got back in touch with her best friend from high school, Jeff Lewis, by sending him a postcard while she was travelling on a train with Maria on their way back from Brighton, England. Both of my daughters came with me to London while I attended Le Cordon Bleu in London. Terri and Jeff started dating soon after we got home from England (much to Joe's chagrin) and they've been together ever since.

Terri and Jeff moved into one of my apartments above the restaurant. We not only worked together, we lived one floor apart later on when I moved into the upstairs apartment. Terri worked as my assistant in the cooking classes, helped with the catering, and was the business manager as well.

Joe and I had separated for good in early 1985, and in November that year, Terri and

Terri was quiet, well organized and a hard worker. As a child, she loved to cook and bake. When she got older, she became a great teacher.

Jeff were married at the historic Alice Austen House, in Staten Island. We prepared the food and desserts at the cafe. I finished the wedding cake at 7:00 in the morning on the day of their wedding! Their wedding cake was a Zuppa Inglese Cake—a hot milk sponge cake with vanilla and chocolate pastry cream, four tiers high. I used fresh fall flowers, and decorated it with Chantilly cream. It was very difficult to be there catering the wedding as the mother of the bride, recently separated wife, and former daughter-in-law. Les and I were now a couple, and he assisted me in the kitchen.

Once we opened the restaurant, we were working many hours together. Terri was in the front of the house, managing all aspects of the business, and I was the back of the house running the kitchen. Terri worked as a waitress, caterer, party planner, and restaurant manager; she taught her own classes, and assisted me in mine. Students liked that we were so different. Terri was quiet, well organized, and a hard worker. As a child, she loved to cook and bake. When she got older, she became a great teacher. I was outrageous, funny, and loved to tell stories about my experiences with my family and my adventures at cooking schools while traveling to France, Italy, and England.

Terri did not want me to do a monologue at the beginning of the classes, and just wanted me to get to the cooking lesson. The classes were more efficient, and ended on time. It was not the same anymore, because my students

Terri teaching a Christmas Cookie Class.

were not the same. When I started teaching at the new location, the classes ran very late into the night. The students developed close friendships with each other and wanted to cook, eat, and socialize. Over the years things changed. The students wanted to come to the classes to learn, but not to hang out. Most of my students had to get up early and go to work the next morning, so we tried our best to be done by 11:00 PM.

While in the past the classes were always full, now many classes were cancelled when they didn't reach a minimum of 10 students. There were many reasons for this. First there was the Food Network and other cooking channels. Second, there was more competition on Staten Island. Many restaurants started giving demonstration classes although I didn't consider them to be of the same caliber of what Terri and I offered. My classes were hands-on, which meant that you helped prepare, and cook or bake the recipes, unlike every other "cooking lesson" offered on Staten Island.

The most important change that affected my cooking lessons was the Internet. Once the Internet really took hold, you were able to access any information needed about recipes, cooking, and baking techniques with just the click of a mouse. What people failed to realize is that having a recipe is not enough, it's only a guideline, like all of the demonstration classes the local restaurants offered. What we taught in our

Terri and I both miss teaching very much, and especially miss the relationships we developed with our students.

classes was so much more than that. We gave the students the opportunity to make and taste the food that we all made together in class. Terri and I both miss teaching very much, and especially miss the relationships we developed with our students, some of whom became our close friends.

As interest in the cooking lessons began to decline, I tried to keep the cafe as new and interesting as I possibly could, by adding new food items to the cafe's menu, and hosting special dinners. It was difficult to be different. If I just served Italian food, it would have been easier and more profitable for me. That was not what I wanted to do. Having a reputation of being an eclectic restaurant does not help your business when you're located on Staten Island.

The way I structured my restaurant's menu was the same way that I taught my classes—by offering new and exciting dishes from all over the world. People found the eclectic menu confusing. It was also confusing that the restaurant was not open full-time. A full-time restaurant is open six to seven days a week, for lunch, dinner, and sometimes breakfast. The cafe was only open from Wednesday through Saturday, with Monday and Tuesday nights reserved for my cooking lessons.

Originally when I purchased the building, we designed it to be a gourmet shop with great take-out food, and cooking equipment in the front room. My cooking school was to be located in the back room, which we converted into a huge kitchen. The kitchen had an enormous 12-foot mirror

The front of the restaurant showing the large tree blocking my neon sign.

hanging over my workstation and demo cooktop, so that all the students could see what was being prepped and cooked on the stove below. It took six men a few hours to hang that mirror. I went from teaching six classes a week when I was in my basement, to only two classes a week when I opened the cooking school/gourmet shop.

My gourmet cookware shop did very well for a couple of years, but then Macy's decided they would open up their own gourmet cookware section, and combined with the stock market crash in the late '80s, my cookware shop ground to a halt. That's when I decided that I had to do something new, and exciting, with that huge front room. Terri came up with the idea of opening a cafe, just serving coffee and desserts, but I thought we would do better as an upscale restaurant. I had no idea what running a restaurant would do to my life.

The building that I purchased was not a good location for a restaurant at all. The street in front of the building curved up a hill, making the building difficult to see. The tree that the city planted in front of my building became a big problem, growing to 30 feet high, which was just tall enough to cover my beautiful neon sign. I did not have a great deal of money to spend on advertising, so I could not compete with the Mafia restaurants that came and went in the neighborhood. What I had was my reputation, but that did not make up for the lack of advertising.

We had only three parking spots in front of my building, along with a few additional parking spots on the street, so that only added to our problems. Almost every restaurant has a parking lot for their customers, so not having one was a huge detriment to our business.

We maintained our reputation as one of the best restaurants on Staten Island, in spite of the traffic problems, which had become unbearable, only adding to our lack of parking, which was mentioned in every review. Another problem was that the cafe was always listed as being expensive. The cost of food just kept going up but I would not change the quality of our food. I did try dishes on the menu that were affordable. My Stuffed Burger, Spaghetti and Meatballs, and Spaghetti with Shoulder Lamb Chops, were all

Jeff and Terri tasting the Zuppa Inglese cake that I made for their wedding.

popular entrées on my menu that were moderately priced. No more foie gras and amazing wild game dishes. We offered buffalo and quail, which were doable, but still somewhat pricey.

My son-in-law, Jeff Lewis, tried to help me out by designing and publishing my website for free, from beginning to end, since I couldn't afford to pay anyone to do this for me. Of course, I started speaking to my ex-husband at this time, and he suggested that I needed a new professional website. Joe said that Maria would design and maintain a new website for me for $5,000. My daughter Maria was one of the leaders in the website design industry at the time, even having written one of the first books about web design. Jeff told Joe to go ahead and ask Maria what she'd charge. Maria told Joe she couldn't design a site for me for less than $25,000 because it would be done

We had many laughs over the perverted pictures he would send me that he threatened to put online.

through her company. So the website stayed as it was.

Jeff also helped me produce and mail the Carol's Cuisine Cooking School brochures after I finished writing them, and the brochures were later turned into my website. When designing the website, he was able to add pictures to the class descriptions, which enhanced their appeal. We had many laughs over the perverted pictures he would send me that he threatened to put online for the class descriptions. The website had to be updated constantly, with my seasonal and holiday menu changes, and my new class brochures, which I offered at least twice a year.

No one realized the amount of work that went into creating, writing, and producing the class brochures. I would work through the night researching recipes, and typing up the class descriptions after working all day. Each brochure had to be new and exciting. I had to create new classes to keep the old students, my "regulars," happy, and still offer a few of my classic classes to appeal to the newer students who didn't have the chance to take those classes yet. Lessons entitled "Thanksgiving Turkey," "Christmas Eve Seafood Feast," and "Techniques & Theory of Cooking," were part of my greatest hits, and were always included in my brochure. In the end, the work was well worth the effort. This was a formula for success for many years, until the introduction of free online cooking lessons, and TV's Food Network changed everything.

In April 2016, I had a terrible accident in my home. I did not know that I had hypertension and suffered a recurrence of vertigo. When I bent down at the top of the stairs to get a part for a computer repairman, I blacked out and fell down 10 steps to a cement floor in the basement. I fell on my face and fractured my wrist and cracked the C4 vertebrae in my back. My knees and my face became very swollen and black and blue. I had to wear a cast on my left wrist for more than six weeks. I was in severe pain for months and was only able to return to work at the end of September. Even then, it was very difficult for me to stand for long periods of time because of my back pain.

After my injury, Terri had to take my place as head chef while I recuperated.

After my injury, Terri had to take my place as head chef while I recuperated. She called Sal and asked him to come back to work with her. We could not have kept the restaurant open without his help. The two of them were very successful in running everything and they made a good team.

What my fall did for Terri (because she had to take over completely for five months) was show her what a talented chef she really is. But when I came back the September before we closed, I no longer felt needed. I was discouraged and started to lose interest in the business because I wasn't in charge anymore. I just came in to cook or teach. I felt my personal touch was gone. Many of my dishes were being done differently. Several nights, I got off the line because I did not feel wanted or welcome. In order to expedite the preparation of my famous mussels, Terri came up with the idea of starting the sauce in advance. The onions, shallots, and garlic were slowly sautéed for at least 15 minutes and then refrigerated in individual portions. Then when the mussels were ordered, she would continue the recipe from that point on. It was a good idea and it worked. Customers were happy and they did not have to wait as long, but in my mind they weren't as delicious.

When I first opened Carol's Cafe, it was one of a handful of fine-dining restaurants on Staten Island. As time went by, more and more places opened up that offered diners so many options and this affected our business. Two doors over, a fine-dining Italian restaurant opened. They had a few partners and more money than I had. They had a bigger place, better air conditioning, a DJ, a good chef, and a big staff in the kitchen. They had a different crowd—a bar crowd—and that made money. People went there to meet people. They also could afford to advertise and they had a beautiful color ad in the *Staten Island Advance*.

Two blocks down from us another Italian restaurant opened up, and they had a good reputation, with a good chef/owner. He was doing fine-dining in one area, pizza in another, and take-out food in another area. A mile away was a very good Japanese restaurant called Fushimi. The Mafia restaurants went in and out of business.

Many of our customers for off-premises catering and cooking lessons left Staten Island and moved to New Jersey. Todt Hill was now occupied with Indian doctors and their families, alongside Polish business people, and Russian families. Our wealthy Italian families moved out to Annadale and Tottenville (which is at the end of Staten Island, about a 30–40-minute drive), where they built beautiful estates to live in. Todt Hill, the area known for being exclusive, was going down financially, and there were many empty stores for rent now on Richmond Road.

> **The outrageous fines from the Board of Health were simply ridiculous.... They would fine you if your spoons were stored in the wrong direction.**

The summers were very difficult because a lot of my customers had summer homes and traveled all over the world. We were always in trouble financially, and at the end of each summer my daughter Maria had to help by loaning us money to survive. We had trouble paying our utility bills, but our electric bills during July, August, and September were especially debilitating. Our monthly operating costs, including payroll and insurance along with the expenses from our food and liquor vendors, were excessive. The cost of maintaining all our old equipment, particularly our walk-in refrigerator and freezer, and the rising costs of doing business continued to hurt us.

Another hidden cost—which no one outside of the food industry knows about—is the New York City Department of Health. The outrageous fines from the Board of Health (they never left an inspection without making money!) were simply ridiculous. I always had to run around when the health department came for inspection, and put my chef hat on. Sometimes I didn't run fast enough, and was fined dearly for it. It's as if they were your business partner. They would fine you if your spoons were stored in the wrong direction, or if you didn't have a label on something that you had just cooked, and for any other nonsense they felt like making up on the spot, in order to make money for the city of New York.

We could no longer afford to have entertainment and the pub was not doing well anymore. More often than not, it remained empty. When we had a heavy rain, the pub had water leaking from the tin ceiling. We had to take down our beautiful wallpaper, and repaint the entire wall many times. The reason for this was that the building was very old and the roof over the pub was flat, so it leaked constantly.

I decided that I was going to rent out the space that I used as my pub. After being packed with customers for years, once NYC passed the "No Smoking" law in restaurants, business in the pub died down dramatically.

I called the realty firm that was owned by Connie Profaci, the wife of John Profaci, who owned the Colavita Olive Oil company.

When a real estate agent showed up, I was very upset. My dog Truffle, a Shih Tzu, only 2½ years old, had died that day. I knew when he was eight months old that he was sick.

My dog Truffle, a Shih Tzu, only 2½ years old, had died that day. I loved him and I was crying. I was not thinking clearly at that moment.

I took him to be fixed and they told me he had a liver and blood problem, and would not live a full life. I loved him and I was crying. I was not thinking clearly at that moment.

She said, "Why don't you put the building up for sale? It will take a long time to sell." I was shocked when the building was sold in a few months time for the price that I was asking. The new owner of the building charged me $2000 a month rent for the cafe, which I personally paid because the business could not afford to. When the 18-month lease was up, the landlord planned to raise the rent to $5000 a month. This was the last straw, so I had no choice. I decided to close my business and retire.

At the very end, we had probably borrowed $50,000 dollars from Maria, which will be paid back to her when I leave this earth. I know I put all that money back into the business, to keep my family employed, and because I loved my restaurant and cooking school. My daughter Terri, my grand-daughter Amanda, and my grandson Keith all worked for me at the end. My office manager, waitress, and bartender, Carol Ann, worked for me for over 20 years. She was very upset when I closed the restaurant. I feel very bad about this, but it was time. I could no longer afford to keep it open.

What finally brought the people back to the cafe was the announcement in the *Advance* that we were closing our doors, and that I was going to retire.

Terri and my grandchildren, Amanda and Keith, in the early days of the cafe.

Customers who I hadn't seen in years were clamoring for reservations. Our main dining room could only seat around 45 people at a time so it was impossible to accommodate everyone in those last few months. The restaurant became jam-packed again, like the old days, and the cooking classes were filled to capacity, with waiting lists. Terri and I couldn't help thinking, where were all of these customers before we got to this point? I'm sure all the people that are forced to close their businesses ask that question.

I think Terri now knows what a talented chef she is, and that she could get a job anywhere.

I think Terri now knows what a talented chef she is, and that she could get a job anywhere. Even though she was successful at running the cafe in my absence, she doesn't want the responsibility or the tremendous stress it takes to be a working chef. She said, "All I want to do is cook at home for my family." Currently she is working in a couple of restaurants as a waitress, and tells me the stories of mismanagement that she experiences. She does miss teaching very much, as do I. I also miss every moment that I am no longer cooking for my customers and my interaction with them in the cafe.

My last dinner service was on New Year's Eve on December 31, 2016. It was one of the most depressing nights I ever spent in the restaurant. I tried to put on a brave face for my patrons who were there to celebrate the holiday

but I couldn't believe it was going to be the last time I would ever cook in the cafe. I don't know how I made it through the evening.

I only returned to the restaurant once or twice during the month of January because it was too upsetting for me. Terri, Amanda, and Keith worked together to do the massive cleanup. It took Terri weeks to reduce my huge recipe collection. Sal came to help as well and also moved a few filing cabinets to my home so I could continue to store my favorite recipes. We had a "Going Out Of Business Sale" and many of our students and restaurant customers came and purchased some of the equipment that we used during our many years in business. Whatever was left after the sale, we donated.

We finally vacated the building at 1571 Richmond Road on January 31, 2017. Carol's Cuisine Cooking School and Carol's Cafe Restaurant touched so many lives, in so many different ways. I am still getting letters saying they "cannot find a restaurant like Carol's Cafe," and "There will never be a restaurant like Carol's Cafe again on Staten Island." A person even referred to me as "the Julia Child of Staten Island."

Left: I was honored to be one of the "Women Of Distinction" at the New York State Women's annual event.

Right: Terri and me at the New York State Women's Luncheon.

Zuppa Inglese Cake

Prepare pans: Spray or grease a 12×2 inch round cake pan or two 9×2 round cake pans. Line bottom with parchment paper, and spray or grease again. Parchment paper should not go to the edge of pan.

Preheat oven to 350 degrees. Bake on center rack.

Hot Milk Sponge Cake

2 cups sifted cake flour	2 cups sifted sugar
2 teaspoons baking powder	12 large egg yolks (room temperature)
½ cup unsalted butter, melted	
½ teaspoon pure vanilla extract	1 cup milk, scalded

Sift together flour and baking powder. Add melted butter and vanilla to scalded milk and keep hot. Beat egg yolks until thick and lemon-colored; gradually beat in sugar.

Quickly add flour mixture and stir just until mixed. Gently stir in the hot milk mixture.

Place batter into prepared pans. Test 12-inch cake, after 40 to 50 minutes, with a toothpick that should come out clean, or until done. For 9-inch pans, test for doneness after 30 minutes.

Cool thoroughly on a cake rack. When completely cool, run a spatula around the edge of the pan and turn over onto a rack to finish cooling. Wrap cake in plastic wrap or foil and place in the freezer to partially freeze. It makes it easier to cut into three thin layers.

Vanilla Pastry Cream

6 tablespoons of flour, carefully measured	1⅛ cup sugar
1½ cups cream	12 large egg yolks, room temperature
1½ cups whole milk	Vanilla bean, split and scraped or 3 teaspoons pure vanilla extract, or to taste
⅛ teaspoon salt	

Combine cream and milk. Combine flour with ¾ cup of the cream and milk mixture, and whisk in. Gradually add the remaining cream and milk combination.

continued

Zuppa Inglese Cake, *continued*

Place in a heavy saucepan. Stir in salt and sugar. Add scraped vanilla bean if using. Cook over low-medium heat, stirring until mixture becomes as thick as a medium white sauce. Stir a little of the hot sauce into egg yolks to temper. Then pour egg yolk mixture into saucepan, stirring briskly. Return pan to low heat for several minutes to thicken; it should start to bubble.

Stir constantly, being careful not to let the sauce boil. Remove from heat, add vanilla (if not using a vanilla bean).

Have ready a bowl of ice. Place a clean bowl into ice with a strainer on top. Pour mixture into strainer and push through strainer. Leave bowl in ice to cool as quickly as possible. Cover with plastic wrap pressed into pastry cream, so skin does not form.

To make vanilla and chocolate pastry cream for Zuppa Inglese Cake, divide finished vanilla pastry cream in half. In one half, add nine tablespoons of dark, unsweetened sifted cocoa—or you can use three to four ounces, melted bittersweet or semi-sweet dark chocolate to the other half of finished pastry cream.

Strain into chilled bowl and press plastic wrap into top of pastry cream, so skin does not form. Refrigerate until completely cold and set.

Rum Syrup

¾ cup water	A strip of orange zest
1 cup sugar	½ cup light rum

In a small saucepan combine the water, sugar, and zest. Stir constantly over moderate heat until the sugar dissolves and the mixture is clear. Once it starts to boil, lower to a simmer and set a five-minute timer. Remove from the heat and add the rum.

Cool and refrigerate until ready to use.

Chantilly Whipped Cream

For a 12-inch cake you will need: 4 cups heavy cream, 12 tablespoons sifted confectioners' sugar, 12 teaspoons pure vanilla extract or to taste, ½ teaspoon almond extract (optional). Combine well, taste for seasoning and adjust. Chill overnight, at least in refrigerator in the bowl you will whip it in.

To make Chocolate Triangles

Melt a pound of semi-sweet dark chocolate over hot water in a double boiler.

Line two or three large cookie sheets with parchment paper. Pour melted chocolate on cookie sheets, and spread with an offset spatula, as thinly as possible. Refrigerate or freeze until set.

Toasted Sliced Almonds

Place almonds on a cookie sheet in a preheated 350-degree oven. Stir occasionally, cook just until golden brown, about 10 minutes. Set aside to cool.

Unsalted green pistachio nuts, toasted and cooled, are also suggested. Sugared roasted almonds are also wonderful.

Assembling and Decorating the Zuppa Inglese Cake

Take partially frozen cake out of freezer and very carefully, with serrated knife, cut into three layers. Examine layers and use the most symmetrical for top. Remove excess crumbs, and, if needed, skin from top layer.

Place bottom layer in center of a flat serving dish with at least a two-inch border. Brush generously with rum syrup. Spread with stirred Vanilla Pastry Cream, leaving an inch border.

Place second layer evenly on top of bottom layer, and brush generously with rum syrup. Spread with stirred chocolate pastry cream. It is a good idea to take the chocolate pastry cream out of the refrigerator an hour before placing on the cake layer. It may be too thick if you use it straight out of the refrigerator.

Place top layer on as evenly as possible, brush with rum syrup. Cover and refrigerate overnight if possible. The cake should age, so the rum syrup seasons the cake.

Decorate the cake with Chantilly Cream, Chocolate Triangles, and Long-Stemmed Red Cherries, rinsed and dried well on paper towels. The sides of the cake are decorated with the toasted almonds or green pistachio nuts.

Cover the cake with Chantilly Cream. Decorate with stars and rosettes, if you like. Place a red cherry on each rosette.

Quickly break the chocolate into large pieces and place on the center of the cake. Quickly place the leftover chocolate back in the freezer in a plastic bag. Place nuts of your choice on the sides of the cake.

Refrigerate until served.

2016 Big Hungry Awards

I READ THIS ENTRY by Big Hungry Shelby who was one of my customers:

"Light as air"
Chocolate Soufflé.

"I do have one list for you every year, and it's my own little awards show in a post: The Big Hungry Awards. Annually, I pick the best of what I ate and where I ate it in New York State the previous 12 months...

My next winner is, sadly, a restaurant that is about to say good-bye. It's a favorite of my family's, so I'm bummed to see Carol's Cafe go. But Carol, the chef at the helm of this Staten Island institution, is retiring, and more power to her! I will miss her quaint cafe stuck in the middle of that bustling island, and I will miss her absolutely singular caramel shrimp appetizer, which has won my Best Appy accolade in the past. So this year, Carol's gets my award for Best Dessert for her gorgeous, light as air chocolate soufflé. Like Carol's Cafe itself, this dish is a masterpiece—a rare treat to find on a menu anymore, and something most chefs just aren't willing to bother with. Now that Carol is retiring, we will have one less spectacular soufflé in this world, and we will be the poorer for it.

I'm a sentimental sort of fool. I know this about myself. I'm sad to see Chef Carol retire and close up her Dongan Hills landmark in Staten Island. And so, in celebration of her decades of excellence, I am awarding Carol's Cafe Best Restaurant of 2016. We took new friends there over the summer, before learning it was closing, and I'm so glad we got a last visit in. If you read this and live downstate, there is still time—she's open until December 31st, so run, don't walk, to get your chocolate soufflé, liver and onions, and caramel shrimp. Thank you, Carol, for feeding us so well all these years, and enjoy your retirement!"

—Shelby Cohen
Big Hungry Shelby

Garlic Herb Pizza Dough

Makes 8 (7-inch) rounds

2 tablespoons extra virgin olive oil

1 tablespoon minced garlic

1 teaspoon finely minced fresh herbs
(thyme, rosemary, oregano, basil,
sage, or tarragon)
Use what you prefer.

¼ cup warm water

1 package dry yeast

1 teaspoon sugar

3 cups Hecker's flour

¼ cup cornmeal

2 teaspoons salt

1 cup cool water

Heat two tablespoons oil in a small skillet; add next three ingredients and cook over low heat until garlic softens, about five minutes. Do not let the garlic brown. It should be golden in color. Set aside to cool.

Sprinkle yeast and sugar over ¼ cup warm water (105–110 degrees) and let stand until yeast starts to foam, about five minutes. Mix flour, cornmeal, and salt in a food processor. Add one cup cool water and herb oil to yeast mixture. With the processor running, gradually pour the liquid ingredients into the dry and combine until a rough ball forms.

If the dough is too sticky or dry, you can adjust by adding flour or water, one tablespoon at a time. Let dough rest for five minutes, then continue to process until dough is smooth, about 35 seconds.

Knead dough by hand for a few seconds to form a smooth round ball. Place in a lightly oiled bowl covered with plastic wrap and let rise until dough doubles in size, about two hours.

Punch dough down and divide into eight equal pieces. Roll each portion into a smooth, round ball. Place the balls on a parchment-lined, lightly floured cookie sheet. Cover with a clean dish towel, and let rest until they puff slightly, about 30 minutes.

When you are ready to fry your pizzas, roll each ball of dough into a seven-inch round, flouring work surface and dough as necessary. Place rounds on a floured surface and cover again with a dish towel until you are ready.

NOTE:

- When I made the dough for the restaurant, I would make four times the amount of the recipe. Instead of a food processor, I would prepare it in a large KitchenAid mixer. After the dough had risen, I would weigh out 3½ ounce balls and individually wrap them in plastic wrap. At that point they were put in Ziploc® bags and frozen for later use. When I needed to use the dough, I would defrost it in the refrigerator.

Pizza Fritta

Carol's Fried Pizza with marinated fresh tomatoes, basil, and fresh mozzarella

3½ ounces of Garlic Herb Pizza Dough (page 344)

2 ripe fresh plum tomatoes

½ cup fresh mozzarella, chopped small

2 tablespoons freshly grated Parmesan cheese

½ teaspoon dry oregano

1 heaping teaspoon minced shallot

1 level teaspoon minced garlic

A few fresh basil leaves, cut into a chiffonade

1 tablespoon chopped flat-leaf parsley

Extra virgin olive oil and balsamic vinegar to dress tomatoes

Salt, pepper, and sugar to taste

Bring a six-quart pot to a boil. Fill a bowl with ice and water. Blanch the plum tomatoes for 20 seconds in the boiling water. Remove them with a slotted spoon and shock in the ice water.

Immediately peel the skin from the tomatoes. Cut them in half, crosswise, and squeeze to remove the seeds. Dice them into ½-inch pieces and place in a small bowl. Dress the tomatoes with the olive oil and balsamic vinegar to coat. Add shallots, garlic, dry oregano, and fresh herbs . Season with salt, pepper, and sugar to taste.

To fry pizza, use a 10-inch frying pan, preferably cast iron. Heat about ¼ inch of olive oil with a basil leaf until it begins to sizzle. Then place the rolled-out disc of dough (see previous recipe) into the hot oil. Fry until golden and lightly brown on one side, then turn over to cook the other side.

Place your fried pizza shell on a small cooling rack over a cookie sheet.

Using a spoon, place your marinated tomatoes on top. Do not add too much liquid or the pizza will be soggy. Carefully place the chopped mozzarella and grated Parmesan over the tomatoes.

Preheat your oven to broil. Lower your oven rack so that the pizza is not too close to the flame. Place your pizza in the rack under the broiler. Watch carefully and bake until the cheese melts.

Garnish the pizza fritta with additional fresh basil on top and serve immediately.

Note: This recipe is for one pizza only. You may multiply the recipe to suit your needs. However, you must only fry one pizza shell at a time or the shells will be oily.

Carol's Cafe Caramel Shrimp

The shrimp recipe that caused a phenomenon was called "Carol's Cafe Caramel Shrimp with lots of Garlic and Ginger." I never taught it or shared the recipe with my customers. It was technical, and I wanted to keep it for the restaurant. Many customers asked me for the recipe and asked me to teach it. It was so easy to make a mistake or burn your caramel or overcook the shrimp. I brined the shrimp in ancho chile powder (not hot, available at Penzeys or Amazon), sugar, and water. I was lucky if it was in the brine for five minutes. It should have been in the brine about 15 minutes. I used this spice for many dishes and it was kept on the line in the restaurant. If a customer wanted it spicy, I would add serrano chile, minced to taste.

Serves 2

¼ cup kosher salt

3½ tablespoons sugar

3 tablespoons mild or medium ancho chile powder

1 quart warm water

¾ pounds large shrimp, deveined, remove shell, but leave the tail on

20 cloves garlic, smashed to flatten

4-inch piece fresh peeled ginger, sliced thinly into quarter-sized rounds or more to taste

Sugar to taste! *I like to put 4 heaping teaspoons of sugar per side on each shrimp.*

Kosher salt as needed. *(Do not use iodized salt.)*

4 tablespoons or whatever is needed of extra virgin olive oil

Freshly ground black pepper to taste

2 teaspoons unsalted butter

Mirin (about ¼ cup)

⅛ cup light soy sauce

Chili oil to taste

Sesame oil to taste

½ cup scallions cut thinly into a 2-inch julienne

Chives to garnish

In a medium stainless or glass bowl, blend the salt, sugar, and ancho chile powder in the warm water. Drop in the prepared shrimp and let stand 15–25 minutes while you set up the rest of the meal. Drain the shrimp, and pat dry. Sprinkle all the sugar on the shrimp and season with salt and pepper.

Heat the oil in a 10-inch straight-sided sauté pan over medium-heat. I prefer cast-iron pans.

Stir in the garlic and ginger and lower the heat to low. Add a sprinkle of salt and sugar. Cook about 10 minutes or until golden brown.

Add the butter to the pan and add the shrimp with all the sugar and stir for another one to two minutes. The shrimp must be completely melted and caramelized and barely firm. The sugar should be a golden-brown caramel.

Add the mirin and cook about a minute or two. Add the soy sauce, chili oil, and sesame oil. Add the scallions.

Turn the shrimp into a serving dish. Sprinkle with chopped chives. Taste them very carefully for seasoning; do not burn your tongue.

Serve immediately! Do not let it sit! Garnish with scallion flowers.

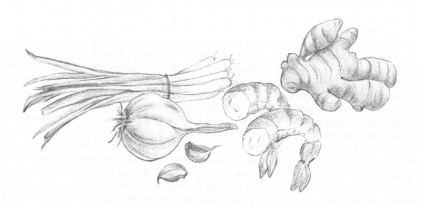

Chocolate Soufflé

⅓ cup, plus 1 tablespoon granulated sugar

Sugar to coat the soufflé ramekins

7 ounces of good quality semi-sweet chocolate, finely chopped

6 large egg yolks

11 large egg whites *(Must be room temperature)*

½ cup heavy cream

2 tablespoons flour

1½ teaspoons pure vanilla extract, or to taste

2 tablespoons unsalted butter

¼ cup confectioners' sugar

¼ teaspoon cream of tartar

Butter well two one-pint soufflé ramekins or four eight-ounce dishes, and sprinkle the inside surfaces with granulated sugar.

In a small pot, bring the heavy cream and the granulated sugar to a boil. As soon as the mixture boils, turn off burner and remove the pot from the heat. Add chopped chocolate and butter to the hot cream, whisking until the butter and chocolate are completely melted.

Using an electric mixer, beat the yolks with the flour and vanilla extract until light and pale yellow. Add a few tablespoons of the still-warm chocolate mixture to the egg yolks in order to temper the mixture. Making sure the mixture is not too hot, add the yolk mixture to the chocolate, and mix well to incorporate. This mixture can be prepared several hours ahead, but should be used at room temperature. If you refrigerate it, take it out of the refrigerator an hour before, to bring it back to room temperature.

Preheat oven to 400 degrees. Add the cream of tartar to the egg whites and whisk at high speed until stiff peaks form, then gently fold ¼ of the whites into the chocolate mixture. Carefully fold the rest of the egg whites into the chocolate mixture. **Do not overfold.** It is okay to leave small bits of egg whites in the folded mixture. Pour the mixture into the prepared soufflé ramekins.

For two one-pint dishes: Bake in the preheated oven for about 20 minutes. Then, raise the temperature to 475 degrees and, through a strainer, sprinkle the tops of the soufflés with half of the confectioners' sugar. Return the soufflés to the oven for an additional three minutes or until caramelized. Serve immediately. May be served with sweetened whipped cream on the side.

For four eight-ounce ramekins: Bake in a preheated oven for about 11 minutes. Then, raise the temperature to 450 degrees and, through a strainer, sprinkle the tops of the soufflés with half of the confectioners' sugar. Return the soufflés to the oven for an additional two minutes or until caramelized. Serve immediately. May be served with sweetened whipped cream on the side.

So Long, Farewell, Auf Wiedersehen, ...Goodbye!

WHENEVER I RUN INTO former customers, they tell me how much they miss our restaurant, and that they can't find a place to eat on Staten Island that is as good as our cafe was. Our cooking school students write me and ask if I would teach classes in my home. I wish I could continue to teach, but it's too much for me physically after my fall. I found out that I suffer from hypertension only after I got hurt, and I now take medication for it.

It's hard for me to express how I feel about my business ending because it was my whole life for over 44 years. I thought my daughter Terri said it best when she posted about it on Facebook:

January 31, 2017

Today marks the real end of Carol's Cafe for me. Although we officially closed our doors on New Year's Eve, the past month was spent cleaning, donating and discarding. You can only imagine how much can be accumulated after so many years.

I should be sad, but I'm happy, because so much of what was Carol's Cafe and Cuisine, has now found a home all around Staten Island, and beyond. Food donated to City Harvest, cookware and bakeware to the Port Richmond High School Culinary Program, and the N.Y.C. Fire Department, and the historical photos of Staten Island that hung on our walls, are now in the homes of our restaurant customers and cooking school students. As of today, the giant plants from the Cafe will continue to thrive at the Clove Lakes Nursing Home.

We also have the legacy of so many people that have learned how to cook and bake. There's nothing more important than teaching, and instilling confidence in someone. We know that every Christmas, students will be baking cookies that they were taught at Carol's Cuisine Cooking School, and then their children will bake them with their children when they grow up.

It was always my profound hope that Carol's Cafe would finish like the Mary Tyler Moore show; on a high note. I feel confident that we accomplished that. It is not lost on me that Mary Tyler Moore's passing coincided with the closing of our business.

I have always believed in fate.

"It's a long way to Tipperary"

—Terri

I WROTE THIS to my daughter: "I am overwhelmed by your talent and love for Carol's Cafe and Carol's Cuisine Cooking School. What I loved the most is teaching with you for 44 years. We were quite a team. I will miss that the most! I love you so much!"

The response from my customers and students was both heartwarming, and overwhelming to me. I decided to include a few of the messages that I received about our closing:

VINCENT BUZZETTA is a pastry chef that began studying with me when he was nine years old.

He wrote, "So beautifully said! The restaurant will be missed so much, but all the memories and recipes will be cherished for a lifetime! I am who I am today because of the foundation you and your Mom gave me, and I'm sure so many others feel the same way! I'm so honored I got to take a part of Carol's Cafe to my kitchen, I'll always cherish it and think of you both!"

Vinny has my 20-quart KitchenAid mixer, that I did most of my baking with for the restaurant, cooking school, and catering.

ANNE DITIZIO, a customer whose father-in-law was "Vinny D," a renowned jazz guitarist who played the guitar on Saturday evenings at Carol's Cafe, said, "Carol's WAS fine dining and a renowned cooking school on Staten Island for decades. God bless you and your family for your amazing contribution to Staten Island. God bless you in a future that promises to continue your legacy of success."

KEISUKE HARADA is a wonderful chef who said, "Last time when I was there it was Maria's wedding party."

JOHN FRANCIS MEROLA said, "I fondly remember my parents celebrating their 50th wedding anniversary at Carol's Cafe."

NOREEN VITOLO said, "I loved Carol's Cafe, you were all my second family. I love to bake! We always laughed as we learned! Carol was my mentor and is a dear friend to this day!"

Letters From My Customers

NOTHING MADE ME HAPPIER than the letters my customers took the time to write about our catered parties and cooking lessons. I chose a few letters that made my heart happy:

Chocolate Cloud Cake with chocolate whipped cream, raspberry preserves, candied almonds, and chocolate triangles. This was the most often requested cake for private parties.

Dear Carol,

I want to express our appreciation for the wonderful job you and your staff did in catering our affair last Saturday. The food was excellent and so beautifully prepared. So was the service.

How can anyone in a kitchen that small be so quiet and get the job done?

The next few days we received calls from most of the guests raving about the food and asking what herbs or cheese I thought you used.

Dear Carol,

No reason you should remember me. I'm Joe—Dr. Lou's brother. We both are aware that the delicious menus didn't suddenly materialize out of space. Much hard work and love lies behind this. What we both know Carol (and not enough others do), is the number of hours you spend in your kitchen between midnight and dawn, thinking of ways of preparing your meals even better—as though that is at all possible.

Congratulations Carol!

You and your restaurant deserve all the pleasant words written in your praise, and more.

Well done Carol!

I've sung your praises before, and will continue to do so in the future. It's an honor for me to say, "I know Carol."

Dear Carol and Terri—

With sincere thanks for making the Oneg Shabbat celebrating our son's Bar Mitzvah so special. The desserts you prepared were scrumptious, matched only by the presentation and service. We've received many calls from guests, all lauding the desserts, with everyone stating their particular favorites. Our own favorite was the Chocolate Cloud Cake (which I didn't get to eat until the next day—hungry for leftovers!) Again, thank you both for your part in making this cerebration so special for us.

Dear Carol, Les, Terri and Staff—

Words on paper cannot express the feelings we had during the celebration of our 40th wedding anniversary. It was a fabulous party, the menu, food, music, flowers (real) ambiance, the planning was excellent. We have received nothing but great reviews from everyone; they are still calling. We were surprised, not only because it's so great that you and Les were able to be a major part of our special day. Now all our family and friends know why we always say that "Carol's the best." Thank you for taking the time to create a very special cake for our very special day. It not only was delicious but very beautiful as well... It was the exclamation point to a great party!!!

We love you,

—Louise and Teddy

I received this note from Doctor Gianvito and it meant a lot to me:

"The Miracle At Carol's"

When my wife died, it was unbearable. I not only missed her tremendously but I also lost my personal cook. I didn't even know how to turn the stove on! Then I was introduced to Carol's Cuisine and her cooking classes. As a result Carol taught me how to prepare adequate meals for my table without too much stress.

If my wife could only see me now, she would never believe it.

Thank you Chef Carol!

—Lou Gianvito

I thought Terri should have the last word in this story of my life. She was there at the beginning of Carol's Cuisine, which she named as a young teenager, and literally locked the door of the building that housed my cooking school and restaurant, since 1983, for the last time.

We're all familiar with the expression, "Recipe for success." Sometimes in your life you're handed a box of ingredients that just don't seem to go together—yes, this is a "Chopped" reference. It's how you take something that is difficult and seemingly impossible, and turn it into something great that shows what you're made of.

This is an analogy for my mother's life. As a child and young woman growing up in Brooklyn, she had little encouragement or emotional support from her family, and later, my father. Despite having to face these obstacles she prevailed by sheer determination, strength of will, hard work, and talent.

I have fond memories as a child at P.S. 48 when the school would have a bake sale. They asked all of the mothers to prepare a cake or dessert and donate it to raise money. I remember that my mother's contribution was always the best, and her cakes looked as delicious as they tasted. It was a precursor of what was to come.

As far back as I can remember, I loved to eat my mother's food. I can still almost taste the individual fruit tarts she would make every Thanksgiving. They looked like little jewels, strawberry or blueberry, with vanilla pastry cream and a shiny glaze on top.

Now that I am older, and I'm the one preparing the holiday meals for my family, I understand the tremendous amount of work it takes to plan and execute a Thanksgiving or Christmas dinner. I don't know how my mother did it. Every year, she catered for all her clients, and then made a delicious dinner for us. She taught me how to carry on that tradition, and I feel that I make her proud with my attempts at coming close to what she achieved.

The business may have ended, but my mother's passion for cooking and baking still burns brightly. They always say to do what you love. My mother did what she loved for over four decades and had a very successful career. I am very proud of what she has accomplished, and I know that I will carry on cooking with all the knowledge that she has instilled in me, and the thousands of students whom she has inspired for over 44 years.

PHOTO BY PETER DAMIANI

INDEX OF RECIPES

For more recipes visit: chefcarolsrecipes.com

ACKNOWLEDGMENTS

I WANT TO THANK everyone who helped me along the way with *Kitchen Bitch*.

In the early stages of the book, my first editors were Elise Macintosh and Christopher Ireland.

The original design was done by Anagraph.

My friend and professional photographer, Bill Higgins, helped me prepare many of the photos for the book.

Thanks to Julie Connery and my granddaughter Amanda Lewis for top editing and Sue Moore Stevenson for her delightful illustrations.

I appreciate the tireless work done by David Van Ness and his patience with the constant changes to make the book the best it could be.

I want to give special thanks to my family.

My son-in-law Jeff Lewis got this project back on track with his intelligence and great organizational and technical skills.

My daughter Terri edited both the content and the recipes, and was the only one I trusted to interpret my vision. Without her commitment and determination, my memoir would never have been realized.

My daughter Maria, who has always supported me in my career and business, dedicated herself to getting the book done, and without her I could not have succeeded. She has always believed in me and that is not something that I am familiar with in my life. I love her and am very proud of all her accomplishments.

Without the support of my family, Carol's Cuisine and Cafe would not have been so successful.

Terri was with me from the beginning. When I got hurt, she had to take over the reins and become the executive chef in my absence until I was well enough to return.

My son Joe was a talented chef and offered advice about the restaurant business over the years even when he was no longer working for me. I love him and his wife Theresa, who has the patience of a saint.

Jeff was my office manager for several years and designed and maintained my website. In addition to helping with the business, he often did needed renovations and repairs on my building which housed the restaurant.

My eldest grandchildren grew up in the cafe. Amanda and Keith came to work with Terri and Jeff from the time they were babies until they were old enough to attend preschool. When Amanda was a young woman, she worked in the kitchen preparing divine soufflés and plating our desserts. Keith started as a busboy (which he hated!) and later became a dishwasher. Both of my grandchildren were with me on the night the cafe closed.

There were three employees who I want to mention who were like family to me: Margaret Strauss, Sal Estudillo, and Carol Ann Moore.

Margaret and I worked closely together; she was my assistant for many years. I would yell at her, and she would yell back! We were great friends and she kept me going. I miss her dearly.

Sal was a talented chef who was faithful to us until the end. If it wasn't for his willingness to return to the cafe and cook alongside Terri, we couldn't have operated the restaurant while I recuperated after my injuries. Sal has a good heart and is one of the hardest working people I know.

Carol was a long-time employee who ran the office and was a great waitress who worked alongside Terri until she moved into the kitchen. She was also the best bartender, and invented and made the most delicious cocktails. She had many regular customers who came to the cafe just to see her. She was like a daughter to me.

Running a successful restaurant and cooking school is not easy, but without the help of family and close friends, it is almost impossible. I recognize and appreciate everyone who gave me their love and support throughout the years and that includes those who made *Kitchen Bitch* a reality.

CAROL FRAZZETTA was born and raised in Brooklyn, New York. She founded and operated Staten Island's first and longest running cooking school, Carol's Cuisine, where she was the head instructor for over 44 years. She was the owner and executive chef of Carol's Cafe, a critically acclaimed fine dining restaurant for 22 years. She is the author of *Carol's Cafe Pasta Sauces*.

The prestigious Zagat Restaurant Guide called Carol's Cafe "the best restaurant Staten Island has to offer." Carol's Cafe was also listed in the Michelin Red Guide. Her recipes also appear in the *James Beard Celebration Cookbook* and the *International Association of Cooking Professionals Cookbook*. Frazzetta's biography was featured in the 2004–2005 edition of *The International Who's Who of Chefs*.

Frazzetta was the first female chef to prepare and serve dinner at the prestigious James Beard House, for a private party of 90 guests. In 2011, Frazzetta was featured as a guest chef for a fundraising event hosted by then-Mayor Michael Bloomberg to aid in the restoration of Gracie Mansion. Her culinary education includes The Cordon Bleu, London; La Varenne, Paris; Marcella Hazan's School, Italy; John Clancy's School of Baking, New York City; Wilton School of Cake Decorating, Chicago; The Culinary Institute of America; The New School, New York City; L'Academie de Cuisine in Bethesda, Maryland; and Windows on the World, New York City.

Carol is the mother of three and the grandmother of four. She is now retired and currently resides in Staten Island with her Yorkie, Meatball.

For more recipes visit: chefcarolsrecipes.com

Printed in the USA
CPSIA information can be obtained
at www.ICGtesting.com
LVHW071514121123
763714LV00028B/1504